SMART MONEY

Understanding and Successfully
Controlling Your Financial Behavior

SMART MONEY

■

JERRY & RAMONA TUMA
AND TIM LAHAYE

"To God Be the Glory, Great Things He Has Done"

To our children, Samuel Ernest Tuma and Hannah Gail Tuma. Nothing in life has been so rewarding as watching the two of you benefit from what we have taught you. You have learned from our failures as well as our successes. Though we teach hundreds or thousands, our greatest joy will be seeing you grow in the ways of God and continue in His will.

To Lee Ann Austin. You are a part of us. Your faithfulness through all these years has made you one of the most valuable foundation stones in the building of Cornerstone Financial Services. We love you.

Contents

Acknowledgments

To Dr. Tim LaHaye. Words cannot express enough thanks for the impact you've had on our lives. We first learned of the threat to undermine our society's moral and spiritual underpinnings by reading *The Battle for the Mind.* When we faced stress in our marriage, we read your books on temperament and, in the muddle of our miscommunication, a light dawned. We discovered ourselves and each other. Nothing has meant more to our marriage than your teachings. Finally, thank you for your input on this book. Literally every chapter reflects your influence. As we have written, we have marveled at how your teachings have been integrated into our lives.

Our prayer is that another generation will discover your valuable insights on family life and will find financial freedom. May God bless you richly.

To Carol Bartley, our editor. You made us rethink and retype. You made us search our souls and bare our hearts. We gave you the material and you made it readable. You continually amazed us. No matter how close our deadlines got, you continually calmed us, encouraged us, and made us believe we could face the challenge. This is truly "our" book!

To Judy Borneman, our nimble-fingered typist who stayed up late and rose early in order to meet our deadlines. Thanks also to your husband, Jim, who loaned you to us in the wee hours of the night. Thank you both for being so committed to our ministry.

To Roberta Watson and Brandon Fibbs. Your hours of making everything fit the English language will be appreciated by all who read this book. Thank you, Brandon, for writing some of the creative stories within these pages.

To Kent and Barbara Froom. Thank you for reading manuscripts and encouraging us along the way.

To Karen Grazier. You are our prayer warrior.

To our pastor, Roger Yancey, and his wife, Pauline. Thanks for your prayer support and guidance.

To all of our staff at Cornerstone Financial Services—Lee Ann Austin, Joan Austin, Gena Skipworth, Bill Nevius, David McCord, and David Welch. Because you have kept all the wheels turning at Cornerstone, we have been able to take time away to write. Without all of you, we are nothing.

To the KCBI listeners in Dallas and Fort Worth, Trinity Oaks Baptist Church, and all the people tested by Dr. Tim LaHaye. Thank you for participating in the testing and interviewing process. Without you, there would be no book.

CHAPTER ONE

Our Pilgrimage

"Wisdom is supreme; therefore get wisdom."

PROVERBS 4:7

A couple of years ago Mona and I took a trip to a quaint bed-and-breakfast hotel about an hour and a half's drive from Dallas to celebrate our wedding anniversary. Part of the purpose of our getaway was to rest, and part was to begin work on our newest project—writing a book in conjunction with Tim LaHaye on temperaments and how they affect people's financial decisions.

While we were there, the Lord confirmed in many ways that this project was of Him. The first night we were sitting out on the back porch reading and enjoying the quiet when an exuberant man burst upon the scene. I wanted to be polite, but frankly I am an introvert anyway, and I was there to work and read. Yet this man's gregarious personality was not to be denied. So despite my initial reluctance to spend time with a stranger I probably would never see again, we began to talk.

I quickly found out he was not only a fellow Christian but he had heard us on the Dallas radio stations discussing finances and was very interested in the topic. He, in fact, had taught financial courses for Christians. As we talked, we quickly pegged this guy's temperament—an obvious sanguine. He was enjoyable, witty, and fun to be around, the type of guy who can make friends with anyone. As we discussed our upcoming book and the financial conferences we do, he made a comment that has stuck with me ever since. He said, "I studied all the principles. I even taught courses on biblical stewardship and handling money, but it wasn't until my wife and I made a commitment and had a change of heart to get holy that we really saw a change in our finances."

The next morning Mona and I went down to the dining room to have breakfast, and even though we realized we were probably being selfish, we wanted to have a quiet breakfast, just the two of us. As we were sitting there sipping our coffee, the hostess came over and asked if someone could join us for breakfast, and we politely, but grudgingly, agreed. Who should she lead to our table but the son of one of our long-time clients. As an odd coincidence—God has a funny way of arranging circumstances sometimes—he and his wife had also decided to take a couple of days of R&R at this same bed-and-breakfast. Although I had met this man, I had not known him well. It turned out that he and his wife had come down for this break because they desperately needed it. They had just opened up their own printing company and were having a tough go of it. As a matter of fact, the stress was about to eat them alive. We ended up spending almost the entire day counseling with them about their business and their marriage.

The husband, an obvious sanguine, was good at sales. He was a visionary. He was always planning new things they could do, new projects to start, and new ways to increase business. His wife, a quiet, introverted person, was the glue that was keeping the business together. While her husband was out making sales calls and formulating grandiose plans, she was at home taking care of the books and worrying about how they were going to pay the rent next month or how they were going to pay for the printing machine her husband had ordered on the spur of the moment or how they would keep the creditors away. Both they and we learned an important lesson that day. It's critical to understand your mate's temperament, especially if you are in business for yourself. God was validating the principles of the book.

The Black Hole of Financial Problems

We have counseled many such unfortunate couples who feel they are at the very edge of a black hole and cannot crawl out. We have seen husbands so far in debt they felt they could no longer remain in the household and so ultimately abandoned their wives and children. We have counseled single moms desperately trying to make it after a devastating divorce, wondering how they are going to feed their children and praying that God will keep the tires on their car from exploding. We have counseled widows who have been left financially ignorant, not knowing where their insurance policies are, what their husband's financial dealings were, nor whom they could trust for financial counsel. We've seen couples who have gotten out of debt and, within two or three years, have found themselves back in the same predicament without a clue as to why it happened.

All these people are desperate people. All of them truly desire solutions. Many of them have read the financial books. Most of them know they should be on a budget. At one of our seminars, I asked a large group of people how many knew how to budget. Over 90 percent of the audience raised their hands. When I asked how many of them lived by a budget, all but 5 percent of the hands went down. People know what they need to do, but they don't seem able to do it.

Within the last few years, we've interviewed and tested over seven hundred people concerning their financial behavior. Over and over in that testing, we asked if they were able to stay on a budget and what they believed was their worst financial habit. Virtually everyone confessed they had difficulty staying on a budget.

Finding the Way Out

With these facts in mind, several years ago we began to pray and ask God to develop a simple way of demonstrating to people the weaknesses of their own personalities that kept them continually in personal debt and financial devastation. Through a series of events, eight years ago we met Dr. Tim LaHaye, but he had already had a strong impact in our lives. In our early years as Christians, we were strongly influenced by his book *The Battle for the Mind* and his temperament books. When we were going through difficult times in our marriage, we read these books and found answers for our relationship as we began to understand temperament differences. Not only were we able to have more patience with each other, but we became more aware of our own shortcomings and failures. As we applied the information about temperaments not only to our lives but also to other people's lives, we began to realize that here was the answer for those people who are perpetually in financial difficulty. So, over three years ago, we contacted Dr. LaHaye, talked with him about our idea, and began testing and interviewing people about their finances.

When we first started this study, we weren't certain whether this theory about the temperaments' influence on finances was valid or not. But as we tested and interviewed, we found to our amazement that at least 80 percent of the people we dealt with fell into the patterns described in this book. We were amazed at the consistency of the patterns. Most melancholies, but few others, can stay on a budget. We were stunned to discover that many sanguines balance their checkbooks in the same bizarre way. We were astounded that so many cholerics divorce. We were surprised at the stinginess of the phlegmatics. Truly, solutions to people's financial pain began unfolding before us.

Through the years of Dr. LaHaye's ministry, some have resisted the concept of the temperaments. Some have even said it is not biblical. We strongly disagree. The temperament principles don't take away from the individuality of every precious human being that God has created. Every star is different. Every blade of grass is unique. No two snowflakes are the same. So also, every human being is unique. But every star has certain characteristics that make it a star, and every snowflake has qualities that make it a snowflake. As we have studied the temperaments and used them in counseling, we have been impressed with God's amazing sense of order in the way He created mankind. He didn't just throw us out there. He designed us. He created us. He created four temperaments that complete each other and make a whole. Without the sanguine, there would be no joy in life. Without the choleric, there would be no destiny in life. Without the melancholy, there would be no music in life. Without the phlegmatic, there would be no humor, and all the rest of the temperaments would be running off half-cocked because phlegmatics are the people who put the brakes on the others. We see within the temperaments that God has created an amazing wholeness as we relate to one another.

Your temperament affects your financial decisions, and it affects your marriage. In fact, almost all divorces can be traced either to financial problems or temperament differences ("irreconcilable differences" as the courts would say). So often opposites tend to attract, and while the quiet, introverted person is often attracted to the gregarious, outgoing person, once they get married, the weaknesses of each of the temperaments drive them apart. Without a strong understanding of what each temperament is like and the ability to accept each other as you are instead of trying to change each other, most marriages face a tough row.

By the same token, each temperament handles finances differently. In this book, we will give you the tools, first of all, to discover both your primary and secondary temperament. And once you have discovered your temperaments, you will see what your typical strengths and weaknesses may be. We will show you how to get on your feet financially and how to make the best decisions, the way God intended with the husband and wife working together cohesively. If you are single, the principles will work just as well.

"Please Help Me!"

The urgency of these issues was brought home to us again just a few days ago when we received a letter that began, "Please help me. I have a very desperate and complicated situation and I don't know where to turn." At the top of her stationery was printed, "I can do all things through Jesus Christ." Her letter told us how she had been married and divorced and remarried to the same man two times. When she was divorced from the man for five years, she completely put her finances into order, despite the fact that she made only one-fifth of what her husband made. She paid off all her credit cards. She had no debt except her car and her brand new home. She had no loans.

Then her husband talked her into coming back to him. He promised she could take care of the household finances because he was convinced she was better qualified. Everything went well for about three months. Then she discovered they had over forty thousand dollars in credit card debt and loans, not including her car or their monthly house payment of twenty-five hundred dollars. He refused her suggestions to sell stock to pay off the debts or to go for credit counseling. "He was in denial about the problem....I was butting into sacred territory and he withdrew and isolated himself from me. Things went from bad to worse....The credit was deteriorating rapidly. I felt devastated by another failure, by the 'dirty trick' God had played on me. I was now over my head in debt, no husband or relationship, and had no hope of getting out of it. The last thing he has done is take me off his checking account and deny me any money....On top of everything else, our house is more than $30,000 in negative equity, and we can't really afford the monthly payments and maintenance, but we can't sell it without coming up with that money that we don't have. Every month he takes cash from his credit cards to cover his expenses and it is a vicious circle. He wants to appear to be Mr. Generous to his kids so he is paying our married daughter's tuition at college and lending to his family and I feel trapped and hopeless and angry. I sold my home, I quit my job to try to make a go of this marriage and all I have is debts and problems."

After reading this letter, Mona felt this woman was so desperate that she needed to contact her. Indeed, the woman was at the end of her rope. She wanted to leave her husband but felt God had closed off all her options. She said she wanted to die. When Mona asked her if there was any other area in their life that was making her feel so desperate, she said absolutely not, that the whole problem of their marriage was finances. She felt that their financial responsibility had brought her to the edge of the cliff, and she was ready to jump off. She frantically declared, "It's all financial, every bit of it. The whole reason for all of our fights, all of this devastation in our family, is because of money."

We Know This Works

This woman's letter is not an isolated case. Nothing seems to bring more devastation in a household, nothing puts more pressure on a household than decisions over money. We know from personal experience. And we have used these principles in our own pilgrimage to become financially free. We disciplined our lives for seven years and got both our company and our household completely out of debt. For this we give God the glory.

It was not easy! There were times when to save money we ate beans and rice and rice and beans! We learned control. We learned to wait on God and determined that a need really wasn't a need until God supplied the answer. We did without. We planned and budgeted and watched God honor our decision to step out of this world's system and do it His way. We allowed God to creatively meet our needs, determining not to trust in plastic but rather in the Almighty God.

As we determined to live our lives this way, we changed! It no longer bothered us to buy pre-owned vehicles. Shopping at bankruptcy sales and auctions became a form of recreation. We learned to barter and recycle and bargain shop. It became a challenge to do it right.

Riches don't last forever; neither does poverty. If we learn how to handle finances with the principles in mind, we will guard the way we spend our money when we have it and truly rest in God when we don't.

We have lived by these principles of discipline and over the years have taught them to other people. One thirty-five-year-old man recently was laid off. Because he had properly prepared for future hardships, he is weathering this storm more successfully than others in his same position. He writes, "I am currently out of work. I have not had a paycheck for nearly three months, but because I have saved money and listened to Jerry on the radio for the last seven years, I feel God has prepared me for this time. I am trying to do consulting/contract work until I find the right job, or continue consulting if I'm successful. If I am careful with my resources and unemployment, I should have enough money for a year before dipping into my investments. I have my first contract job in June."

Problems will occur, but following God's ways makes life less difficult. Proof of this is in the testimony of the couple who owned the printing company. We hadn't seen this couple since meeting them at the bed-and-breakfast two years ago. To our surprise and joy, we "ran into them" again just recently. Once again, we had been secluding ourselves in order to write this book. Deciding to take a break, we went to a local restaurant for breakfast. What a pleasant surprise to see this man who had been our first interview and to spend four hours discovering the successes and failures they had experienced since our last meeting.

He had learned that being a sanguine meant he had managed by the seat of his pants. He learned that he is great at getting things rolling, but his wife is great at keeping things rolling. He takes less offense as she shoots down his ideas, realizing that he has a tendency to "give away the seed corn, instead of waiting for the harvest." He realized that he hates detail; she loves it. He has to have people around him; she works best alone. He comes up with ideas for expansion but has come to trust her methodical, melancholy mind as she declares what will or will not work. They have made seemingly little changes, transferring to each other tasks more suited for them.

Now there is a sweet balance between them. Instead of two rocks beating each other to death, they have become two cogs turning, fitting together, working in unity, making it all come together. And together they are accomplishing their goals.

Overall, we were thrilled at their progress. Her physical appearance had changed from someone heavily burdened to someone who was beginning to have a handle on life. He was a joy! A true man of character, he had painfully assessed his sanguine weaknesses and was doing everything possible to overcome them, getting wise counsel and making himself accountable to other people. He's on his way to being a very successful businessman.

We were able to counsel them further concerning who should hire their employees. He tends to hire friends. She, on the other hand, is able to hire based on their needs. We were also able to recommend that all business contracts should be done jointly since the sanguine in him wanted to "cut great deals" for the other guy.

Two years ago, we had been privileged to be used by God in their lives. Just sharing a simple truth about temperaments and finances changed the whole direction of a marriage, a family, a business, and two individuals.

Our prayer is that this book will be a "hinge point" of change for you, as she described our visit with them two years ago. We pray this book will assist you in bringing order out of chaos, that it will teach you about your weaknesses and give you hope that you can change. You can have financial order in your household and in your business. If you are married, you and your spouse can work together in unity toward your goals and dreams. The principles of God remain the same, and His only desire is that we seek Him and walk in those ways.

■

Your Temperament and Your Money

CHAPTER TWO

What's Your Temperament?

by Dr. Tim LaHaye

*"Now you are the body of Christ, and each one of you
is a part of it."*
1 CORINTHIANS 12:27

Your inherited temperament is *the* most powerful influence on your behavior. It influences everything you do, including the way you earn, manage, and spend your money. Of course, many things influence your behavior, from childhood experiences and training to education. But although you can change your behavior through learning, you will never change your temperament. Like the color of your eyes, you are born with it.

The good news is that you do not have to be ruled by the weaknesses of your temperament. That is what this book is all about—to acquaint you with the oldest theory of human behavior known to us, to confront you with each temperament's strengths and weaknesses in handling money, and to offer biblically sound principles for improving your spending and earning habits.

I didn't invent the temperament theory, although I have written six books on the subject. Actually, the theory as conceived by Hippocrates is over twenty-four hundred years old and has been embraced and expanded upon by students of human nature, both Christian and secular.

The principles of the temperament theory presented here are based on my books, including the *Spirit-Controlled Temperament* which has over one million copies in print and has been translated into more than twenty-seven languages, the LaHaye Temperament Analysis that I have administered to over twenty-seven thousand people, and thirty years of using the theory in counseling. I am even more convinced today of the validity of this ancient tool for diagnosing people's temperament than I was when I first became acquainted with it. While no theory is perfect, I have found nothing that compares with it in helping people overcome their inherited weaknesses.

Why Christians Embrace the Temperament Theory

The temperament theory does not come from the Bible. However, Christians have gravitated to it because it does not violate any known biblical principle and is supported by many others. For example, the theory assumes that people have a sin nature that accounts for their weaknesses. Unlike humanistic psychology, it does not teach that human nature is "perfectible" with the right environment and education.

The temperament theory presents our weaknesses in helpful detail so that we can summon God's aid and do something to correct those weaknesses. As Christians, we recognize that we need God's help. Contrary to humanism, we are not able to raise ourselves by our own bootstraps, but we need God's power to overcome those inherited weaknesses that lead to bad habits and drag us down into sin. That is where the indwelling ministry of the Holy Spirit becomes practical in our everyday lives, by maximizing the positive side of our temperament—our strengths, talents, and abilities—and enabling us to overcome what we would otherwise be helpless to change.

What Is Temperament?

Temperament is the combination of traits we inherited from our parents, and it combines with other human characteristics to produce our basic makeup. Most of us are more conscious of its expression than we are its function.

It is a person's temperament that makes him outgoing and extroverted or shy and introverted. It is temperament that makes some people art and music enthusiasts while others are interested in sports or industry. Doubtless you know both kinds of people who were born to the same parents. In fact, I have met outstanding musicians whose siblings were tone-deaf.

While early home life, training, education, and motivation powerfully influence our actions throughout life, temperament is the number one influence. It is the first thing that affects us, and, like body structure, color of eyes, and other physical characteristics, it escorts us through life. Extroverts are extroverts. They may tone down the expression of their extroversion, but they will always be extroverts. Similarly, although introverts may be able to come out of their shells and act more aggressively, they will never be transformed into extroverts. Temperament sets broad guidelines on everyone's behavior. On one side are strengths; on the other are weaknesses. The primary advantage to learning about the four basic temperaments is to discover your most pronounced strengths and weaknesses so that with God's help you can overcome your weaknesses and take advantage of your strengths. In this way you can fulfill your personal destiny to the maximum.

To properly understand temperament's control of our actions and reactions, we should distinguish carefully between temperament, character, and personality.

INHERITED TEMPERAMENT
+
CHILDHOOD TRAINING
+
PARENTAL LOVE
+
LIFE'S EXPERIENCES
+
HABIT
+
EDUCATION
+
SELF-DISCIPLINE
+
MOTIVATION
+
MENTAL ATTITUDE
+
HEALTH

YOUR BEHAVIOR

Temperament is the combination of inborn traits that subconsciously affect our behavior. These traits are passed on by the genes. Some psychologists suggest that we get more genes from our grandparents than our parents, which could account for the greater resemblance of some children to their grandparents than to their parents. The alignment of temperament traits is just as unpredictable as the color of eyes, hair, or size of body.

Character is the real you. The Bible refers to it as "the hidden man of the heart." It is the result of your natural temperament modified by childhood training, education, basic attitudes, beliefs, principles, and motivations. As such, it is made up of the mind, emotions, and will.

Personality is the outward expression of ourselves, which may or may not be the same as our character, depending on how genuine we are. Personality may even be the pleasing facade we present to disguise an unpleasant or weak character. Many people go through life acting a part on the basis of what they think they should be, or how they want people to see them, rather than as they really are, which is a formula for mental and spiritual chaos.

In summary, temperament is the combination of traits we were born with, character is our "civilized" temperament, and personality is the "face" we show to others.

Which Personality Type Are You?

The heart of the temperament theory divides people into four basic categories, which Hippocrates named sanguine, choleric, melancholy, and phlegmatic. Once people diagnose their own basic temperament and know its natural tendencies, they are better equipped to ascertain what vocations they are best suited for, what natural weaknesses they must work on, what strengths they can build on, and even what problems they may have with their finances.

Do not be surprised if you fail to identify yourself under only one of the temperament types because no one is 100 percent sanguine, choleric, melancholy, or phlegmatic. We are all a combination of at least two and perhaps three temperaments. In fact, don't be surprised if you feel like you are one temperament sometimes and another temperament at other times. Actually, most people have a dominant temperament and a secondary one. Your secondary temperament may have a strong influence on how you handle financial decisions (more on that intriguing subject later). The more you know about your primary and secondary temperaments, the better you will understand how they influence each other and contribute to your total makeup. However, your predominant or basic temperament, the one that influences you the most, should not be too difficult to diagnose.

At the end of this chapter is a temperament test which you should be able to take in about fifteen minutes in order to determine your dominant and secondary temperaments. Since it is a short overview, it won't be exact or scientific, but it should give you a good indication of your temperaments. Keep in mind that if you are in an unusual mood (fearful, depressed, angry, or worried) when you take the test, it can affect the outcome. Try to take the test when you are calm and relaxed.

For further confirmation, have your spouse, best friend, or parent take the test for you as well. Sometimes others see us more clearly than we see ourselves.

1. Read through the four lists of characteristics. Once you've read all four, come back and place a checkmark beside the characteristics that you think best describe you.

2. After placing checkmarks by the appropriate characteristics, total the checkmarks for each list

3. The list with the highest number of checkmarks should be your dominant temperament, and the list with the second highest number of checkmarks should be your secondary temperament. Answers to the test are in the Appendix. Again, this will not be exact but should give you a good indication of your temperament. For more exact and thorough results, we recommend you take the LaHaye Temperament Analysis. Information on this test is available in the Appendix.

Remember that no one is totally one temperament; most people are a combination of two. As you learn more about the various temperaments, you may find that your first selection is really your secondary temperament. That usually happens when people are balanced between their primary and secondary temperaments. Test results will be only as good as the answers you have given. In other words, you have to take an extremely honest look at yourself to come up with the correct answers.

No temperament is either good or bad. They all have strengths and weaknesses. The objective is to find out what we are and then to use our new understanding to handle our finances better, improve our work, and gain greater peace and fruitfulness in our families.

One caution. As you find yourself identifying with a temperament, don't allow it to become an excuse for not taking responsibility for your actions. It would be easy to excuse a behavior by saying, "I can't help being impulsive. I'm a sanguine." Or, "God made me a choleric, and that's why I have a problem with anger." The proper use of temperament teaching is to help us recognize and understand our weaknesses and learn how to overcome them, as well as build on our strengths. Rather than passively declaring, "I can't change," which leaves us hopeless, we should say instead, "With God's help, I will change." Temperament teaching can be a tremendous tool in the hands of Christians who really desire God's best for their lives.

Why Is This Important to Our Finances?

As we have said, temperament influences everything we do, from driving a car to choosing a vocation. And it certainly influences how we spend our money. As I write, a dear sanguine friend is in prison for the way he handled money. He is a master salesman who has made and lost two fortunes. I don't believe he ever intended to cheat anyone, but his carelessness regarding detail made it appear to a jury as if he did, and he was found guilty. Although that is an extreme case, most Christians spend their lives far below their financial potential because they do not recognize their inherent financial weaknesses and do not practice God's principles for financially maximizing their potential. That is why I am glad to recommend this material developed by Jerry and Mona Tuma, two excellent financial counselors who know and understand the temperament theory and how it influences behavior. Everyone can benefit from their application of biblical principles of personal finance to the twelve blends of temperament.

Once at a conference, I heard a financial management expert say, "In a recent survey it was revealed that no more than one person out of eleven uses right money management techniques." He went on to say, "It has been proven that the other ten could relearn the proper use of money in a very short time. It would only take twenty minutes a day to develop good money management habits." Knowing your personal temperament will help you improve the financial habits of your life. And if you are married, knowing your temperament and your spouse's temperament, can not only improve your financial habits but also your marriage.

Now let's take a close look at the four basic temperaments and how they handle finances.

	TEMPERAMENT #1		TEMPERAMENT #2
	Perfectionist		Talkative, popular
	Analytical		Loud, sometimes brash
	Industrious		Emotionally volatile at times
	Musically inclined		Persuasive
	Enjoys art, music, things of beauty		Quick tempered
	Detail oriented		Colorful, exciting personality
	Precise, exact		Fun loving
	Introspective		Low self-control
	Self-sacrificing		Impulsive
	Excellent planner		Low sales resistance
	Supportive of others		Compassionate
	Self-disciplined		Emotionally responsive
	Serious		Warm friendly
	Gifted, multi-talented		Outgoing, extroverted
	Aesthetic		Enthusiastic
	Worrier, fearful		Loves people
	Critical and picky		Great encourager
	Indecisive		Not well organized
	Pessimistic		Loves approval of others
	Deeply emotional, moody		Restless
	Creative		Optimistic
	Sensitive		Sometimes late to appointments
	Loyal, faithful		Not good at details
	Frozen by fear, worry, depression		Sensitive
	Harbors resentment		Not well disciplined
	TOTAL		TOTAL

	TEMPERAMENT #3		TEMPERAMENT #4
	Calm, cool		Strong willed, determined
	Laid back		Time is most valuable asset
	Easy going		Driving personality
	Quiet, reserved		Impatient—wants it done yesterday
	Inactive, sometimes lazy		Sometimes bossy
	Tendency toward passivity		Direct, forceful
	Avoids and dislikes conflict		Values tasks over people
	Slow to make decisions		Natural leader
	Peaceable, peace loving		Likes to be in control
	Quick, dry wit		Sometimes intolerant of others
	Diplomatic in conflict resolutions		Decisive
	Dependable, reliable		Strongly opinionated
	Objective		Independent, hard working
	Efficient		Self-motivated
	Orderly		Confident
	Agreeable, likeable		Self-reliant
	Hard to motivate		Self-assured
	Frequently waits until last minute		Goal oriented
	Often indecisive		Aggressive driver
	Fearful, worrier		Risk taker
	Self-protective		Prone to anger
	Saves everything		Sarcastic
	Introverted		Argumentative
	Stubborn		Insensitive, unsympathetic
	Works well under pressure		Practical
	TOTAL		TOTAL

CHAPTER THREE

Sanguines:

The Last of the Big Spenders

"The plans of the diligent lead to profit as surely as haste leads to poverty."

PROVERBS 21:5

I f you were to sit in the lounge area of your bank to simply watch people, you would discover an astounding thing. You can pick out a sanguine every time. He's the guy in the blue suit standing in the corner with his papers. Pen in hand he flies through the forms he needs to complete to withdraw his funds from the bank. The questions are familiar to him; he filled out these same forms six months ago. Inside his briefcase is his checkbook. Although checks have been written liberally, the register in the back barely has an entry. He just doesn't have time to figure it all out. And why should he exert himself when the bank can figure it out for him?

After depositing his money into the new bank, he leaves the building and catches a glimpse of himself in the window. "Pretty sharp," he admires. He certainly does look the part. He sure likes his new diamond ring, even though he would have liked the stone to be a little larger. Too bad gold chains are out of style; he used to wear five or six of them—real gold ones.

He's a salesman, and a good one at that. He can sure haul in the money. The only problem is he cannot figure out where it all goes.

The other day he and his wife got into an enormous fight over a new color photocopier he bought. He couldn't believe she was so upset. He needed the copier for his business. Doesn't she know that appearances are everything in the advertising business?

Speaking of his wife, she sure has been irritable lately. The car payment hasn't been paid in two months, and the credit card company has been calling and giving her fits. He thought if he bought her a real nice tennis bracelet that would make her happy with him again.

To his utter shock, she flew into an absolute rage when he handed her the beautifully wrapped package. He didn't understand. This approach had worked before. What's all the fuss about the bills? Don't I make a lot of money? Doesn't she know the Lord will provide?

He suffers a momentary bout of depression but picks right up when one of his best friends calls and invites them to a dinner party at one of the best restaurants in town. And he is the life of the party. When the meal was finished, as always he reached for the tab. Why is she kicking him under the table? He whips out his gold card one more time. So what if his wife figured out they were almost $10,000 in debt. If it's already that high, what's one more charge going to matter? It's worth it to be liked.

What's a Sanguine?

Sanguines are warm, buoyant, and lively people. They are so outgoing they are usually considered superextroverts. They have a great capacity for enjoying themselves and generally pass on this fun-loving spirit. The moment they enter a room they tend to lift the spirits of everyone present by their exuberant conversation. They are fascinating storytellers, and their warm, emotional nature almost allows you to relive the experience as they tell it.

Sanguines never lack for friends. They can genuinely feel your joys and sorrows, and they have the capacity to make you feel important, as though they are your special friends. And they are, as long as they are looking at you. Then they fix their eyes with equal intensity on the next person they meet.

Receptive by nature, they are easily impacted by external impressions and will respond with an outburst of feelings. Feelings rather than reflective thoughts control their decisions.

The Apostle Peter in the Bible was likely a sanguine. Every time he appears in the Gospels he is talking. In fact, Dr. LaHaye once read through the Gospels with the specific purpose of verifying his suspicion—that Simon Peter talked more than all the other disciples put together. That is typical for sanguines. As one sanguine minister says, "A sanguine always enters a room mouth first." Their noisy, blustering, friendly ways make them appear more confident than they really are, but their energy and lovable disposition get them over the rough spots of life. People will even excuse their weaknesses by saying, "That's just the way they are."

Sanguines typically have the greatest level of faith of any temperament. They, like Peter, are the first ones to walk on water! Their hearts compel them to walk in God's way. If sanguines think God has told them to do something, they will leap at the opportunity while everyone else stands around thinking about it. Sanguines are frequently the first to step forward when they see someone else in a financial bind. They will be the ones to boldly declare to others in a crisis that God will supply all their needs. They say this from experience, because sanguines have a way of keeping God on "red alert." And God has proven himself faithful in their lives. Sanguines truly believe the promise of Malachi 3:10: "'Test me in this,' says the LORD Almighty, 'and see if I will not throw open the floodgates of heaven and pour out so much blessing that you will not have room enough for it.'" And test God they do!

Sanguines are the life of the party at social gatherings, church functions, and office parties. They're able to charm the socks off a grasshopper. Possessing a great sense of humor, they rarely get depressed. One woman we tested said, "What are black moods? I've never had one!" Because sanguines are extremely responsive to their surroundings and to the moods and feelings of those around them, they are able to bring the saddest person out of the doldrums. But the people skills that are the sanguines' best asset often become their worst handicap to good stewardship of their finances.

True romantics, sanguines frequently sweep their mates off their feet with just the right gift or surprise them with an exciting place to go. In fact, sanguines delight in accommodating people in general. They will be the first to remember secretary's day, boss's day, an anniversary, or a birthday. They will remember your favorite flower, candy, or anything else that's important to you. They are often generous to a fault.

Sanguines can make great salespeople. They can sell swamp land in Florida, and everyone will love them for doing it. They are able to earn great amounts of money, and they are equally able to spend great amounts of money.

Sanguines usually have little analytical ability (unless their secondary temperament is melancholy) and are not given to self-examination or intro-spection. But when they finally have the courage to truly look at themselves as God sees them, they are the first to break into godly sorrow and repen-tance. Once sanguines grasp what is truly expected, they will give their whole heart to be not only hearers of the Word but doers also.

Strengths and Weaknesses

Sanguines Act First, Think Later

The root of most sanguines' financial problems is easy to pinpoint because sanguines are the most open of all temperaments. They are also the most impulsive. They rarely think before they speak or act. They tend to be impulsive in everything, including their financial dealings, which often results in consumer debt, lack of savings, or tax problems.

One woman we surveyed said her worst financial fight with her spouse occurred when she charged $129 for a purse. She knew it was foolish. She normally didn't spend that kind of money on a purse. She had no particu-lar reason for buying it, except an impulse. That incident was merely indica-tive of the root problem. She had accumulated over $25,000 in credit card debt and eventually had to file for bankruptcy.

Because sanguines are likely to buy impulsively, they tend not to worry about the bill until it comes due. Or worse, they spend again simply because they owe so much anyway. A forty-nine-year-old man observed, "I spend money on hobbies and foolish things the same when I am out of work for several weeks or a month as when I am working full-time."

In their impulsiveness, sanguines often enjoy buying gadgets or adult toys, usually high quality, expensive items. Said one man we surveyed, "I impulse buy audio-visual equipment, camera equipment, computers, etc." Another person commented, "I am an impulse spender. I have excellent taste in everything from clothes to food, and I spend accordingly." One sanguine summed it up by saying, "I enjoy spending money more than saving it. I call it recycling to help the economy!"

Sanguines could profit from the wisdom of Proverbs: "It is not good to have zeal without knowledge, nor to be hasty and miss the way."[1]

Sanguines Can't Say No

Closely linked with impulsiveness is a lack of self-control, which drastically affects sanguines' finances. As suckers for the latest gadget, they may spend tremendous amounts of money on things that other temperaments would consider junk. They frequently buy unnecessary items, often spending twice as much as another temperament by buying more expensive items.

Our years of observation and testing indicate that sanguines have the lowest sales resistance of any temperament. The business world has an old saying that "the easiest person to sell is a salesman." It could be said that "the easiest person to sell is a sanguine." With sanguines' love for people, natural talkativeness, and ability to make people like them, they tend to enter and excel in the field of sales. But by the same token, their impulsiveness, lack of self-control, and desire for approval make them the easiest to sell to. Several sanguines we tested described themselves as the "last of the big-time spenders." But they are not really a dying breed!

Regarding the worst financial fight of her marriage, one lady said it was caused by "my spending at a dress sale (really low prices!) when my husband had told me that week to be careful about spending money. I know I was wrong. I haven't even worn a couple of the dresses I bought. I don't even like them!" Another said, "Because of compulsive buying, if I have a hundred dollars, I'll spend ninety in one day and have to live on ten dollars for a week." Other sanguines would typically comment, "I don't seem to be able to help myself," or "My worst money habit is spending all I have and wanting the best money can buy."

Even when there is no salesperson around, sanguines have difficulty controlling their spending. Sanguines sometimes go crazy at garage sales, buying all sorts of stuff because it is so cheap. Much of this junk will land in the trash, an unused closet, or a corner of the garage until they decide to have their own garage sale because they have too much stuff.

Proverbs 25:28 describes a person without self-control as being like a village without walls. At the time this verse was written, a village without walls was defenseless, helpless to fight off an enemy attack. This principle remains true today. Without self-control, we are constantly tugged in this direction or that by our own desires and by enticements fed to us through the media, salespeople, or even our spouses. Without self-control, we are financially defenseless.

Sanguines Want Approval

Sanguines are easy to spot because they usually have the broadest, brightest ties, the hottest pink skirts, the glimmering sequined jackets, thick gold chains, and the massive cubic zirconium rings (unless of course they can get real diamonds!). Everything asks, "Look at me. Do you like me? Do you approve of me?"

Their desire for approval shows up in their desire to be part of the "in crowd." The type of fountain pen they use, the brand of sunglasses they wear, the brands of clothing they buy are usually influenced by others' opinions. A clever salesman will use this to his advantage by emphasizing that "everybody has one" or by appealing to the sanguine ego by telling them how good they will look in that new car or that new suit. They will be especially susceptible to ads or sales pitches that feed their egos or appeal to their desire for approval—ads depicting success, fun, or anything that makes them the life of the party. They need to be someone everyone loves.

They are the people most likely to blow their budget, and even go into debt if necessary, just to impress others with their new house, car, clothes, or jewelry. And therein lies their downfall. One very successful sanguine businessman destroyed his marriage and his business with irresponsible financial decisions. He owned a limousine with all the trappings and an $800,000 mansion and produced flashy ads for his business. He earned money and he spent it, sparing no expense in any area of his life. And his flashiness did attract attention. When the IRS turned their attention toward him, he lost everything. He was humiliated and sentenced to prison for filing a false tax return.

Sanguines Fly by the Seat of Their Pants

Sanguines rarely plan ahead. Their zest for life and natural optimism promote a carefree attitude toward the future. They fly by the seat of their pants the majority of the time, living only in the present and rarely considering the consequences of their actions. Instead, they react to a situation when it arises, which frequently leads them into financial difficulties. Uncontrolled spending that results in credit card debt is a common by-product of this sanguine trait.

Sanguines frequently find that money which should have been saved for the future is not available when needed. One sanguine lady stated, "I could have planned for my children's education. Instead I frivolously bought collector figurines." Because of their tendency to spend impulsively and not to plan, they rarely have a large nest egg at retirement. Unless they work for a company that forces them to save a large percentage of their income, they may have little to show for a lifetime of generally excellent earnings.

This lack of planning can cause job and career problems, too. One sanguine man stated that he impulsively quit his job, assuming he could find another one at the same salary. But he didn't. Some advance planning to determine job availability in the same income range could have saved this man and his family unnecessary suffering.

Because they hate the discipline of working for someone else, sanguines often go into business for themselves. Being rather creative, they find appealing ways to start various enterprises. However, because of a lack of forethought and proper planning, they rarely see any possible pitfalls. As a result, they frequently fall into craters and go bankrupt. Of all the temperaments, they particularly need to remember this verse in Proverbs: "A prudent man foresees the difficulties ahead and prepares for them; the simpleton goes blindly on and suffers the consequences."[2] As one man said, "I am always chasing another dream. Sometimes I wish I could shake off this drive so I could find some peace."

For them to be better stewards of the financial resources God has entrusted to them, they must learn either to plan ahead or to network with someone who does. This includes planning for purchases and career changes, as well as budgeting and debt elimination. As Jesus said, "Suppose one of you wants to build a tower. Will he not first sit down and estimate the cost to see if he has enough money to complete it?"[3]

Faithful Givers

When reviewing the results of our financial testing, we noticed the most common positive financial habit listed by sanguines is tithing. Sanguines are usually faithful in this area of biblical stewardship. In fact, we have seen sanguines tithe and even give beyond tithing while owing creditors and remaining consistently behind on their bills. (Perhaps sometimes we subconsciously try to bribe God into bailing us out after we have messed up!) While tithing is certainly a biblical practice, paying taxes and bills on time is also important. The sanguines' desire to give must be controlled so that it doesn't cause them to neglect other obligations.

Sanguines are also soft-hearted and trusting and, therefore, are the most responsive to others' pleas for help. They will donate to a ministry, provide a loan for a relative, or even cosign a note. But sanguines should be cautious in responding to pleas for help. While there are genuine needs in the body of Christ and the world to which we should respond, we must be discerning and respond to the pleas to which God would have us respond. Sometimes bailing out an individual or a ministry can be detrimental to their long-term maturity.

Because the warm-hearted sanguine can be counted on whenever help is needed, this tendency can lead a family into severe financial difficulty if it is not controlled. It can drive spouses crazy and lead to a continual lack. One sanguine said, "I am currently unemployed but somehow always have enough to share with someone else."

One wife lamented, "My husband can't say no to anyone." A friend was in financial difficulty, so her sanguine husband "took a table saw off his hands." Shortly thereafter he shocked his wife by backing into the driveway with a horse trailer and two horses. She declared they had no place to put the horses and asked why on earth he bought them! Again the same story— "The guy needed a break, so I bought the horses." Sanguines must learn sometimes to say no even if it hurts.

God has not called us to give away money that we don't have or to help others when we can't pay our own bills. As Christians we have an obligation to pay our bills in a timely fashion. If we are giving money to needy causes while letting our bills go unpaid, we bring reproach to the name of Christ.

Sanguines are sometimes gullible and lack keen discernment into the character of others, so they are especially vulnerable to being conned. With this trait and their desire for approval, they should never be bill collectors. One sanguine we tested owned his own business but was unable to collect receivables from his clients because of his desire for approval. Combined with a high level of debt, his bankruptcy was inevitable.

A soft-hearted, fifty-eight-year-old sanguine we interviewed really got "taken for a ride." Unfortunately, she didn't get to enjoy the drive. She and her husband allowed a friend to talk them into charging tires for his eighteen-wheeler on their American Express card. They had previously loaned him money, and he had always repaid it. But this time he stuck them with a five thousand dollar debt. He didn't pay one penny of it and acted as though nothing had happened, never acknowledging the damage he had done.

She said every month they paid on that debt "was like opening the wound deeper and deeper....My spouse and I knew Proverbs 6:1-5 forwards and backwards. It warns against the folly of cosigning, and we wound up the fools. Bad debt, lost friendship after ten years, fussing between my husband and me over the loss, and being angry with ourselves. We knew better. We sowed folly and reaped folly."

The Danger of Debt

Sanguines, as much as any other temperament, must learn not to presume on the future. This is especially true for sanguines in sales or other careers where income can vary. When business or income is at its highest, we normally make our greatest financial mistakes. We assume our income will grow indefinitely and we'll always have it so good. But business, like the weather, tends to move in cycles. The time for grandiose spending is not after a big harvest, nor is it the time to acquire debt to finance those big plans. In reality, during times of great harvest we should continue to live our lives simply, putting back surpluses so that we will have provision for future times.

God's Word encourages us to save during good times so that we'll have extra to fall back on in lean times. But the optimistic nature of sanguines rarely allows them to see future problems, so they may spend everything they make based upon their present level of income. In our testing, sanguines had the largest credit card indebtedness of any temperament, with many owing as much as twenty-five thousand dollars, and some even more.

Sanguines Are Gift Givers

As you would expect, sanguines love to give gifts. Their love for people and generous nature, combined with their desire for others' approval, make them excellent gift givers. However, since sanguines are the temperament of excesses, they are particularly vulnerable to having their positive traits become problem traits. Like all other sanguine traits, this area must be governed by the Holy Spirit so that it doesn't become excessive.

A common remark from sanguines is they have learned they can't gain the love or approval of others by buying gifts. One stated, "I allowed the pressure of others and my world view to make me think that buying for others could make me and them happy." Sanguines, eager to regain the approval of their spouses after a fight, will frequently buy expensive gifts, even if the fight was about their overspending!

Like everyone else, sanguines must determine what motivates their behavior. If they find that their gift giving is prompted by self-seeking motives, such as gaining someone's approval, then they may reconsider what they are doing.

One sanguine man we interviewed learned this principle the hard way. He was in love. He wanted to prove his love for his fiancée, so he responded in the typical sanguine way—he bought her the biggest, most expensive engagement ring he could find. In addition to spending way too much on the ring, he failed to consider the cost of their long-distance relationship. As the combined expenses significantly deteriorated his financial position, he realized that she would have been just as happy with a ring that cost half as much.

Sanguines Enjoy Eating Out

The sanguines' impulsive nature combined with their frequent use of credit cards often causes them to spend much more than necessary when eating out. Something about putting it "on the plastic" leads them to think this type of overspending is no big deal. The attitude of many seems to be "I'll never get this credit card paid off anyway, so what's the difference?" or "If I have four thousand dollars charged on my Visa card, what's an extra twenty-five or fifty?" This type of thinking gets people, especially sanguines, into trouble as all those purchases add up.

Sanguines are quick to splurge on expensive restaurants or, when eating out in a group, to pick up the tab or to buy appetizers and desserts. This type of spending can easily run into hundreds of dollars per month.

Although there is virtue in being generous, sanguines often blow their budget since they tend to excesses.

Because of our fast-paced world and more women joining the work force outside the home, eating out has become a larger part of everyday American life. While eating out is much less trouble, it can be three to four times more expensive than eating at home. We all need to evaluate the impact of this habit on our budgets, but especially the sanguines since they are prone to spend excessively when they eat out.

Sanguines Hate Details

Sanguines are notoriously poor at recordkeeping because they hate details with a passion. That contributes to their tendency to overspend because they don't know how much money is in their bank account or what they owe in bills. Sanguines tested the highest—by a large margin—in not knowing where the money they spent last week had gone. If it weren't for their ability to make an excellent living, more sanguines would go broke. In fact, our survey indicates that more sanguines do go broke than any of the other temperaments.

With their dislike for details and their trusting nature, many sanguines rely on the bank's figures, instead of their own, in balancing their checkbooks. They may find themselves so burdened with uncompleted paperwork and forms that they feel they'll never have their check register in order. Instead of sorting out the paperwork, they frequently withdraw most of their money from one bank and deposit it in another. Then with their next statement from the old account, they can find out their balance. If it's lacking, they will pay it off, and if not, they will probably take what money remains and go celebrate. While other temperaments may find this approach to money management absurd, our studies show it is common among sanguines.

Since they are the least detail-oriented temperament, sanguines don't make good accountants. And they most often rely on others—their spouse, a friend, or an advisor—to tend to the details of financial planning.

Otherwise, the fly-by-the-seat-of-the-pants sanguines find themselves just one step ahead of the creditors. Unless there is help and discipline, the lack of attention to budgeting, balancing the checkbook, and recordkeeping will keep the family's finances in disarray.

Prescriptions for Sanguines

To combat their impulsive, fun-loving, trusting nature, sanguines should make some shopping rules.

1. Never buy anything over ten dollars on the spur of the moment. Plan your purchases and ask God to direct your spending. You will be led either by God or by your human nature. And your human nature, if given full rein, will spend you right into the poorhouse. Resist the desire to spend impulsively, and instead learn to plan ahead.

Many couples have committed not to spend more than a certain pre-set limit—perhaps as little as five dollars or as much as fifty—without first consulting each other. This immediately stops most impulse spending. When we "submit to one another" as we are directed in Ephesians 5:21, we find much better balance. Husbands and wives work better as a team when both partners are rowing the boat in the same direction. Submitting to one another in financial decisions promotes greater harmony in the home and a better stewardship of the resources God has given.

2. Never purchase anything with a credit card. Many sanguines have learned to combat their impulsive nature by no longer using credit cards. Research has found that, on the average, people spend 34 percent more when using a credit card, even if they pay the balance off every month! The temptation to buy on the "easy payment credit plan" normally makes us spend more on items that we would never buy if we had to save ahead of time for them.

Sanguines should begin to save money for the things they intend to purchase. By saving a little at a time, they will eventually have the money they need. As Proverbs 13:11 says, "He who gathers money little by little makes it grow." This is also an excellent way to develop more self-control.

And it solves two other problems. Once we have saved our hard-earned money and delayed gratification, we may find we really don't need or want the item after all. We can then use those resources in more fruitful ways. And, by forcing ourselves to save for every major purchase, we may find a comparable item which costs much less than the intended purchase. As we become more watchful over our spending, we will search for bargains and sales. By shopping seasonally, we can save 20 to 50 percent on most purchases, and we will save even more by not paying 18 to 21 percent interest on our purchases.

3. Become accountable to somebody. Sanguines tend to justify their actions rather than face their weaknesses. Corrective criticism is regarded as disapproval and fended off. But as Proverbs 27:6 says, "Wounds from a friend can be trusted." Each of us must allow others to bring corrective insights to us concerning our own nature. Sanguines especially must be willing to allow their lives to be laid open for examination by godly friends who love them and have their best interests at heart.

A wise businessman, fully recognizing his sanguine weaknesses, hired the right people to make him successful. He had a choleric do his collections and a melancholy to keep his books. He followed the advice of another fellow sanguine who declared, "Don't be embarrassed to ask as many people as possible for the most sound advice when dealing with money. Listen carefully, and do not make decisions on the spur of the moment." That says it all. Having accountability to God and to others who are strong in this area can be the greatest financial asset to sanguines.

4. Pray about all spending plans. Ask God for guidance before you act. Ask in faith, believe, and act accordingly (more on this in chapter 11). If we find an item is really necessary and deserves the investment of the precious resources that God has entrusted to us, we can buy it with a clear conscience, certain we have done our very best to be good stewards of the Lord's money.

5. Learn to wait on the Lord. To combat the natural tendency to buy impulsively and make quick decisions, sanguines must learn to wait on the Lord. We must understand we are not our own. We were bought with a price, and all that we have is His. Our money is His money—not just 10 percent, but all of it.

Waiting on the Lord means we surrender our will to His. We must be willing to die to our earthly desires, goals, and objectives, and accept His desires for us. While this cuts across our natural grain, it will fulfill us and sustain us far better than our own actions and plans ever could. God sometimes makes us wait on things to build godly character into our lives. For a sanguine, this often means delaying a purchase until the right time—God's time.

If the Lord has not provided money to pay cash for something, He may be saying no to that purchase. To truly be His obedient children, we must be willing to obey, even when He says no. Waiting on the Lord can save a lot of money.

6. Develop more self-control. Self-control is one of the fruit of the Spirit: "the fruit of the Spirit is love, joy, peace, patience, kindness, goodness, faithfulness, gentleness and self-control....Those who belong to Christ Jesus have crucified the sinful nature with its passions and desires. Since we live by the Spirit, let us keep in step with the Spirit."[4] As in other areas of our lives, we must exercise self-control over our purchasing decisions, large and small.

When we crucify our sinful natures, we no longer live by its desires but by God's. This means we must get to the point where we are neutral as to the outcome of the matter. Then we should ask God to show us His will. As we submit ourselves in a deeper way to Christ and His discipline, and as we submit our daily decisions to Him and follow Him with all of our hearts, we will see our desires begin to change. No longer will we be driven by our flesh. When His desires become our desires, we are submitting to the headship of Christ in all areas of our lives. "In the house of the wise are stores of choice food and oil, but a foolish man devours all he has."[5]

7. Plan ahead. All in all, sanguines are the most likely of the temperaments to find themselves in financial difficulties, and we literally mean find themselves. Since sanguines rarely plan ahead, they are truly surprised when their spending gets them into trouble.

Planning usually saves a bundle, especially when you consider all the money we spend over a lifetime. We should pray about the direction and timing and then make the best decision we can. Planning is easier when done in conjunction with a spouse, especially a melancholy spouse.

As Proverbs 21:5 says, "The plans of the diligent lead to profit as surely as haste leads to poverty." If we are diligent in planning our future, our purchases, our savings, and our investments, then our plans should lead to profit.

8. *Take encouragement from Peter.* While God may have created sanguines with certain tendencies, He didn't say they had to be controlled by them. Let's take another look at the sanguine with whom we began this chapter—the Apostle Peter. Peter, who was as unstable as water, was renamed by the Lord in anticipation of his being filled, empowered, and changed by the work of the Holy Spirit. This volatile extrovert became Petros, "the solid rock." Once God transformed him, Peter became a man of character and peaceful moderation—a faithful, prayerful, courageous man of God. Steadfast in God's ways and courageous even unto martyrdom, Peter gave all the glory to God.

It is no coincidence that Peter had some outstanding things to say about transforming our natures: "Make every effort to add to your faith goodness; and to goodness, knowledge; and to knowledge, self-control; and to self-control, perseverance; and to perseverance, godliness; and to godliness, brotherly kindness; and to brotherly kindness, love."[6]

The transformation in Peter's life should encourage every sanguine. God used the oratory skills and the natural strengths of Peter to build and empower the early church. But God also worked in Peter's life to change his weaknesses and flaws into strengths. Just as He did for Peter, God desires to use our natural strengths and replace our weaknesses with His strengths.

CHAPTER FOUR

Cholerics:

The Movers and Shakers

"If I have the gift of prophecy and can fathom all mysteries and all knowledge, and if I have a faith that can move mountains, but have not love, I am nothing."

1 CORINTHIANS 13:2

As a young man, Jim knew exactly what he wanted out of life. He wanted to be successful and to retire in style by his early forties. He met a rather passive young woman, set up house, and began to steamroll through life.

He worked long hours, longer than anyone else around him. He did whatever it took to climb the corporate ladder. Those who worked for him continually felt the pressure of his conquering spirit. They were driven to be the best achievers, with very little reward. His sarcasm made his co-workers back away, and his kindness appeared only to be a means to an end.

Home life for his wife was dark indeed. She had no input into future plans and lived in fear of Jim's dying. She knew nothing about their finances. He told her what to spend and how to spend it. He queried her on every little expenditure.

She watched as her husband got sucked into several get-rich-quick schemes. Then he started a business on his own, risking all of their savings. If she had not threatened to leave him, he would have mortgaged the house also.

He went to his corporate job during the day and then slaved nights and weekends trying to keep his own business afloat. He realized almost too late that he should have taken his losses and gotten out, but he just couldn't let go. He could not admit failure.

When almost all was lost, he pulled out of his own business and was promoted to vice president of his corporate division. It required a change of location but that was okay. The opportunity to reach his goal was set before him. It was now or never.

As always, this diligent worker found himself in a profit position again. He began to save and invest his money. He saw his opportunity for the big break by trading in the commodity futures market. In a short while his losses totaled tens of thousands of dollars. Again he found himself behind in his goal. The clock was ticking. Forty was behind him.

Although he began to have nagging health problems, he ignored them and pressed on toward his goal. And he reached it, a little later than expected, yet still young for most people to retire.

Once retired, he took stock of his life. His children no longer lived at home. They had become self-centered and demanding and had little interest in helping others. Where had they learned that? And his wife had long ago developed her own interests.

Finally, his health failed. He had three heart attacks. Now this man, who had spent his life, family, and his health to get wealth was spending all of his hard earned money simply to stay alive.

What Is a Choleric?

Cholerics are quick, active, practical, strong-willed, self-sufficient, and very independent. In any relationship or situation, they will be the ones to take control. They tend to be decisive and opinionated, making decisions both for themselves and others. Like sanguines, cholerics are extroverts but are not quite as outgoing.

Cholerics thrive on activity. They do not need to be stimulated by their environment but rather stimulate their environment with their endless ideas, plans, goals, and ambitions. They do not engage in aimless activity but rather invest their practical, keen minds in planning worthwhile projects. They do not vacillate under the pressure of what others think but take definite stands on issues and can often be found crusading against some social injustice. Cholerics are not frightened by adversities; in fact, adversities tend to encourage them, which usually allows them to succeed where others would fail.

Invariably they seek utilitarian and productive values in life. Not given to analysis, but rather to quick, almost intuitive appraisal, cholerics tend to look at the goal for which they are working, without recognizing the potential pitfalls and obstacles in the path. Once they have started toward their goal, they may run roughshod over anyone who stands in the way. They tend to be domineering and bossy and do not hesitate to use people to accomplish their ends. They are often considered opportunists. In essence, cholerics can get so blinded by the goal of getting the best buy, making the most money, or getting the best deal, that they sacrifice relationships.

The cholerics' emotional nature is the least developed part of their temperament. They are not sensitive to the needs of others and so do not sympathize easily, nor do they naturally express compassion. In fact, they often are embarrassed or disgusted by others' tears. They reflect little appreciation for music and the fine arts, unless their secondary temperament trait is melancholy.

The Choleric Paul

The most obvious biblical illustration of the choleric temperament is Paul. Before his conversion, he was Saul, possibly a member of the Sanhedrin. At the stoning of Stephen, the first recorded Christian martyr, the accusers laid Stephen's clothes at the feet of Saul. Many have suggested this indicates Saul's leadership of the group. He was a zealot with a cause who demonstrated his passion by persecuting the church. He was strong-willed, self-sufficient, and willing to kill for his cause.

God had to supernaturally bring Saul to his knees in one devastating blow. God struck him blind. Since cholerics see exactly where they are going and depend on no one but themselves, God hit Saul where it counted. Suddenly, this self-reliant young man had to depend on his companions literally to lead him by the hand to Damascus. Saul's independent days were over, and he had learned a great lesson: Unless God leads, you may see, but you are really blind.

Saul became Paul and threw himself wholeheartedly into his new cause, eventually enduring floggings, imprisonment, and shipwrecks because of it. In him, we have a blazing example of the power of a person sold out to God. After his conversion, he remained the epitome of self-discipline and self-control. He declared, "No, I beat my body and make it my slave so that after I have preached to others, I myself will not be disqualified for the prize."[1] He understood every thought and action had to be "brought into captivity" in obedience to Christ. Strong willpower, decisiveness, and high motivation made this choleric apostle a dynamic and powerful leader.

Obviously, Paul was not a perfect Christian; he experienced failure too. However, he was willing to give his life to reach the goal set before him. This is a common thread for cholerics: When they choose a cause, they are willing to die for it.

Strengths and Weaknesses

Goal-oriented Visionaries

Cholerics are the true visionaries in life. They see what can be done, and they proceed full steam ahead to do it. With all their hearts they believe "where there is no vision, the people perish."[2] If you want something accomplished, ask a choleric to do it. With their incredible leadership ability, they are the "movers and shakers" of this world.

Cholerics who have visions of being financially successful and debt-free often are in the best financial condition of anyone. One choleric man we interviewed had, in his twenties, designed a detailed and stringent plan for retiring early. At the age of forty-nine, he had completed every goal on his list and retired in relative comfort.

It's typical for cholerics to begin working at a young age, and if they learn good money habits then, those habits will stay with them throughout life. One choleric we know made pot holders and peddled them in her neighborhood at the age of ten. Another young man began providing his own clothing and school supplies while in the sixth grade and continued to do so throughout junior high, high school, and college.

Cholerics can suffer every kind of tragedy, setback, or failure and bounce back because they are always looking forward, striving toward the goal before them. Their life's verse could be Philippians 3:13-14: "But one thing I do: Forgetting what is behind and straining toward what is ahead, I press on toward the goal to win the prize for which God has called me heavenward in Christ Jesus." Obstacles may provide an opportunity to change course, but, for cholerics, they are no reason to quit. Although many cholerics said they had never faced a financial crisis and their financial affairs were in order, they also shared a series of tragedies they had overcome.

As a youngster, one choleric woman we interviewed had saved enough money to go to college. Using that money, she completed her freshman and sophomore years without any additional financial assistance. In her junior year when she went to the bank to withdraw money for the next semester, she discovered her parents had been "borrowing" money from her account and using it for themselves. Unfortunately, they didn't have the money to repay her, so she had to make it on her own again. True to the choleric's nature, she did make it on her own. She worked her way through college, accomplished her goal, and obtained her degree.

Cholerics are able to weather almost any financial storm because once they decide to get their finances in order, they are as tenacious as bulldogs. One choleric woman commented, "If I feel we are getting too tight on money, then I pull in the credit cards and insist we pay off everything. I really hate being in debt. Besides our house and car payment, I am always figuring out how to get the bills paid. I get a lot of satisfaction when I can pay off any bill." Many cholerics establish short- and long-term plans to most efficiently manage their money. They will find the shortest path to pay all their bills, including the mortgage. Although cholerics have weaknesses in their temperament that often cause severe trials, cholerics also tend to have the greatest testimonies of God's deliverance simply because they weather such great tests.

When choleric women become widows and discover their husbands were not frugal, they are often able to become debt-free quickly. One woman said, "My husband has been dead for seven years. I sold our properties and paid off all bills. I used what was left and the insurance money to remodel my home and to buy a car. I now am debt-free and have enough income to get by on. Social Security provides enough for me to get my BS degree in education." In typical choleric fashion, she had the determination to overcome all obstacles even after her husband's death.

While cholerics' goal orientation is a positive trait, it can also create difficulties in their marriages. Cholerics commonly demand a dollar-for-dollar accounting of their spouse's spending. One wife of a choleric said she couldn't even buy a tube of lipstick without first getting permission. As one choleric husband admitted, "I want to know what she wants ten dollars for." Even the smallest amount his wife spends affects his ultimate goal.

One choleric man we interviewed had been in business for many years and had faced financial losses and even divorce. When we asked him to describe the greatest failure in his life, he mentioned a missed opportunity—not his divorce, not any of several serious setbacks. He described in great detail how much he regretted his failure to enter the construction business after World War II. He believed that if he had gone into construction at that particular time it would have made him a very wealthy man. Cholerics are constantly looking for the opportunity of a lifetime.

Cholerics Are Practical

As stated before, cholerics are highly practical and utilitarian. If you want to make them happy, give them a gift they can use. If you want to absolutely dumbfound them, give them something useless. One choleric wife we talked to had received a "sleep machine." No matter how hard she tried to use it, every "soothing" noise sounded like racket and static to her, so she exchanged it for a warm, useful sweater. If you really want to please cholerics, just give them the money, and let them pick out what they want because you aren't likely to please them anyway.

A friend of ours confessed that his practical, opinionated, choleric nature got the better of him last Christmas. As the family was exchanging gifts, one of the children received a toy with lots of small, plastic parts. Before our friend could stop himself, he blurted out, "Great! A million tiny parts to step on in the carpet!"

They Reach Their Potential

Combining their vision and practicality, most cholerics reach their full potential. You won't often find cholerics on the welfare rolls. If they are forced to receive aid, they won't do so indefinitely. One young, single mother had to take refuge in a home for battered women and accept assistance rather than let her children starve. However, she concentrated on putting her life back together and was totally self-supporting within three months.

One choleric man we know survived the depression by standing in line, watching other carpenters pound nails, while saying to the foreman, "See that man over there? I can work harder and faster than he can." As a result of his drive and his willingness to work harder than anyone else, he got the jobs and was able to feed his family.

Cholerics Are Self-sufficient

If this book depended upon obtaining information from the time-conscious choleric, we would not be writing anything. Cholerics do not have time for financial surveys, interviews, or any other human interest function. They have people to see and places to go—yesterday! Many began our interviews by declaring, "You've got ten minutes." We solved this problem partially by interviewing their spouses, who not only had time to talk with us but were often thankful for the conversation we added to their lives.

The more successful that cholerics become, the more their self-sufficiency is revealed. They are often considered loners. One choleric woman stated, "I'd absolutely rather do things alone. Nobody meets my expectations." Their self-sufficiency does not allow them to seek the counsel of others. With their desire to remain in control, they usually have the attitude of "I can do it better myself," and they will do it until they run full force into a brick wall.

The cholerics' self-sufficiency exacts its highest toll in marriage. Unless they have had really good training on marriage, cholerics tend to be non-communicative and anger-driven people who frequently do not make great spouses. Beyond all other temperaments, over and over the cholerics we interviewed declared their worst financial disaster was when they got divorced. Many times the spouse could not accept being "locked out" of the choleric's life. On the other hand, the choleric didn't know anything was wrong because the spouse was afraid to confront him or her. And the choleric couldn't understand the spouse's viewpoint anyway. After all, cholerics do whatever is necessary to be good providers, even working two or three jobs at times. Their philosophy is if they work harder, they will make it. While having a work ethic is positive, life must be balanced. Not only is divorce catastrophic personally, but it is catastrophic financially, and cholerics are all too vulnerable to it.

Cholerics may discuss financial decisions with their spouses but make their own decisions anyway. One choleric man "talked" with his wife about purchasing a neighbor's five hundred dollar canoe. By the end of the discussion, the wife thought they had agreed not to buy it. To her dismay, within a week she realized the canoe was no longer in her neighbor's yard but in her own. The husband couldn't understand why his wife was so upset; they had the money to buy the boat. He didn't understand that he had violated her trust. She thought they were partners who would communicate with each other before making such a purchase. Ironically, this same choleric requires his wife to clip coupons to save twenty-five cents on a bottle of shampoo.

Another choleric husband unilaterally decided to spend $250 on a basketball hoop. When he brought it home, his wife became really angry. His response was, "I don't have to ask anyone how I can spend my money!" When the spouse is ignored in financial decisions, problems in the marriage are inevitable.

When wives of cholerics are asked to describe their greatest financial fear, they quickly respond, "If my husband dies, I am afraid I will have no financial solutions for my household." True to their self-sufficiency, many choleric husbands fail to prepare their wives for handling the finances after their death.

Cholerics' self-sufficiency may even affect their relationship with God. One choleric woman declared, "Sometimes it is easier to trust myself than to trust God." Indeed, God often must bring them to complete destitution before they will cry out to Him for help. One woman we surveyed became a Christian only after her fifteen-year-old child was killed in a horrible accident.

Cholerics Have High Expectations

Cholerics have high expectations of themselves and everyone around them, an attitude that seems to be partially responsible for many of their divorces. While high expectations can be a positive motivation, cholerics expect everyone else to be just as efficient and driven and capable as they are. Since other temperaments aren't like that, cholerics have difficulty accepting them. And as the cholerics continue to drive their spouses as hard as they drive themselves, their spouses often refuse to live under this kind of pressure.

One fifty-year-old man stated, "I am learning a lot about bondage. Being a workaholic, I realize how much it is cutting into my family life." Cholerics, in particular, need to realize there is more to life than money and power so that they don't lose their relationships along the way.

Since cholerics have such high expectations about every area of life, it should be no surprise that this extends to their finances, too. For cholerics, it is often important that their financial successes are reflected in the things they wear, their cars, and their houses. They want people to note their success.

These high expectations often carry over into investment performance. If cholerics hire an investment manager or invest in a mutual fund, they will expect to get the highest performance available, even though this is not always possible since all investments go through cycles.

Their Problem with Anger

One choleric woman we know had a set of bookcases built. As the cases were being designed, she made her Christianity known to the contractor. But when the bookcases were delivered, several things did not meet her choleric specifications. Before she could control her anger, this choleric called the contractor and flew into a verbal rage. After she hung up, she began to realize what a poor testimony she had given to her Christianity—the man's soul was worth much more than the fifty dollars she was arguing over. So she tearfully called him to repent. She now has a bookcase as a daily reminder of what God thinks of her anger and her fifty dollars. That woman is Mona Tuma.

In our testing, cholerics often admitted anger. One woman with an exceptionally bad temper was given an expensive boat. She then spent enormous sums of money refurbishing it. She described in minute detail the exact color for the pinstripes. When she returned to check on the boat, she discovered the color of the pinstripes was off just a bit. She blew her fuse and declared she would never ride in that boat as long as she lived.

If restaurants serve bad food to cholerics, they will be the first to send it back with a loud and long explanation. If you waste cholerics' time or show any form of inadequacy or ineptness, they will tell you in no uncertain terms. Combining their anger with their tendency to be cruel and sarcastic, cholerics have a way of upsetting everyone around them. So they may find themselves continually mending fences.

Just Get There—Now!

As we said earlier, cholerics are visionaries. However, these people of great vision can often find themselves ensnared by get-rich-quick schemes, unstable franchises, limited partnerships, speculative investments, and futures markets because they also have a "Get there now!" mentality. The end justifies the means, and they want to get to the end fast!

Many cholerics declared they had great visions for the future and were willing to go to the limit to finance those visions. They also admitted their potential for destroying their dreams by taking risks and assuming debts. Cholerics, like sanguines, have a history of high debt. Some cholerics we tested have as much as fifty thousand dollars in credit card debt alone! Some owe banks millions of dollars. The reason behind their debt? Spending money and risking debt are justifiable means to reaching their ultimate goal.

In our testing, rarely did any temperament other than a choleric mention investing in speculative markets. The cholerics' comments indicate the downside of this trait. Said one respondent, "I invested twenty thousand dollars in commodity futures and lost half of it." One farmer who had invested in the futures market to protect himself in the event of a severe drought said, "Since 1984, my losses versus my gains have exceeded a hundred twenty thousand dollars."

When cholerics think they see a good deal, they will jump right into it before considering the whole cost. Another choleric farmer bought additional land because he envisioned a much larger farm. He nearly lost everything because the market dropped and interest rates went sky-high.

A common crisis among cholerics occurred when they decided they wanted a new house. Rather than waiting until their old house sold, most would purchase and move into a new one. They either expected the house to sell or decided to live with the headaches of renting it in the meantime. Instead, they often found themselves with two house payments.

In addition to these extremes, cholerics need to be aware of blowing their budgets in little things, such as long-distance phone calls and eating out. Cholerics hate to write letters because it takes time and there is no immediate feedback. One choleric suggested, "I wish the phone company could keep a running total of my charges so when I get close to my budget amount, I could just stop." Since preparing a meal takes too much time, they would rather eat out. In our testing, many cholerics responded that eating out was their worst money habit.

Always on the Move

Never content with what is happening around them, cholerics demand change. They change their lifestyles. They excel to greater heights. They are always on the move, which can be financially devastating. One choleric who found his business in trouble explained, "We made too many moves at one time. We moved to a new and larger building, hired another person, leased another vehicle—all in one year. Then the business slowed down. We learned not to take too many steps at one time and to keep a closer watch." Another man assumed a debt of more than sixty thousand dollars to acquire an existing business, although he had no previous experience in operating such a business. He just thought it was a good deal. All good things take time, and if cholerics allow themselves to do too much too fast, they can dig themselves into a deep hole.

A young pastor at a board meeting had just outlined very aggressive building plans and other church programs when one of the older board members reminded him that Rome wasn't built in a day. This choleric pastor's response: "Yes, but I wasn't foreman on that crew!" That pastor was Tim LaHaye.

Their Attitude toward Giving

Unlike melancholies who must give the perfect gift, cholerics consider time their most valuable asset. Therefore, shopping for gifts is merely a task which must be finished, and quickly. They also believe that what is good for one is good for all. A choleric Christmas shopper may leave a store with his arms full of the same gift for everyone on the list.

Cholerics may stockpile money, putting their trust in it rather than in God. Said one choleric we interviewed, "My worst money habit is that I tend to hoard money, and at times I find my security in dollars instead of in God." For this reason, it is difficult for them to spend money on other people.

Unless cholerics have the secondary temperament of sanguine, they find tithing extremely difficult. Typically cholerics tithe on what is left after paying the bills. Only when cholerics are absolutely convinced they are following God's command and must give to receive God's blessings will they be faithful in tithing.

Prescriptions for Cholerics

1. Learn to walk in love. Interestingly, a choleric wrote 1 Corinthians 13, the greatest chapter on love. Paul knew from personal experience that love is the most important characteristic for a choleric to acquire.

First Corinthians 13:1 says, "If I speak in the tongues of men and of angels, but have not love, I am only a resounding gong or a clanging cymbal." Cholerics can be gongs and cymbals. They tend to justify their bulldog tenacity by believing the end justifies the means, but Paul declares that love must be the controlling factor in a Christian's life, including the choleric's life.

When cholerics weigh all of their actions on the scales of love, they will see their lives come into incredible balance. One choleric who admitted to a very poor marriage said, "In dealing with relationships, either business or personal, it is important to communicate and know what the other one needs. Love communicates. Love lays down its life for the other person. Love is patient. That kind of love keeps cholerics from jumping ahead of themselves and perhaps jeopardizing their family's financial security. Love waits. Love is not inflexible."

Love is patient and kind. This will keep cholerics' anger under control so they do not destroy their Christian testimony with their mouths.

Love is not proud. Love doesn't desire power or position.

Love is not self-seeking. Love wants to know what the other person thinks and desires. Love communicates.

2. Make people a priority over goals. Although the following scripture is taken a bit out of context, the principle is an important one for cholerics to remember. Matthew 19:30 says, "Many who are first will be last, and many who are last will be first." Cholerics are often the ones speeding down the track while everyone else is eating their dust. If they are unable to slow down and bring other people with them as they meet their goals, they will have truly failed in the long run.

3. Learn to be patient. Patience is a virtue in every aspect of life but especially so in handling money. Impatience normally will lead us to take more risks than we should or acquire more debt than we should in order to reach our goals more quickly. And it is one of the most dangerous aspects of cholerics' temperament concerning money.

4. Beware of greed. Because of the cholerics' impatient nature, they may succumb to greed. Learn to recognize when risk is too high. Learn to bounce ideas off other people who are not cholerics. Simply let them look at the opportunity without having any input from you, and allow them to give you their opinion. Then listen. This may keep you in balance and prevent trouble in the long run.

5. Along with your spouse, set reasonable limitations for the various areas of your budget. Then delegate the shopping to the spouse who is most willing to take the time to shop frugally. Because cholerics are so determined not to waste time, they often end up spending more money simply because it is the fastest solution. Either learn to develop frugality and take more time to shop wisely, or delegate the responsibility to another person in your family who will.

6. Don't compromise on what is right for expediency's sake. Cholerics tend to cut corners in order to save time. Although as Christians cholerics don't want to do anything which is illegal, immoral, or unethical, they may find that bending a rule a little bit is easier than going to extreme lengths to ensure that all requirements have been fulfilled. One unfortunate result of all of these seemingly small compromises is that the children may lose respect for their high-roller choleric parent. In the children's minds, if their parent did it a little, why can't they do it a lot? Take the time to do things right and avoid problems down the road.

7. Involve your spouse in your financial dealings. Since cholerics like to be in control, they must learn to slow down and listen to their spouses. Pray with and involve your spouse in your plans and financial decisions. You will not only have a much more fulfilling relationship, you will also make better business decisions because your mate can see your weaknesses and can help you with your blind spots. As spouses submit to each other, they will achieve God's proper balance.

8. Stay out of debt and avoid risky business ventures. Typically, cholerics are supremely confident of their own abilities and, therefore, sometimes shoot themselves in the foot. Avoiding high risk business ventures will allow you to keep more of what you earn and may prevent you from having to start over every few years. The Living Bible states this clearly in Ecclesiastes 5:13-17: "There is another serious problem I have seen everywhere—savings are put into risky investments that turn sour, and soon there is nothing left to pass on to one's son. The man who speculates is soon back to where he began—with nothing. This, as I said, is a very serious problem, for all his hard work has been for nothing; he has been working for the wind. It is all swept away. All the rest of his life he is under a cloud—gloomy, discouraged, frustrated, and angry."

9. Be motivated by eternal values. Colossians 3:2 exhorts us "to set your affection on things above, not on things on the earth." Since cholerics are especially goal oriented, they need to be careful not to allow their own earthly financial goals to become the driving force of their lives. We must remember to keep God's values first. For example, one choleric donated five million dollars toward the production of the Jesus film, which has been translated into over seventy languages and, according to estimates, has been responsible for half a billion decisions for Christ. Even though he suffered financial reversals later, he had the satisfaction of knowing he had made an investment in God's kingdom.

10. Beware of pride. Cholerics are especially tempted to overestimate their own wisdom and not listen to others, which can lead to poor financial decisions. Pride is particularly dangerous when the stakes are higher, as in investments and major business decisions. Cholerics need to remember that pride causes them not just to resist human wisdom but God himself: "God resisteth the proud, and giveth grace to the humble."[3]

CHAPTER FIVE

Melancholies:

Balancing It to the Penny

"For God did not give us a spirit of timidity, but a spirit of power, of love and of self-discipline."

2 TIMOTHY 1:7

Sitting in her new apartment, Janet was enjoying the moment. Beautiful music surrounded her. Her favorite books were stacked neatly on the shelf. True, she only had one chair in her little living room, but it was the best money could buy. She would rather do without than live with a discount store imitation.

She had just landed her first job. How she loved lining up those wonderful numbers in a row. What satisfaction she derived from each balanced column. Yes, she would enjoy this job, just as long as her boss did not expect too much from her. She hated challenges that didn't have an absolutely observable outcome.

Her boss quickly gave her a raise. He wanted to keep this diligent worker. The company's finances had never been so ordered. All the accounts were up to date. No project was too much to ask of her. Plus, she dressed exceptionally well. From her earrings to her shoes, every inch of her was scrubbed and well manicured. What a jewel he had found.

Then Janet met a wonderful man—attractive, outgoing, the life of the party, in fact, everything she was not. She was drawn to him like a magnet. He was funny and romantic. He planned extravagant outings. So what if she ended up helping him pay? For the first time she was happy.

The wedding was beautiful. Her dress was beautiful, covered in pearls just as she had dreamed. She spared no expense. In fact, it cost her most of her savings, but after all she was only going to get married once in life. What if she felt guilty as she walked down the aisle? It was worth it.

Three months later, she wondered what had possessed her to marry this irresponsible man. He made a good living, but he spent every dime he made. Even with their two incomes, each month they just barely covered their bills and made the house payment.

Then she discovered she was pregnant. She had trouble with the pregnancy, so the medical bills piled high and she was forced to quit her job. Fear absolutely drove her to distraction. She worried about everything. She couldn't even sleep at night for fear of what the future might hold.

Her fear made her even more critical of her husband. He told her he would take care of the money, but he would forget to pay the electric bill. He used credit cards, spending money they did not have. One morning she went to make a telephone call, and the phone had been cut off.

After her husband had had enough of her complaining, he decided to let her manage the money. As she began to sift through the shoe box full of receipts, she wondered how could this have happened to her organized world. Bank statements hadn't been reconciled in months, and to her shock, they were thousands of dollars in debt. Never in all her life would she have believed she could be in such a mess. She wanted to die. She saw no way out.

What Is a Melancholy?

Melancholies are the richest of all the temperaments. They are analytical, self-sacrificing, gifted perfectionists with a sensitive emotional nature. Because they can sense and understand other people's emotions, they often make good counselors.

No one gets more enjoyment from the fine arts than they do. They appreciate beauty and esoteric values, are often musically inclined, and are usually very intelligent. Occasionally, in a mood of emotional ecstasy or inspiration, melancholies may produce some great work of art or genius, but these accomplishments are often followed by periods of great depression.

In addition to being analytical, they are detail oriented, so they make wonderful computer programmers, accountants, or engineers—anything requiring detailed analysis. Their analytical minds diagnose accurately the obstacles and dangers of any project they have a part in planning. However, this trait also makes them reticent to initiate a new project or puts them in conflict with those who do.

By nature, they are prone to be introverts, but since their feelings predominate, they are given to a variety of moods. Sometimes these moods will lift them to heights of ecstasy that cause them to act more extroverted. However, at other times they will be gloomy and depressed, and during these periods they become withdrawn and can be quite antagonistic.

Melancholies make faithful friends, but unlike sanguines, they do not make friends easily. They seldom push themselves forward to meet people, but rather let others come to them. They are perhaps the most dependable of all the temperaments, for their perfectionistic and conscientious tendencies do not permit them to be shirkers or to let others down. Their reticence to put themselves forward is often taken as an indication that they don't enjoy people. However, they not only like others but have a strong desire to be loved by them. It's just that they find it difficult to express their true feelings. Disappointing experiences make them reluctant to take people at face value, so they are prone to be suspicious when others seek them out or shower them with attention.

Melancholies spend more time planning than anyone else. As a matter of fact, they often carry this strength so far it becomes a weakness. They will plan for days, finding the easiest and most efficient way to accomplish any task. And the job will be done extremely well—when it is finally done.

Melancholies usually find their greatest meaning in life through personal sacrifice. They seem desirous of making themselves suffer and will often choose a difficult life vocation that involves great personal sacrifice. They may even take a reduction in salary for humanitarian reasons. One woman we interviewed was offered a job at several thousand dollars less than her current salary. For any other temperament, the decision would have been made right then. But they appealed to her altruism. They needed a strong secretary to compensate for the deficiencies of an aging man who was gradually being replaced. Because she is so relationship oriented, once she knew the circumstances, she was torn between wanting to protect this man and meeting her own financial needs.

Once a vocation is chosen, melancholies are prone to be thorough and persistent in pursuing it and more than likely will accomplish great good if their natural tendency to gripe throughout the sacrificial process doesn't get them so depressed that they give up altogether. No temperament has so much natural potential when energized by the Holy Spirit as the melancholy.

The Melancholy Moses

The most obvious biblical character with melancholy traits was Moses. In the books of Leviticus, Numbers, and Deuteronomy, Moses recorded God's detailed instructions regarding the tabernacle, the priests' robes, and the exact way gold would overlay the wood. Obviously, the Lord chose an extremely detail-minded person to instruct. Heaven help us if he had asked a sanguine to follow these instructions. A sanguine would have said, "Hey, guys, let's have some fun. How about we build a tabernacle!" with no advance planning and little attention to detail.

God also used Moses to lay down the law for His people. Melancholies can be rigid, and sometimes legalistic, Christians. With their perfectionistic nature, they will almost always abide by the law, making the law much stronger than it really is. It is no coincidence that the Lord used Moses to lay down the law for the people of Israel.

Another interesting aspect of Moses' character was low self-esteem. Despite their capabilities, melancholies have difficulty accepting new challenges and facing new tasks because they typically have the lowest self-image of any temperament. Apparently Moses had this problem after his forty-year respite in the desert tending sheep. God personally chose Moses from millions of people to deliver the Israelites from the hands of the Egyptians. He knew Moses had the necessary character and traits to execute the task, yet Moses repeatedly told God he couldn't handle the job. If Moses had so much trouble with his self-esteem, then certainly we're not exempt.

While Moses had a number of negative characteristics, he was ultimately successful in accomplishing the task God had given him. The children of Israel were delivered from Pharaoh and brought into the promised land although Moses couldn't accompany them. When controlled by the Holy Spirit, melancholies can be one of the most effective tools the Lord uses to accomplish His purposes. Yet, when paralyzed by their own weaknesses, they can become almost completely debilitated. Yes, Moses was definitely a melancholy.

Strengths and Weaknesses

Melancholies Can Budget

The temperament with the greatest natural financial strengths and the greatest ability to control spending is the melancholy. It is, by nature, the most self-disciplined and detailed of all the temperaments.

It is the most likely temperament to budget successfully over the long run. Sanguines can't possibly follow a budget (so they say) because they are impulsive, dislike details, and can always find something more fun to do with their time. Phlegmatics rarely get around to budgeting. Cholerics, like sanguines, just buy what they want because planning and following a budget take too much time. Melancholies, however, enjoy the detailed analysis of developing a budget. Being introspective by nature, they like determining where they spend their money, so they generally manage their checkbook well, even to the point of balancing it to the penny. Their disciplined nature allows them also to follow a budget rather easily by regulating their spending and avoiding exceeding their income.

Melancholies Battle Fear

On the down side, no other temperament battles fear as intensely as the melancholy, who can become absolutely paralyzed by it. This fearfulness often causes melancholies to sell themselves short in their career goals. They may even perform below their capabilities, perhaps at barely acceptable levels, because they are afraid they can't handle additional responsibilities. Since they always see the negatives in a job, they will frequently choose to remain in a less demanding position because they are comfortable there.

The melancholies' fear of the unknown and the desire for security will not let them take advantage of a new business opportunity, even when it is staring them in the face. Even if the opportunity is in their chosen field or with their present employer, they may fail to go for it for fear of making a wrong decision. In order to reach their potential in career goals and salary, melancholies require encouragement.

Because of their fear, melancholies take few risks with their money. They are afraid of the unknown. They are afraid of whatever they can't control. What if something happens to adversely affect the investments? So they may be content to leave their money in a guaranteed account which earns only 3 percent interest—even though they may not need it for thirty years—because their security is not threatened. Even though they may not be making any money because of inflation, they aren't losing any either.

Analysis Paralysis

A strength of melancholies is that they usually make good decisions about purchases because they take so long to analyze them. The other side of the coin is that because of their penchant for thorough analysis and perfection, melancholies rarely get things done quickly. Frequently, they don't get anything done at all. Since they are satisfied only by perfection, they will not attempt a job until they can do it perfectly. When this tendency is combined with fearfulness, melancholies fall into "analysis paralysis." They will use every available resource to study a situation from every possible angle.

Yet, because they fear overlooking a key element, they are still afraid to make a decision because it might be the wrong one. While a sanguine or choleric will make a decision, right or wrong, and jump into action, the melancholy may take action only when forced.

Certainly every temperament needs carefully to consider all aspects of a situation before making a financial decision, but melancholies must also have faith. James 1:5-7 says, "If any of you lacks wisdom, he should ask God, who gives generously to all without finding fault, and it will be given to him. But when he asks, he must believe and not doubt, because he who doubts is like a wave of the sea, blown and tossed by the wind. That man should not think he will receive anything from the Lord." This would be a good passage for melancholies to memorize and to remember when paralyzed by fear and analysis.

They Are Critical and Uncompromising

Melancholies are critical. When their boss assigns a new project or new responsibilities, melancholies will typically voice a thousand and one reasons why they cannot do it, why it should not be done that way, or why it cannot be done at all. They see so many overwhelming problems, they may refuse the project if given a choice. For this reason, melancholies often need choleric bosses who will not accept no as an answer.

When Henry Ford (probably a choleric) told his engineers (probably melancholies) to build a V-8 engine, they analyzed the project and said it couldn't be done. Ford would not accept such negativism. He said, "Gentlemen, build me a V-8 engine." Within a short time, they had overcome all the "insurmountable" problems and had built the V-8 engine.

One of the melancholies' greatest strength-turned-weakness is the ability to see problems—even those which don't exist. Perhaps ten of the twelve spies the Lord sent into the promised land were melancholies, seeing only the difficulties ahead and forgetting about God's promises for the future and His provisions in the past.

Even though melancholies' low self-confidence sometimes makes them feel inadequate, they can, on the other hand, become proud of their strengths. Since melancholies tend to be critical of themselves and others, they are often judgmental, especially toward those who lack the strengths they possess. For example, the sanguines' impulsiveness and lack of self-control frequently cause them to put their foot in their mouth. Melancholies don't understand a lack of self-control because they have been generously endowed with it. Since melancholies carefully plan their every move, they don't easily tolerate someone plunging into a task without first setting the course. Consequently, melancholies have little patience with a sanguine, especially if the sanguine is their spouse.

Melancholies Expect Perfection

As a matter of fact, melancholies demand the impossible—perfection in an imperfect world. Anything short of perfection is failure. For this reason, they often overspend on their purchases, wanting the "perfect" thing.

According to our test results, melancholies tend to spend excessively on clothing; their desire for perfection makes them buy the best possible. Because they love art and literature, they also spend excessively on books and video equipment. If they are musically gifted, they will tend to overspend on musical instruments and peripheral equipment. They most likely own the most expensive stereo system on the block. With their fascination for tinkering with technological gadgets, they also have a hard time resisting computers and VCRs. Male melancholies' desire for perfection sometimes extends to their automobiles. In fact, one melancholy man we tested admitted to impulse spending on Lincoln Continentals.

Female melancholies love beauty. They love to be surrounded by the finer things in life and spend accordingly. Unless they are governed by pre-planned spending limits, they will buy gourmet foods at the grocery store, designer clothing at the boutique, diamond rings and furs, or whatever makes them feel good. Because they desire the best quality in everything, they will often purchase the most expensive item available even when one of lower quality and price would suffice.

We know one melancholy housewife with four children who refused to buy a dishwasher for six years. When we asked her why she waited until her children left home to buy the dishwasher, she said, "Are you kidding? I wouldn't buy one of those cheap pieces of junk. I wanted one with all the top-of-the-line features." Now she has a top-of-the-line dishwasher, and she and her husband can very effectively wash the two dishes and three glasses they dirty every day.

Recently I [Mona] was out shopping with her when we came to a store that sold hats. Just for the fun of it we decided to go in and try some on. We found a beautiful hat that was perfect on her, but she said, "I couldn't possibly buy this hat." "Why not?" I asked. "Well, if I bought this hat, I would have to have a new car. I couldn't wear a hat like this in the dumpy old car I have!" Such is the temperament of the melancholy.

When melancholies apply their uncompromising desire for perfection to the quality of goods they buy, it can bankrupt them. One melancholy we know would not be caught dead in a discount shoe store. His pride will not allow him to buy an inexpensive pair of shoes even if he plans to wear them only once. Rather than admit they have gone too far, melancholies attempt to justify their extravagance by saying, "I can't help it if I overspend my income. I have such good taste."

Melancholies' desire not to compromise their high standards is good when directed by the Lord. However, when it is not directed by the Lord, they can be unreasonable, uncompromising, and legalistic, applying their desire for perfection where it is inappropriate. If they refuse to compromise on unimportant or irrelevant issues, they may undermine their business relationships and perhaps even lose their jobs.

Melancholies Are Moody

Melancholies are moody, with emotions swinging from high to low. Elijah is a good example of the debilitating effects that such mood swings can have. Elijah defeated the prophets of Baal in the duel of fire on Mount Carmel. He outran King Ahab's chariot all the way to Jezreel. He witnessed some of the most spectacular miracles recorded in the Bible. Yet he was so afraid of Queen Jezebel that he hid in the desert and asked God to take his life.

While most melancholies may not go hide in a desert, their moods do affect their spending habits. Many of the melancholies told us that when they are at one extreme of the emotional spectrum or the other, they tend to make rash decisions. If this tendency is allowed to control their spending, financial plans can be destroyed.

While both male and female melancholies are prone to spend when depressed, the female more often shops to relieve depression. Buying may lift the depression temporarily, but because of their low self-image, melancholies cannot justify buying something for themselves. So then they are often overcome by guilt and return items bought on impulse, especially if they were for themselves.

Depression can be debilitating to melancholies because it leads to inactivity and poor work quality, thereby hindering their productivity and advancement. They may not ever receive a promotion. Even worse, they may be dismissed from their job.

Melancholies' Shopping Habits

The female melancholy is content to spend all day at the mall, wandering from store to store, examining the goods, feeling fine materials, and admiring quality construction. A choleric, on the other hand, considers shopping a miserable waste of time to be completed as quickly as possible. A phlegmatic is too lazy to spend the day shopping, preferring to watch television or to relax. And a sanguine, being more interested in people than things, usually buys something very expensive after a great talk with the salesperson. But the melancholy can shop all day long.

Since wives are usually more interested in their home, they often spend excessively, or convince their husbands to spend excessively, on the house itself, the furnishings, and occasionally the car. One word of caution to melancholy women: Don't watch the home shopping channels. When you need something, determine the best place to buy it. Constantly watching the shopping channel tempts us to buy impulsively and unwisely.

Ironically, melancholies may buy impulsively even though they are self-controlled individuals. Apparently they spend when they allow their emotions to gain the upper hand. Spending reduces their stress level and makes them happy, and once the impulse-buying habit gets started, it is difficult to break. Discontent can be a major hindrance to melancholies' staying on budget.

Prescriptions for Melancholies

1. Don't give way to fear. Worry and fear are the greatest enemies for melancholies. Once they have analyzed a situation and prayerfully made a decision, they must take action. Instead of selling themselves short, they must walk in faith and not let fear, low self-esteem, or procrastination hold them back.

A good scripture for melancholies to memorize is 2 Timothy 1:7: "For God did not give us a spirit of timidity (of cowardice, of craven and cringing and fawning fear), but [He has given us a spirit] of power and of love and of calm *and* well-balanced mind *and* discipline *and* self-control"(AMP). Melancholies must use this spirit that God has given us to conquer the fear within them.

First Peter 3:6 is a great verse for female melancholies, in particular. In discussing what wives should be, Peter exhorts them to be like Sarah. The Amplified Bible says, "You are now her true daughters if you do right and let nothing terrify you—not giving way to hysterical fears or letting anxieties unnerve you."

Our word to melancholies: You can do more than you think you can! Risk it!

2. Overcome depression with praise for God and love for others. In order to combat fear and depression, melancholies have to learn to depend upon God and to be filled with His Spirit. Ephesians 5:18-20 says, "Be filled with the Spirit. Speak to one another with psalms, hymns and spiritual songs.

Sing and make music in your heart to the Lord, always giving thanks to God the Father for everything, in the name of our Lord Jesus Christ." There is a direct connection between being filled with God's Spirit and having an attitude of praise, and one of the sure ways to be filled with God's Spirit is to praise Him through singing and making music in our hearts to the Lord.

The Messianic prophesy in Isaiah 61 has encouraging words, especially for the melancholy:

> The Spirit of the Sovereign LORD is on me, because the LORD has anointed me to preach good news to the poor. He has sent me to bind up the brokenhearted, to proclaim freedom for the captives and release from darkness for the prisoners, to proclaim the year of the LORD's favor and the day of vengeance of our God, to comfort all who mourn, and provide for those who grieve in Zion— to bestow on them a crown of beauty instead of ashes, the oil of gladnesinstead of mourning, and a garment of praise instead of a spirit of despair. They will be called oaks of righteousness, a planting of the LORD for the display of his splendor.[1]

God says He will give us praise instead of despair, gladness instead of mourning, and beauty instead of ashes so that we may become strong and show His splendor.

Another way to overcome depression is to love one another. Jesus said in John 15:9-11, "As the Father has loved me, so have I loved you. Now remain in my love. If you obey my commands, you will remain in my love, just as I have obeyed my Father's commands and remain in his love. I have told you this so that my joy may be in you and that your joy may be complete." Since melancholies have a particular problem with a critical spirit, they need to work on loving others, and by so doing they will find that God's love will well up in their hearts and their joy will be full.

3. Act in faith. Melancholies, more than any other temperament, need to seek the Lord's wisdom, practice sound financial principles, and then act! Act in faith.

Ecclesiastes 11:4 has good advice for melancholies: "He who observes the wind [and waits for all conditions to be favorable] will not sow, and he who regards the clouds will not reap"(AMP). Melancholies tend to go overboard with analysis, whether it is self-analysis or analysis of decisions. By waiting until all conditions are perfect, they rarely take action. Melancholies need to study the problem, seek the Lord's wisdom and sound financial advice, and then *do* it.

4. Lower your standards. Melancholies must be willing to lower their standards for the quality they demand and for the perfection they desire in every area of life. This does not mean compromising on godly principles but tempering the tendency to go overboard. Seek godly counsel from someone you have confidence in who will be able to advise you if your standards are attainable and if your desires for perfection are from the Lord or from your temperament.

When you are considering something to buy, ask yourself: How often will I use this item? Would an item of lesser quality work just as well? Could I find a better use for the financial resources that I will have to spend on this item? How much more does the highest quality item cost than the one of lower quality, and what could I do with those financial resources?

5. Stop selling yourself short. Understand that God can do mighty things when working through melancholies. Other good scriptures for melancholies to memorize are Philippians 4:13—"I can do everything through him who gives me strength"—and 2 Corinthians 12:9-10—"But he said to me, 'My grace is sufficient for you, for my power is made perfect in weakness.' Therefore I will boast all the more gladly about my weaknesses, so that Christ's power may rest on me. That is why, for Christ's sake, I delight in weaknesses, in insults, in hardships, in persecutions, in difficulties. For when I am weak, then I am strong." Don't sell yourself short in thinking you can't accomplish something or you don't measure up. Keep in mind that this is a tendency of the melancholy temperament, and counter it by saying God is mighty and He can do all things through us.

6. Network with people of other temperaments. If you are unwilling to make compromises at work, seek the advice of phlegmatics, who are more easy-going. Perhaps an elder in your church or an older co-worker you respect could help you maintain a proper balance.

When you need to get something done quickly, network with cholerics. Cholerics, of course, want everything done yesterday and can get a project off dead center. Don't resent a choleric boss or a choleric spouse, because the melancholy's inclination to overplan, to wait, to study everything beforehand can benefit from the dynamic tension created by the choleric's impetuousness to get things done.

When it comes to shopping, consider taking a phlegmatic friend with you. The cautious spending habits of the phlegmatic will help balance your desire for perfection.

Whenever you feel down or as if you can't handle the task, network with sanguines. They have the highest expression of faith and are excellent at exhorting others and building them up and lifting their spirits. Develop sanguine friends.

7. *Be flexible.* While the strong discipline you possess is great for working on a budget, your spouse may not be as well endowed. The best balance occurs when you learn to occasionally concede to your spouse. Remember, God has given you your spouse to complete you and to balance you in areas where you may be extreme. Compromise is far more important than potentially jeopardizing your relationship with your spouse.

8. *Resist pride.* It may seem contradictory to tell melancholies, who are plagued with low self-esteem, to resist pride, but often they become prideful in areas where they are gifted, such as self-discipline or intellect. In financial decisions, pride can lead you to make poor decisions by blinding you to your weaknesses and causing you to overestimate your own wisdom—a deadly combination.

CHAPTER SIX

Phlegmatics:

The Great Relaxers

"He who gives to the poor will lack nothing."

PROVERBS 28:27

There he sits, Mr. Couch Potato, the great relaxer. Mr. Potato has a good steady job; in fact, he has had the same job for fifteen years. Life is comfortable, routine, nondemanding. He does his job well because he knows it's expected of him, but he is out of there at five o'clock sharp. That gives him just enough time to make it home, grab a bite to eat, and then relax in front of the television just in time for his favorite show.

If the truth were told, he is a bit bored with his job, but even though he is quite capable of advancement, he doesn't want the added responsibility. Management positions require conflict, and he hates conflict. In fact, he could make a lot more money if he would just put the effort into it, but it's just not worth it.

Besides, his boss would just put more pressure on him, and his boss was already complaining the other day about how shabby his clothes looked. What's wrong with a wide, brown striped tie? It goes well with the suit, which is ten years old. But it's still in good condition. It will do for a few more years.

Yesterday when he came home from work, the lights were off. He had forgotten to pay the bill—again. It galled him to pay to have it turned on, but what could he do? It wasn't that he didn't have the money. At least he was pretty sure he had the money. He just hadn't taken the time to reconcile his bank statements in months. And then there was the credit card bill that was piling up. Maybe if he waited awhile he could scrape up some more money to pay it. Maybe if he put off dealing with the problem it would go away. Maybe he would just let his wife take care of it.

But the real problem is the prices of things these days. When he went out to eat with the office crew last week, he couldn't believe they left such big tips. A dollar was plenty to leave anybody for any meal. And the prices of food! He could remember when a hamburger cost only fifty cents.

He has lots of hobbies that he loves to tinker with. In fact, he has a train set that he started buying years ago. Someday he's going to put that train together.

His wife subtly reminded him this morning that today was their anniversary. She wrote it in red lipstick on his bathroom mirror! He'd have to remember to pick her up a rose at the street stand on the way home.

What Is a Phlegmatic?

Phlegmatics are the calm, easygoing, never-get-upset individuals with such a high boiling point they almost never become angry. They are the easiest type of person to get along with and are, by nature, the most likeable of all the temperaments.

Phlegmatics derive their name from what Hippocrates thought was the body fluid which produced that "calm, cool, slow, well-balanced temperament." Life for phlegmatics is a happy, unexcited, pleasant experience in which they avoid as much involvement as possible. No matter what circumstances surround them, they are always consistent. Yet beneath this cool, reticent, almost timid personality, phlegmatics have a strong combination of abilities and good, retentive minds.

Phlegmatics don't lack friends because they enjoy people and have a natural, dry sense of humor. They can have a crowd in stitches yet never crack a smile. Possessing the unique capability for seeing something humorous in others and the things they do, phlegmatics maintain a positive approach to life. Usually kindhearted and sympathetic, phlegmatics seldom convey their true feelings but are natural peacemakers and good mediators and administrators.

Phlegmatics tend to be spectators in life and try not to get deeply involved with the activities of others. In fact, only with great reluctance are they motivated to any activity beyond their daily routine. This does not mean, however, that they cannot appreciate the need for action and the predicaments of others. A phlegmatic and a choleric may confront the same social injustice but with entirely different responses. The crusading spirit of the choleric will respond, "Let's get a committee organized and campaign to do something about this!" The phlegmatic will say, "These conditions are terrible! Why doesn't someone do something about them?" Once aroused to action, however, their capable and efficient qualities become apparent. They will not volunteer for leadership, but if it is forced upon them, they prove to be capable leaders.

Phlegmatic Abe

The best illustration of a phlegmatic in the Bible is Abraham. When Abraham walked in the Spirit, depending on the Lord, he was very successful. When he walked in fear and doubt, he was a failure.

God called Abraham to leave his comfortable home, his country, and his family and go to the destination He would show him. Abraham apparently started with good intentions, as most phlegmatics do, but he got only as far as Haran. It was not until his father died that Abraham finally obeyed God and moved on. In typical phlegmatic behavior, Abraham had to face a crisis before he would act in absolute obedience.

Rather than depend on God, more than once this fearful phlegmatic looked for the easy way out. Trying to avoid conflict with Pharaoh, Abraham twice had his wife lie for him, which illustrates another primary downfall of this temperament—abdication of the position of responsibility. Under pressure from his wife, Sarah, he used Hagar to bear a son, Ishmael. Later, again at Sarah's insistence, he sent Ishmael away. In order to keep peace in his family, Abraham allowed Sarah to rule the roost.

After years of struggling with his weaknesses of abdication, procrastination, and fearful unbelief, by the end of his days Abraham emerged a transformed man. Through the years God had revealed more and more of His nature to Abraham, and as a result Abraham began to understand the ways of God. He became a great man of faith, declaring to his promised son Isaac as he took him to the top of the mountain to be sacrificed, "God himself will provide...."

This is the answer to the phlegmatics' weaknesses. When they understand that God can be trusted, no one will be more faithful—as demonstrated by the life of Abraham.

Strengths and Weaknesses

People Skills

Phlegmatics are relationship oriented. Though they will never be the life of the party, they are humorous, easygoing, and pleasant company. They always assume the best of people. Their dry wit gives a cheery side to every crisis, and even during the worst of times, phlegmatics unwittingly make those around them laugh. One phlegmatic, when asked how he could have avoided his financial crisis, blankly looked up and said with a stone face, "By dying."

Much to their chagrin, they may find themselves in a position of great responsibility because they are such good diplomats. They listen attentively, saying very little and weighing all options in their analytical mind. When they finally do speak, they usually have come up with an amiable solution for everyone. They are as faithful and dependable as a hound dog and as logical and unemotional as *Star Trek's* Spock.

Because phlegmatics have an intense desire for peace, they often abdicate their responsibilities in financial circumstances. When phlegmatics get into debt and cannot pay their bills, they may develop the attitude "if you can't pay it all, don't pay at all," which causes bills to mount exponentially. By avoiding the conflict of facing creditors while the debt is still manageable, phlegmatics end up with their backs against the wall. What could have been a matter of negotiation with the creditor now becomes an issue of demand. Some phlegmatics find themselves at "zero hour" wondering how they got into this mess. One woman said of her husband, "He'd give away the farm just to keep peace."

The phlegmatics' desire to keep the peace and to avoid responsibility can prevent their vertical promotion within a corporation. Although boredom with a present job may motivate them to transfer to an equivalent job in another company, they are not likely to expend the effort to earn a promotion. As one phlegmatic declared, "I like to just switch boats. I go from boat to boat because I don't like to rock the boat."

Phlegmatics Are Tenacious

Because of their desire to conform and to do the right thing, few phlegmatics declare bankruptcy. Plus they learn from their experiences. Usually steady and reliable, they may find themselves in a financial crisis once, but rarely will they make the same mistake twice. One woman said, "The first year of our marriage we had to pinch every penny to get out of debt." That was over thirty years ago, and they have never faced a money shortage again. Phlegmatics just clamp down hard on all the spending and "keep the belt tight."

One phlegmatic said, "In all honesty, I have never been through a financial crisis. Sure, money has been tight at times, and we have had to skip a few vacations and fun things, but I have always been able to pay the bills and provide for my family. I do give glory to the Lord for this and praise Him for His provision." Phlegmatics usually try to live within their income. They have a strong work ethic and do their best to keep a steady job.

The negative side of this tenacity is that phlegmatics will stay with something, such as an investment or a job, even if the boat is going down. Sometimes they need to learn to bail out when necessary rather than go down with the ship.

Phlegmatics, especially those whose secondary temperament is melancholy, make good accountants because they enjoy the details and the number-crunching. Their attention to detail helps them keep good records, and they will spend a great deal of time making sure everything is in order. They will keep their desks neat and efficient, even to the point of obsession. The dust on their desks will be organized while piles of work lurk in a closet or file drawer.

Phlegmatics Love to Save

Phlegmatics love to save and hate to spend, unless their secondary temperament is sanguine. They rarely spend money on themselves and then only on things they truly believe they need. On the whole, phlegmatics are extremely conservative and bargain shoppers. Spouses of phlegmatics may even consider them tightwads.

If they had the money, they would shop only once a year since they hate to shop and don't want to expend the effort. When they grocery shop, for instance, they may buy three of everything to avoid going to the store next week. While buying in bulk can save money, they often overspend here.

Not only do they love to save money, they love to save everything. They will keep five different sizes of clothes in their closet because one day they might be able to wear them again. (After all, the bell bottoms and clogs in the bottom of their closet are in perfectly good condition, even if they are from the seventies!) If an item is priced right, phlegmatics will buy it and keep it because they might need it someday. (It's not uncommon to find price tags still on the "great buys" hanging in the phlegmatic's closet.) Hoping to get one more use from it, they will keep a piece of tin foil until it falls apart.

Planner or Procrastinator?

Being organized, logical, and detail-minded, phlegmatics are meticulous planners who are usually aware of their financial status. But they have real problems carrying out those plans. They often want all the circumstances to line up before taking action. For example, phlegmatics may plan an exercise program for themselves. At the urging of their spouse, they may purchase all sorts of exercise equipment or join a health club (one phlegmatic we know has three health spa memberships), but then will rarely use the equipment or go to the club. They have great plans for getting into shape and losing weight, but they cannot bring themselves to act. One lady described her phlegmatic husband as a "great relaxer. He is always the one who says, 'Let's just have another cup of coffee.'"

Phlegmatics will wait, wait again, then wait some more before ever making a decision. There is a saying that you can "never out-wait a phlegmatic." This is positive when applied to sales resistance, but it can also be negative. Phlegmatics often miss great financial opportunities simply because they are unable or unwilling to make quick decisions. This can easily be seen in their investments and savings accounts; they commonly put their money in a savings account earning as little as 3 percent and leave it there rather than research other options. They look for secure savings vehicles, which is commendable, but if the investment doesn't make any money, they really don't care. They have made the decision. The money is invested. Only when a crisis occurs will they make a switch, and by then it may be too late. They look back with regret, wishing they had made the decision sooner but will justify it by saying, "I didn't want to be hasty."

Consider the man who owned two cars. One day his wife saw him come home with two more cars, one being a 1965 Mustang. He planned to restore both and sell them for a profit. He had all the ideas, logic, and plans, but no follow-through. Unfortunately, because he was never able to put his plans into action, that Mustang sat in the garage for fifteen years before he finally sold it. During that time, he had put exactly eight miles per year on the car, driving it once a year to and from the station to be serviced.

Even though phlegmatics usually understand their finances well, we've seen some phlegmatics get as much as three or four months behind in reconciling their bank statements. One phlegmatic we surveyed was regularly as far as ten months behind. Several phlegmatics said they waited until the last minute to pay bills. Most have experienced a utility disconnect or have been required to pay a late charge, not because they didn't have the money to pay the bill, but because they let it slip by.

When confronted, phlegmatics don't admit to procrastinating or to being stuck in the planning stage. They may tell their spouse just to make a list of what needs to be done. To which the spouse responds, "Big deal! I make list after list after list, and still nothing happens." Phlegmatics will pull out old calendars and review past weeks, describing in detail what meaningful duties kept them from performing critical tasks. But the fact remains the same. Until a crisis occurs, phlegmatics won't move. Consequently, they may spend a lot of time on the edge of crises. One woman who is married to a phlegmatic angrily responded, "We don't have any time to live because all we do is put out fires." Phlegmatics must "chew the cud" before making a decision. They must see that everything lines up before acting. So they are constantly putting out fires rather than controlling future events.

Mona's grandmother summed up her phlegmatic husband in this verse: "The house might be on fire, furiously crackling down the stairs. But not a word from dear old Dad. He's playing solitaire!"

Phlegmatics and Giving

Tithing is often a particularly tough task for phlegmatics due to their naturally stingy nature. It may take all the faith they can muster to start tithing, but once they have taken that step, a tremendous conversion occurs. They then become some of the most faithful tithers due to their dependability. Once they have learned to tithe, it can boost their trust in God in every area of their lives.

For some reason, giving money or praise makes phlegmatics feel vulnerable. One woman said of her phlegmatic husband, "You can see how pained he becomes when you watch him give a tip. As he pulls it out of his wallet, he will massage the money with his fingers. He says he does this to make sure there are no bills stuck together, but I think he is saying good-bye to his money."

However, if phlegmatics see a true need and are motivated by the Holy Spirit, they can give sacrificially. One phlegmatic man we know, upon learning that someone needed a coat, literally gave the coat off his own back and did without one for several months.

Influence of Secondary Temperament

When we first examined the phlegmatics' test results, it was difficult to categorize their responses because the answers appeared to be so diverse. Only by categorizing phlegmatics according to their secondary tempera-ment were we able to find definite patterns. After consideration, we realized this made perfect sense. Phlegmatics are amiable, easygoing followers; there-fore, it's logical that of all the temperaments, they are the most strongly influ-enced by their secondary temperament. Said one phlegmatic, "That has to be true. If we didn't have another temperament, we would never spend any money. We are too stingy."

We recommend that phlegmatics, in particular, study their secondary temperament carefully. A phlegmatic might find, to his amazement, that he is a sanguine walking around in a phlegmatic body. One phlegmatic declared, "It's like I have two people running around inside me." For the phlegmatic, this is truly the case.

In the next chapter, we will examine all the combinations of primary and secondary temperaments, especially the phlegmatic combinations so phlegmatics can become more aware of their financial strengths and poten-tial weaknesses.

Prescriptions for Phlegmatics

1. Take on more than you think you can do. Phlegmatics are the one temperament that should accept more projects and challenges than they think they can do. They need the challenge of overcommitment. If you have a phlegmatic in the family, put several things on his or her "to do" list. If there are just a couple of things on the list, phlegmatics will decide to do them whenever they get around to it. When there are a large number of things to be done, they sense more urgency and will more readily attack the list. Although they may not complete the list, they will at least whittle it down.

Once dedicated to a task, they usually meet their deadlines and become more satisfied with themselves. When phlegmatics understand why they must get out of debt, they will be the first to do so and will stay out of debt.

2. Practice crisis intervention. Attack the small things before they become big. If you are in debt, call creditors first; don't wait for them to call you. If you are behind in your payment to the electric company, call them and establish a payment plan before your family has to live without lights. One phlegmatic confirmed, "I have learned to settle affairs quickly. I don't let small problems go into large ones."

3. Put action to your plans. Set financial goals and then allow yourself a fixed amount of time for planning and no more. Set deadlines or have others set deadlines in order to get things accomplished. Then determine what action is needed and move forward. Don't spend more time thinking about a financial decision than it is worth.

4. Communicate with your spouse. Phlegmatics are usually the quietest of all temperaments, so your spouse may not understand exactly what makes you tick. This can lead to big misunderstandings and problems. When you are dealing with finances, communication is a big factor, as compromises must be worked out and the insight of each person must be considered. As Paul told the Ephesians, we must learn to submit one to another. This is extremely important in financial decisions. Your spouse knows you better than anyone else and can help you overcome your weaknesses. Give an ear to your spouse's advice. He or she is frequently right.

5. Determine your secondary temperament. Once you have determined your secondary temperament, study the section showing the strengths, potential weaknesses, and recommended solutions for that combination.

6. Learn to confront, confront, confront. The phlegmatic temperament should develop the attitude "I am going to attack life, not allow life to attack me." Because of the pure hatred phlegmatics have for conflict, they will often let things slide until finally they are boxed into a corner and have no other way out but to face the conflict head on. If phlegmatics will learn to face the conflict earlier, then it will not escalate. Confronting is the only way phlegmatics will overcome passivity and achieve financial freedom.

7. Don't sell yourself short. Much like melancholies, phlegmatics tend to sell themselves short. Because they are unmotivated by nature and often are slow to think things through and act, they don't naturally rise to the top as leaders. However, once forced into a leadership position, they can become exceptional administrators. If you force yourself to take on more than you think you can do or would like to do, you will accomplish much more. Don't sell yourself short.

8. Practice generosity. The conservative nature of phlegmatics often shows up in areas where it shouldn't. Remember that the Lord said in Proverbs 22:9, "A generous man will himself be blessed, for he shares his food with the poor." Phlegmatics are in little danger of going overboard in generosity, so they must especially be sensitive to the direction of the Holy Spirit in their finances and in giving to others. If you allow Him to deal with your nature, He will get more out of you, which in turn will leave you more blessed.

9. Develop faith. Fear, worry, and anxiety are usually the most self-limiting traits of a phlegmatic. As they learn to trust God spiritually, they can begin factoring Him into any project, which makes them more venturesome. One step of faith leads to another.

CHAPTER SEVEN

Temperament Combinations:

The Other Person Inside You

"Now the body is not made up of one part but of many."

1 CORINTHIANS 12:14

While it is important to understand how the strengths and weaknesses of your primary temperament relate to finances, at times it is even more important to understand what your secondary temperament is. While the majority of the time you will act according to your primary temperament, under certain stresses you will respond according to your secondary temperament.

For example, I [Jerry] estimate that I am about 60 percent phlegmatic and 40 percent choleric. However, when I am under intense pressure to get the newsletter published, respond to clients, prepare to leave town, or to put on a conference, and still watch the markets, I become extremely choleric. I run over everyone, I am impatient, I am intolerant. On the other hand, when I am not under time pressures, I generally act like a typical phlegmatic. If I'm not careful, I can be a couch potato, watching endless hours of television, sports, and news. At these times I become passive and appear disinterested.

These conflicting traits can create financial problems. One lady we know is a phlegmatic/sanguine. Most of the time she shops conservatively and stays within a tight budget. True to her phlegmatic nature, she is frugal in almost everything she does. But her secondary temperament, the sanguine, loves to give gifts, frequently extravagant gifts. She will carefully follow her budget to the letter and then suddenly blow it by buying an expensive gift for someone. She can't figure out what's going on. Actually, it's simple and predictable. When it comes to gift giving, her sanguine side overrules her more passive phlegmatic side and blows her budget.

Understanding the strengths and weaknesses of both your primary and secondary temperaments will give you a better grasp of what may beset you financially. This holds true whether you are a choleric, a sanguine, or a melancholy, but it especially holds true for the phlegmatic. Since phlegmatics are the most passive temperament, their secondary temperament can have a greater impact on them than it will on anyone else. For that reason, we will begin with the phlegmatics and look at them in more detail.

The Phlegmatic/Sanguine

Phlegmatic/sanguines have most of the traits of a sanguine, yet they can absolutely be defined as phlegmatics. True to their phlegmatic nature, they are procrastinators who are stubborn, stingy, careless, forgetful, and irresponsible with paperwork. But like Jekyll and Hyde, they have another side. One minute they will be stingy; the next minute they will buy their spouse an expensive gift.

When they are young, phlegmatic/sanguines must submit themselves to the discipline of the Lord to avoid becoming drifters. Often they dislike the discipline of an employer and will jump from job to job. Some phlegmatic/sanguines we tested had held as many as three or four jobs a year. However, when they are in structured jobs, they are more inclined to stay put.

The real tragedy occurs when they decide to start their own business. They have little self-discipline, are easily distracted, and are terrible record keepers. Because they have a double dose of the desire to please people, they find it hard to collect outstanding debts. They will be great salespeople and may make money easily, but they will have great difficulty managing it. If they decide to go into business for themselves, they must surround themselves with people who will hold them accountable for making proper business decisions.

Phlegmatic/sanguines may be content to live with their parents well into their adult years. They don't want to leave home because they don't want the responsibility awaiting them in the "real world." They may also allow their parents to support them long after they finally leave home. One set of parents we know was still buying their phlegmatic/sanguine son his cars when he was thirty-five years old.

The sanguine side influences them to spend impulsively and excessively. The phlegmatic nature tends to buy in bulk. When these traits combine, big problems arise. Even though they needed only one car, many of the phlegmatic/sanguines we tested purchased two or three. When they could afford to do so, they also bought three-wheelers, trucks, and BMWs.

To gain the approval of a spouse, phlegmatic/sanguines will often give lavish gifts, sometimes overlooking the fact that important bills are due. In the first year of marriage, one phlegmatic/sanguine husband bought his wife incredibly expensive gifts for every holiday: a diamond ring on Valentine's Day, a watch for Easter, a dog for Mother's Day, pearls on July 4th, and a twelve-diamond necklace for another occasion. Every single holiday this man produced an enormously expensive gift to make his wife "feel special," and he created a mountain of debt. Phlegmatic/sanguines mean well, but many times they go too far.

Few phlegmatic/sanguines would be caught in a discount store because their tastes are expensive. Males may choose eighty dollar, name-brand shirts. When asked why, one man said, "It makes me feel in style. It builds my self-image, and it meets my spouse's approval." But when we asked if he were aware of style, he admitted, "Not really." The sanguine side wants to be in style, but the phlegmatic part doesn't really care if clothes match.

Phlegmatic/sanguines have a lot of difficulty managing their own money. They may put off making financial decisions until it's almost too late. Because they are prone to extravagant or outlandish financial decisions, they don't stay on a budget. Characteristic of their sanguine nature, they trust the bank with their money and may solve a problem in their account by switching to a new bank. With their lack of organization, they may wait to pay bills until the last minute or until they are overdue, repeatedly incurring late charges or expensive deposits to have electricity or telephone services restored.

Phlegmatic/sanguines may spend to change moods, primarily when they are angry. When one phlegmatic/sanguine would have a fight with her husband, she would go to the toy store to shop for her children. She said she never spent less than a hundred dollars when she was mad, whether they had the money in the bank or not.

When faced with a major financial decision, phlegmatic/sanguines are quick to say, "The Lord will provide." The wife of a phlegmatic/sanguine husband who habitually called upon the Lord to provide declared in frustration, "Yes, he expects it to fall out of the sky." Immediately the husband declared, "It does." Her response? "It happened only one time."

Phlegmatic/sanguines usually cause their spouses to feel insecure. In many cases the spouse will take over just to survive. Phlegmatic/sanguines demonstrate their love with their gift buying, but much to their disbelief and chagrin, they are often sorely rebuked by their spouse. Over and over again in our interviews, an anguished wife of a phlegmatic/sanguine would say all she really wanted was the gift of responsibility. She would be absolutely content to live knowing that the bills were paid on time. Unfortunately phlegmatic/sanguines, like all phlegmatics, have to face a crisis before they will change. When asked what made him seek the Lord and desire to put his house in order, one phlegmatic/sanguine pointedly said, "I didn't realize how selfish I was until my son got sick. God humbled me. He put me in a position where I had to realize that I don't make anything. God gives me everything."

To their credit, phlegmatic/sanguines have an unparalleled trust in God for their future and the future of their families. Such peace makes other temperaments look enviously at these people who always live on the sunny side of life. Phlegmatic/sanguines just don't worry.

One phlegmatic/sanguine man we interviewed said, "Life is not my plan. It is the Lord's plan; there is nothing I can do about it. If a catastrophe hits, God will take care of me." A lady summed up the phlegmatic/sanguine's philosophy by saying, "I decided a long time ago that when you wake up in the morning, you can choose either to be happy or sad. I choose to be happy." Such is the beauty of this gentle nature. These people deal with life as it comes, truly living by the day.

The Phlegmatic/Choleric

Unlike the phlegmatic/sanguines, phlegmatic/cholerics are usually tremendous business people. Most phlegmatic/cholerics we tested were in leadership positions—business owners, department heads, executives. They are wonderful diplomats (the phlegmatic side), which enables them to motivate people. And they have tremendous drive (the choleric side), so they demonstrate a high work ethic to others. Because phlegmatic/cholerics hate to be in limbo, they determine where they are going and where their security lies.

Rarely do they quit. The stubbornness of the phlegmatic combined with the tenacity of the choleric causes phlegmatic/cholerics to press through all obstacles to reach their goals. They demonstrate that a secret of successful business is tenacity. When they think they are right, they will hang on forever. However, once they are convinced they are wrong, they will change course.

Phlegmatic/cholerics are visionaries. When they get to the top of one mountain, they're already looking at the next one. Consequently they have a difficult time enjoying the view from the mountaintop. Their visionary nature encourages them to go to the limit to finance their dreams. Several phlegmatic/cholerics we tested realized they had the potential to destroy their dreams by taking risks and acquiring debt.

When phlegmatic/cholerics see a reason to do so, they will sacrifice greatly. They will live in modest homes, drive modest cars, and put as little as one dollar of gasoline in the tank to go just the next mile. But they must be absolutely convinced of the need.

The phlegmatic's stability and unemotional nature allow these people to survive extremely difficult situations without great mood swings. To quote one businessman, "I look at the future, I hope in the future, I have faith in God. This allows me to fight problems rather than worry about them. I also set myself multiple goals and attain them one by one."

However, as with all phlegmatics, these people are procrastinators and putterers, which can greatly inhibit their productivity. Their desire to please people frequently causes them to take care of the "squeaky wheel" first so that they are constantly tending to what is urgent, not necessarily what is important. They then "hit the wall" with deadlines when important tasks finally have to be done.

The choleric drive mixed with the phlegmatic procrastination becomes lethal to those who work for them. Phlegmatic/cholerics are likely to wait until the last minute before performing any task, but when it's down to the wire, their choleric nature will drive everyone around them into the grave to get the job done. However, in financial matters their timing can actually be an asset. Their phlegmatic nature allows them to outwait anybody else, but their choleric side urges them to make immediate important business decisions when necessary, usually resulting in a successful track record.

Phlegmatic/cholerics absolutely hate to shop. When they meet with a salesperson, they want the person to get right down to business without wasting time. They will often make quick decisions just so they can move forward. Comparison shopping is out of the question unless it is for a major purchase that they really care about. Then the tight-fisted phlegmatic kicks in, and they often shop and shop for the best deal.

Unlike other phlegmatics, they feel secure in handling money. Financial difficulties are not mistakes; they are challenges to overcome. Normally they are totally aware of their financial status and can account for every dollar they spent last week. They hate stress, rarely make long-term contracts, and seldom declare bankruptcy.

In recordkeeping, they demonstrate their phlegmatic side by paying whoever makes the loudest noise. They rarely consider it worth their time to get remuneration for a faulty product or an overcharge. But when they do decide to correct a wrong, they devote themselves to getting exactly what they want.

As with all phlegmatics, they find it difficult to achieve a balance in life. Phlegmatic/cholerics stand on either side of the scale at any given moment. They will either be too phlegmatic, procrastinating and dragging their feet, or too choleric, making quick decisions and diving into something without thinking. They can seem highly motivated one moment and so unmotivated the next that they cannot accomplish anything. They function in the choleric side in the business world yet come home and collapse on the couch in the phlegmatic nature, expecting everyone else to serve them.

They can improve their balance by listening to their spouse's counsel. One man declared, "I need to put more stock in my wife's advice and heed what God is telling me." That is a particularly strong statement for phlegmatic/cholerics to make because, while they may be great business people, they can be weak as parents and spouses.

The Phlegmatic/Melancholy

Phlegmatic/melancholies are at the other end of the scale from the phlegmatic/sanguines. They prefer a calm, steady, practical job that requires logic, such as a librarian, clerical person, or computer programmer. Once they land a job like that, they will keep it forever unless an act of God intervenes. Usually they are meticulous and creative.

However, tragically, phlegmatic/melancholies rarely have the drive to reach their potential. If they are writers or artists, they may stash their creations away, declaring them not good enough. The phlegmatic side will tend to laziness and procrastination, and the melancholy side will be fearful and perfectionistic, a destructive combination for self-motivation. There will always be some reason not to excel.

Procrastination may lead them to bounce checks. One phlegmatic/melancholy we tested said it had been over ten months since he had reconciled his bank statement. Another man admitted that something got disconnected about once a year, not because he didn't have the money to pay the bill, but because he procrastinated long enough to create a crisis. A choleric wife summed it up by saying, "Life with a phlegmatic is nothing but going from crisis to crisis."

However, when phlegmatic/melancholies finally do get around to reconciling the bank statement, they enjoy meticulously recording each transaction and searching for errors. True to form, one phlegmatic/melancholy reported, "I record every penny I spend—sometimes daily—and tabulate monthly totals."

Phlegmatic/melancholies usually find budgeting easier than other phlegmatics. They are conservative in their shopping, an activity they would prefer to do only once a year. This group, more than other phlegmatics, holds on to their clothes—from childhood if possible. In their desire for organization, they tend to shop from a list—when they have to shop—and rarely buy anything that is not on it. They aren't tempted to spend a lot on vacations, which they often find a chore, but instead prefer to stay home and putter around the house.

The phlegmatic side looks for the best deal on the best product within the budget. The melancholy side is interested in quality and beauty. So the tension within phlegmatic/melancholies is that they will declare themselves to be savers—clipping coupons and watching for sales—but never buy less than the best for their family.

Phlegmatic/melancholies usually buy very meaningful gifts. The melancholy side wants a fine, intricate, perfect gift for each person, and the phlegmatic side carefully plans and expends great time and effort to find it.

But they do have one fatal flaw in spending—they may be extravagant when buying musical instruments, computers and computer programs, and gifts. One phlegmatic/melancholy woman we interviewed lamented, "I just do not understand what is blowing my budget." She said she shopped at all the thrift stores, went to garage sales, looked for bargains, bought in bulk, and followed all the rules of smart shopping, but still her budget was blown to bits. After talking with her and examining her check register, we discovered that, although she wouldn't buy anything for herself, she was an extravagant gift giver. She had spent $125 on a tea cup—one tea cup—for a wedding present, just because it "reminded her of the bride."

Many times phlegmatic/melancholies will overspend on gifts for their children, particularly if they were deprived in their own childhood. They want to do everything within their power to ensure their own children are not deprived. One phlegmatic/melancholy we tested, believing he would have only one child, charged his credit cards to the limit because he wanted the best quality, name-brand crib and clothes for his daughter.

Phlegmatic/melancholies will commonly take three or four months to make a purchase because it has to be just right. One man decided to find just the right apartment. His melancholy side had to have the right location (just five minutes from work so he could sleep later in the mornings) on the right floor (just high enough to avoid hearing everybody else's noise but not far away from the parking lot and with not many stairs to climb either). Yet when we asked him after a few weeks what kind of a view he had, he scratched his head and said, "I don't really know. I never bothered to look."

Above all other temperaments they will hold on to what is theirs for the longest period of time to get the most wear out of it. One phlegmatic/melancholy sheepishly admitted he just kept gluing the soles of his shoes back on. He supposed that when the glue ran out it would take just as much effort to shop for a bottle of glue as for a new pair of shoes so he would buy new shoes then.

In comparison with other temperaments, phlegmatic/melancholies' financial crises are minimal because they don't want the stress. Other people we tested described their financial crises as losing their jobs, having $25,000 in credit card debt, and filing bankruptcy. But phlegmatic/melancholies considered themselves in a crisis when they were overdrawn by $150 and were billed $15 in service charges.

The Sanguine/Phlegmatic

Sanguine/phlegmatics tend to be extremely happy, carefree people who take life casually. Tending to see the bright side of everything, these people spread cheer in every area of life.

Sanguine/phlegmatics are interested in people and, with the sanguine influence, love to talk. Because they enjoy helping people, they likely will be happiest in a vocation that allows them to do so.

Since they would rather talk than work, their biggest weaknesses will typically be lack of motivation and discipline. Of all temperament combinations, they have the most difficulty in finishing projects. When the negative traits from both temperaments are combined, these people can become irresponsible and lazy. To combat this, they must develop endurance and patience.

They have absolutely no sales resistance. Salespeople smell them a mile away and rub their hands together with glee. They can be sold land, junk cars, leaky boats, you name it. If they aren't careful, they will buy it all, exclaiming what a great deal they got.

Both temperaments need the approval of others and love giving gifts, so shopping can also be a real problem for them. They will buy a twenty thousand dollar engagement ring in order to sweep their prospective fiancée off her feet. Never mind that after they are married they will have to sell it in order to pay his IRS bill that he neglected to pay.

Perhaps their greatest financial pitfall will be the impulsive buying sprees. Their phlegmatic side will leave bills on the table, ultimately forgetting that they exist. Then their sanguine side will impulsively splurge on whatever suits their fancy, most likely eating out with friends at the best restaurants and picking up the tab.

The Sanguine/Choleric

Since both of these temperaments are extroverts, sanguine/cholerics will be the biggest talkers and the most outgoing of all combinations. Their sanguine side is impulsive and wants to talk quickly, and the choleric side hates waiting for details, so they typically talk before they have all the facts. They are also highly opinionated and particularly prone to anger.

Because their secondary temperament is choleric, these sanguines will be the highest achievers of all the sanguine temperaments. If they are in business, they will be impulsive drivers. They are big thinkers, big talkers, and, if not careful, big spenders. They are the business owners most likely to expand their business in order to look more successful. They will hire the finest architects who have the finest references, the best interior designers, especially those who have decorated some famous person's office, and basically overextend themselves in order to look good to their prospective clients. They will run big ads and rent billboards—anything grand enough to draw attention to what they are doing. If they aren't careful, these dreamers will dream their way right into the poor house.

They are truly amazing people who will accomplish a great deal. More money will go through their hands in their lifetimes than perhaps any other temperament, but if they are not careful, they will be hard pressed to account for much of it at the end of their lives. They appear to be the most together people in the world. They are survivors.

However, both temperaments have a tendency toward pride, causing sanguine/cholerics to try to justify their actions. Rather than incur anyone's disapproval, sanguines will try to shift the blame to someone else when something goes wrong, and cholerics can't see their faults or mistakes. So sanguine/cholerics have difficulty admitting their mistakes.

When it comes to shopping, sanguine/cholerics must be careful. The sanguine impulsiveness combined with the choleric drive to get things done may cause them to make expensive purchases quickly with no remorse whatsoever. Unlike the sanguine/melancholy, who might later reconsider, sanguine/cholerics can always justify their purchases and can drive a more conservative spouse completely up the wall.

They will worry over the fact that they do not have a savings account but then will absolutely blow their budget giving gifts. One single parent divorcée on a limited budget said she bought as many as fifty or sixty gifts a year, not counting those for her own family. Although she said she shopped wisely and rarely spent over ten dollars per gift, that totaled as much as five hundred dollars per year. She loves people, and many people give to her, so she feels that remembering them is the least she can do.

The Sanguine/Melancholy

Sanguine/melancholies tend to be highly emotional because they are dominated by the two most emotional temperaments. Although the sanguine side may temper the melancholy tendency to depression, their combination of anger and depression are dangerous. They, more than other temperaments, may spend to change their moods. Almost unanimously the sanguine/melancholies we tested said that spending brought them out of depression.

Since being admired by others is important to them, sanguine/melancholies may be the best dressed people around. The sanguine's love for attention and approval is balanced by the melancholy's perfection and conservativeness to prevent them from becoming too garish or bold in their clothes or jewelry.

The domination of the sanguine side will cause these people to verbalize the criticisms their melancholy nature generates. So they must be particularly careful to control their words.

When it comes to shopping, both sanguines and melancholies love quality, although for different reasons. Sanguines love the attention and approval they get by wearing expensive and showy items. Melancholies love quality because of their perfectionistic nature. This combination can be dangerous and explosive in shopping, causing great overspending.

Name brands mean a lot to this group. Quality makes them happy, and feeling happy is an important aspect of their lives.

Being wonderful loving parents, they are tempted to overspend on their children. They love to make their children happy. They love to have their children's approval. If their grown children live out of town, their phone bills tend to be sky high. This desire for their children to have the best is a primary source of arguments between sanguine/melancholies and their spouses.

The Melancholy/Phlegmatic

Few people are as sensitive as the melancholy/phlegmatic. These people will be able to go into a room and sense that another person has a problem before anyone else does. Melancholy/phlegmatics are also one of the most introverted of all the temperaments. The mood swings of the melancholy are tempered by the easygoing attitude of the phlegmatic, making these people easy to get along with, second only to those who are primarily phlegmatic. As strong introverts, they frequently have low self-confidence.

The melancholy's desire for perfection is somewhat balanced by the phlegmatic's good-natured, carefree attitude toward life. These people perform well in areas that demand analysis, planning, detailed work, and logical decision-making abilities.

Their greatest weakness is fear since melancholies are the most fearful of the temperaments, and phlegmatics are second. They will be afraid to make mistakes, to take on new responsibilities, or to do anything outside their comfort zone. Because of their phlegmatic nature, they also fear conflict. Their fearfulness and their inclination to "analysis paralysis" cause them to be slow in making decisions.

Of all the temperament combinations, melancholy/phlegmatics take the longest to shop. Melancholies, especially women, not only love feeling the fine fabrics and textures, they are indecisive. They take forever to decide on a purchase. If they are married to one of the more decisive or impulsive temperaments, especially the choleric, conflict is almost certain. Each partner recognizing and understanding these differences is a first step toward preventing arguments.

Melancholy/phlegmatics can do without longer than anyone else. They are the temperament voted most likely to be missionaries to the poor. They find it easier to meet other people's needs than their own, so they are easily taken for granted. If they see a person in need, they will sacrifice to meet that need. While certain people may truly be called to this kind of living, melancholy/phlegmatics must come to a balance in life.

They would rather live with what they have than make any decisions that would effect change. And they can be content with very little. They will be neat and clean. Their homes will be sparse but beautiful. They may only have one classical music album but they will play it contentedly all day long.

Like other melancholies, they suffer greatly from guilt. Melancholy/sanguines may feel guilty just because they made purchases. Melancholy/cholerics may feel guilty because they pushed everyone too hard. But melancholy/phlegmatics often feel guilty just because they have things others don't. So they may find themselves giving away their things in order to meet other people's needs, thereby creating their own financial downfall.

One melancholy/phlegmatic college student who was rooming with several girls less prosperous than she decided to buy the groceries, toilet paper, paper towels, and all of the basic necessities for the household. She discovered to her chagrin that people took her gifts for granted and soon began to expect her to meet their needs. This was a harsh lesson for her to learn at a young age. Melancholy/phlegmatics must discern whom they should give to and determine whether they are taking too much of other people's responsibilities on their own shoulders. The melancholy/phlegmatics' desire to fix everyone's problems around them can cause their financial demise.

The Melancholy/Choleric

For business, the melancholy/choleric is a good combination. The conscientious, hard-working, sacrificial traits of the melancholy combined with the get-it-done-now drive of the choleric create a person who will accomplish a lot. The choleric side prevents the melancholy side from getting too hung up on details. Having the choleric as the secondary nature also helps balance the melancholy's mood swings, making prolonged bouts with fear and depression less debilitating than in other combinations.

A weakness of melancholy/cholerics is their tendency to be critical of themselves, family members, and co-workers. Pride is a natural tendency for cholerics, and melancholies' giftedness, talent, and intellect give them something in which to take pride. If they are not controlled by the Spirit of God, these people can become haughty and derisive of others' weaknesses where they are strong.

Order rules their lives. One melancholy/choleric, when visiting a friend, found herself impulsively cleaning the rather disorderly home of her much chagrined friend. She had to stop and explain that it was not a reflection of the other woman but rather a reflection of her own compulsion for perfection. Another woman told the story of how her husband had gone into her orderly closet one morning, pulled out a blouse to check the size for a gift he was buying her, replaced the blouse on the rack, and had gone to work. After he left the house, she went into the closet and became agitated that someone had been in her closet. How did she know? "One of my blouses was turned the wrong way on the rack." Every single blouse in her closet was hung the same direction.

But perhaps the height of melancholy/choleric orderliness was demonstrated by a young man who lived with us for a while. Every morning he not only arranged his bills in his wallet so that they all faced the same direction and were in order of value, but he also ironed the bills when he ironed his shirt for the day! Some times he even starched them to make them more crisp!

Melancholy/cholerics must be careful not to become critical of the rest of us who don't seem to get it together quite so well. Melancholy/cholerics tend to marry the most disorganized, disordered temperament—the phlegmatic/sanguines. The phlegmatic/sanguines add laughter and joy to these rather sober people, but as the years go by, the melancholies get tired of their mate's apparent irresponsibility. Happy is the couple that recognizes the order and accountability that melancholy/cholerics bring to the marriage and the joy and balance the phlegmatic/sanguines bring. If they learn to recognize and appreciate each other's strengths and weaknesses, they have the potential of a secure financial household.

Melancholy/cholerics also can be uncompromising idealists. The choleric's willpower combined with the melancholy's unyielding desire for perfection in everything may make them immovable when defending their ideals. While this is good when regulated by the Holy Spirit, it will be destructive if it gets out of balance.

In spending habits, the melancholy's desire for perfection linked with the choleric's drive to get it done now can become extremely costly. Melancholies desire high quality but are naturally cautious. Cholerics are driven to do things quickly because they consider time the most valuable asset. When these traits combine, people may spend large sums of money to buy that perfect item right now! A good deterrent is for melancholy/cholerics to stop and pray before they make a purchase and then remain submitted to the Lord.

Melancholy/cholerics usually feel insecure if they are not in control of the family finances. Male or female, they rarely find themselves in debt or out of control financially. They will be the temperament to budget. They balance their accounts regularly and rarely have to pay a late charge. With their orderliness they can find any bill or receipt on a moment's notice. However, they seldom enjoy a sense of accomplishment from this order because in their own minds it is still not good enough.

The Melancholy/Sanguine

Melancholy/sanguines make excellent employees. Their creative melancholy side will shine in all that they finish. But therein lies the rub. The sanguine side keeps them distracted as they spend time with unnecessary conversations and unnecessary tasks, so they complete less. Melancholy/sanguines have to monitor their self-control.

Whatever they put their hand to will be creative and beautiful, and they will have little difficulty selling their creativity to others. But once the sale is made, they may cancel the order because they have no confidence that they can deliver the quality they have promised.

Melancholy/sanguines love to give gifts. However, they are so critical of themselves and insecure in their choices that when they give a gift, it is bathed in excuses. They will point out every flaw and possible problem and declare that they wish the gift could be bigger or more expensive. The recipients have to profusely thank the melancholy/sanguine for the gift, assuring them it is indeed a wonderful gift and just what they wanted.

But when it comes to buying for themselves, melancholy/sanguines are full of guilt. Their sacrificial melancholy side will cause them to utterly deprive themselves, going weeks or months without buying anything for themselves. They will scrimp and save and follow all the rules until they can't stand the deprivation anymore. Then watch out. The impulsive sanguine escapes like a dog breaking free from its leash. They dart in and out of aisles, stuffing anything that hits their fancies into their shopping carts. They will try on every size and shape imaginable trying to find the perfect item. Then suddenly to everyone's surprise, the deed is done. They have picked out the most colorful and often least useful purchases possible. But the suffering begins after they go home. The melancholies' guilt once again gains control as they crucify themselves for spending too much and indulging themselves. Frequently, they may return most of what they bought simply because they feel too guilty.

Cholerics

Cholerics are at the opposite end of the spectrum from where we began with the phlegmatic. If phlegmatics are the most likely to be influenced by their secondary temperament, cholerics are the least likely because the choleric temperament is so domineering. When financial decisions become stressful, cholerics will clearly demonstrate their choleric traits, but their secondary temperament will moderate the choleric extremes.

The Choleric/Sanguine

Even though they have the drive and decisiveness of the choleric temperament, choleric/sanguines will naturally be more loving than other choleric combinations. One very successful choleric/sanguine insurance broker said he was not motivated by power or money but by the needs of the people he served. His ability to understand other people's needs comes from the sanguine's caring and sympathetic nature. However, the choleric/sanguines' more trusting nature can make them easy prey for the get-rich-quick schemes of "well-meaning" friends.

Choleric/sanguines can be very decisive and impulsive, which makes them loaded guns. They rarely take time to investigate business opportunities before jumping right into them, and they will impulsively buy something without taking time to consider other options or possible pitfalls. With smiles on their faces, choleric/sanguines can also force their desires down others' throats as well.

Choleric/sanguines can be the most extravagant spenders. One man wanted to look successful, so at the age of twenty-one he bought his first Cadillac.

Because power and money play vital roles in the choleric/sanguines' lives, they must be careful to submit themselves—and all their desires and expectations—to the will of God.

The Choleric/Phlegmatic

The choleric/phlegmatic is probably the purest form of choleric because the phlegmatic temperament is so docile that the choleric tendencies will overrule in almost all areas. Their primary downfall comes when the phlegmatic's stubbornness merges with the choleric's strong will. Once these people make a decision, it is virtually impossible for anyone to change their minds.

Choleric/phlegmatics are good beginners—full speed ahead!—but weak in following a job through to completion. And if the task is completed, it may be haphazardly done. They will establish a detailed budget and buy an expensive computer program to help them manage it. They will assign each person an area of fiscal responsibility. They will set goals and determine the finish line. Then they will either lose interest or, more likely, delegate the daily drudgery of the project to an unfortunate lesser power.

They will spend money on hobbies and crafts and end up with bags and boxes full of unfinished projects. One woman has a baby quilt, which she started three years ago, still sitting in a bag in her closet. Whenever someone has a baby, she attacks it for a while, thinking she will finish it. But in a short time, her phlegmatic laziness takes the wind out of her sails, and she puts it back in the bag to await the birth of the next baby.

Choleric/phlegmatics are normally the most tight-fisted of the temperament combinations. The choleric vision and the phlegmatic selfishness create an uncheerful giver. They will delay paying bills until the last minute. While they have no intention of paying late charges, they also do not intend to lose any interest their money could earn.

Like their counterpart, choleric/phlegmatics sometimes procrastinate until the last possible moment and then attack a project with a "get out of my way" attitude. When shopping, they become whirlwinds, demanding and complaining, honking their horn at every slow person in front of them. However, if they have time, their phlegmatic nature may surface, and they may "relax" by getting in the slow lane and driving leisurely.

If cholerics didn't have a secondary temperament, they would be tyrants indeed. For these people, the phlegmatic side allows them some relaxation in life. Fortunately for those who have a relationship with choleric/phlegmatics, the phlegmatic's humor and laid-back approach to life lends some balance to the choleric drive.

The Choleric/Melancholy

Choleric/melancholies are not only driven, they are driven to achieve perfection! What a combination! They will stay up all night to get a project done perfectly. They can be the most detail-minded number crunchers who have ever walked on the face of the earth, balancing their bank statements down to the penny. If it is off one iota, they will go to the bank to have it corrected, unless they become concerned with the time it requires. Then the choleric side will refuse to waste the time.

Choleric/melancholies are among the most critical people alive. Not only will they correct the bank, they will correct anybody else around them.

Consequently, this temperament goes through life pointing out other people's ineptness. If they do not control themselves, they will devastate everyone in their wake. And those who have felt the brunt of their criticism will never forget the blow.

As employees, choleric/melancholies are most faithful. They will finish projects simply because they need to be finished. Anything they buy or do will be uncompromised. Usually they are quite successful because they want the finer things in life and are willing to pay the price for them. The melancholy's sacrificial nature linked with the choleric's driver side will get things done. They will bite off more than they can chew—then they will chew it!

Consider yourself privileged if you have a choleric/melancholy friend. You will find they are loyal and faithfully sacrificial. They are willing to lay down their life for someone they love. They also love to give fine gifts. One woman we interviewed made drapes—perfect drapes—for another person's entire house, in one week.

Many choleric/melancholies develop severe health problems, particularly stomach problems, because of their drive for perfection. The resulting medical bills can greatly increase their financial pressures. One of the best remedies for the physical and financial problems of choleric/melancholies is for them to force themselves to relax.

Now that we've looked at the temperaments and how they affect your financial decisions, let's expand our perspective by looking next at the principles from the Word of God pertaining to the handling of finances and then to some practical steps that you can take to achieve greater financial success.

PART 2

God and
Your Money

CHAPTER EIGHT

The Lure of Our Culture

"Therefore, I urge you, brothers, in view of God's mercy,
to offer your bodies as living sacrifices, holy and pleas-
ing to God—this is your spiritual act of worship. Do
not conform any longer to the patten of this world, but
be transformed by the renewing of your mind. Then
you will be able to test and approve what God's will
is—his good, pleasing and perfect will."

ROMANS 12:1-2

Mona and I were fresh out of college, newly married, and were beginning our financial dealings as husband and wife. Since I was getting into financial planning, my first objective was to pay off a few debts that had accumulated during my college years. Using the domino principle, we were out of debt within a matter of months and were determined to stay that way.

Soon afterward, our business and our income began growing as my career took off. As a matter of fact, it grew rapidly. Before long we could afford a big home—"an American dream house"—and two nice cars, all financed of course.

Then our income got pinched. But we still had some things we wanted to buy, even if our cash was running a bit tight. So I borrowed some money, using our credit cards. After all, these were not really large debts, and we would be able to pay them off soon, considering what our income was.

Within several months, we had managed to accumulate several thousand dollars in consumer debt.

One day, I suddenly realized we had done the very thing we had set out not to do several years before: We were deeply in debt. I remember thinking to myself, "How could this have happened to me?"

Sound familiar? This story is repeated time and time again as couples in our culture begin their lives together. Our story continued as we watched our income decline. What had seemed to be relatively insignificant debts when acquired now became major debts. Little did we know we were about to go to debt school, under the tutelage of the Lord. Over the next several years we made another commitment to get out of debt and stay out, a stronger commitment this time because it was based on biblical convictions about debt, not just financial principles. It took a number of years, but we were able to get completely out of debt by following the principles outlined in this book. As you read the book, keep in mind that the stories are real and the principles have been tested. They work.

The Impact of the Culture

If we are truly to achieve financial freedom, one of the most important steps we must take is to understand our culture's impact on our viewpoints and actions. Our culture's values are normally not biblical values, and we must discern between the two in order to follow God's ways.

The secular media and advertisers continually program us with humanistic values concerning material goods, similar to those portrayed by the rich fool in Luke 12:19, who decided he would eat, drink, be merry, and take life easy. It's the philosophy of the bumper sticker that says, "The one with the most toys at the end wins," as if life were a gigantic Monopoly game where the goal is to acquire more than other people can. These materialistic views and other humanistic values advocated throughout our culture have resulted in a society full of strife and anxiety, constant fear and depression, and stressed out, burned out people with no balance to their lives.

Jesus told us in Matthew 6:24 that we could not serve God and anything else: "No one can serve two masters; for either he will hate the one and love the other, or he will stand by *and* be devoted to the one and despise and be against the other. You cannot serve God and mammon (deceitful riches, money, possessions, or whatever is trusted in)"(AMP).When Jesus talked about mammon, He was not talking about just money. In many of the surrounding cultures of Jesus' day, Mammon was a literal pagan god of material gain. So, when Jesus referred to mammon, He was talking about the personification of all materialistic possessions. We will either love and be devoted to God, or we will love and be devoted to the pursuit of material wealth.

While none of us would admit to serving material wealth or mammon, many times we find ourselves running after these things. Although these humanistic attitudes do not represent our conscious values, they have influenced us and the church as well, perhaps more than we realize. We are like the frog in the kettle that is boiled to death because he does not realize the water is ever so slowly being heated. We have gradually allowed the world to transform our Christian values into secular ones so that the fruit of materialism—strife, anxiety, fear, depression, stress, and burn out—is much more evident in most of our lives than the fruit of the spirit—"love, joy, peace, patience, kindness, goodness, faithfulness, gentleness and self-control."[1] As individuals and as the church, we must regain our distinction from the world in our attitudes and handling of money. We must again become salt and light.

Advertising and Sales Techniques

To recognize our culture's attitudes toward money and material goods we need only to look at advertising and sales techniques. Advertising is designed to create discontent and to appeal to our ego. It suggests that happiness and fulfillment are achieved through acquisition. Money is everything. If we follow the pied piper of advertising, it will always lead us into buying more than we should.

Depending on our temperament, we will be particularly vulnerable to certain products and sales approaches. Take, for instance, how an ad for a cruise ship might be tailored to appeal to the four temperaments.

Since time is their most valuable asset, cholerics, or Type A people, will be most susceptible to a sales pitch that emphasizes how a product or service saves time, will help them reach their goals faster, or accomplish more. If advertisers for a cruise ship wanted to appeal to cholerics, they would emphasize the number of sights people can see and what they can accomplish—assuming, of course, they can get cholerics to take a vacation at all. If the cholerics bite, they will pack the vacation with tremendous activity, but they may also take two or three briefcases along so they can get extra work done during the down times.

Sanguines will be attracted to suggestions that a product will make them part of the "in" crowd and will create more fun. They are ideal targets for the cruise. If they see people talking, going to shows, doing aerobics, and playing water volleyball, sanguines are ready to sign up.

Melancholies will be attracted to ads that show the beautiful aspects of life. For them, a cruise is enticing if it is shown to provide beautiful scenery, walks along pristine beaches, and access to museums.

Because the phlegmatics are the most difficult group to motivate, they are the hardest to sell. It takes persuasion over a longer time, or by a spouse, to get them to spend their money. But when they do spend, it will usually be on a product that promises to give them more time for relaxation. Ben Franklin must have been a phlegmatic, considering that most of his inventions were designed to save time or energy.[2] For phlegmatics, the appeal of the cruise would be relaxing on the deck of the ship or taking a nap in a hammock under a palm tree.

Limited-Time Offers

One of the most effective sales techniques is to get us to buy without carefully considering our decisions, without counting the cost. Advertisers and salespeople know that if we truly weigh our decisions, we are more likely either to buy less or possibly not to buy at all. It's a major approach of direct-to-the-consumer sales, such as door-to-door soliciting.

When I [Jerry] was in college, I sold expensive waterless cookware to single, working women. One of the inducements we used was a bonus of an expensive set of china, stoneware, or cutlery—if they bought that day. Of course, the price of the cookware already had the cost of the china factored into it, so people were paying for it regardless.

Salespeople frequently offer a bonus or discount to induce us, or pressure us, into buying today. "This will only be offered for a limited time. If you buy today, you get the bonus (or discount)—but only if you buy today." The objective is to get us to make the purchase now so that we won't stop to think and decide we don't really need it or that it's too expensive. This approach also eliminates comparison shopping. Sanguines, with their impulsive nature, are particularly vulnerable to these offers.

Buy Now, Pay Later

Another common and effective sales approach in America is the "buy now, pay later" plan, which appeals to the lust of our flesh because it says we can have it now. No waiting. No delayed gratification.

Again, since it appeals to an impulsive and optimistic nature, sanguines typically are the most susceptible to this approach also, although the struggle can be equally hard for melancholies because it enables them to get higher quality items than they can truly afford. Phlegmatics may be the least tempted, but, in truth, all of us at times have been bitten by this bug and have given in to the temptation to spend impulsively. The problem with the "buy now, pay later" philosophy is that it discourages self-restraint and encourages overspending our incomes, which over the long term results in continuous lack.

Keep Up with the Joneses

Envy and pride can be strong motivators to buy, especially for sanguines and cholerics. "Buy bigger, buy better, buy the best," the ads cry, and we become unwilling to settle for less than the best.

This mind-set comes from our warped view of success: We measure our success as a person and our place in society by the quality of goods we own. If we drive an expensive car, anyone can see we are successful. When we buy the best items, we show that we are top-quality people. This constant striving for material things and the resultant overspending, tension, and stress portray the worst possible values to our young people—values that stand in stark contrast to the Word of God. Few people can echo the Apostle Paul's words in Philippians 4:12: "I have learned the secret of being content in any and every situation, whether well fed or hungry, whether living in plenty or in want."

The American dream originally envisioned that through hard work, diligence, and savings, each generation could have a better life than their parents had. While there is nothing wrong with that dream, it has become perverted and distorted. Today the American dream is self-oriented. Our goals have become the acquisition of fancier cars, bigger houses, higher salaries, and more expensive gadgets, regardless of the cost to our time, our families, or others who might get in our way. And the stress lines in our culture are beginning to show.

Work Harder and Longer

Another deception we subconsciously buy into is believing that through striving we attain prosperity. We should be diligent in our work "as unto the Lord," but the presence or absence of success over the long run is a direct result of God's blessing or lack of blessing in the lives of believers.

As the Israelites were preparing to enter the promised land, God described the blessings He desired to pour upon them. But He also gave a stern warning, lest they forget He had blessed them and claim that this new wealth was the result of their own handiwork. In Deuteronomy 8:17-18, God says, "You may say to yourself, 'My power and the strength of my hands have produced this wealth for me.' But remember the LORD your God, for it is he who gives you the ability to produce wealth." We can work as hard as possible—ninety hours a week—and still fail, if God's blessing is not on what we're doing. While there is usually a direct link between the quality and quantity of our work and our financial reward, they are not the only factors.

God will give us blessings as He so desires. We cannot grasp them on

THE LURE OF OUR CULTURE

our own. This is one reason Paul tells us repeatedly in the New Testament to be content. Contentment does not mean being lackadaisical or slothful. Contentment comes with hard work and diligence but without the constant striving for gain that accompanies so many of our efforts. It means not being continually dissatisfied with where we are in life, which is a direct contradiction to our culture's constant reinforcement of materialistic values. We would do well to remember God's messages concerning contentment: "Keep your lives free from the love of money and be content with what you have"[3] and "Better a little with the fear of the LORD than great wealth with turmoil."[4]

Get Rich Quick

Another popular enticement of our culture is not only can you get rich, but you can get rich quick and at little cost, as evidenced by the preponderance of sweepstakes and state lotteries. But God says in Proverbs 28:20, "A faithful man will be richly blessed, but one eager to get rich will not go unpunished." God tells us that to be blessed, we should be faithful—faithful to God and the principles of His Word, and faithful to our families.

Wealth in the life of a believer is usually a result of diligence, patience, thrift, hard work, and God's blessings. It is a result of the right heart attitudes and behavior toward material things, over a long period of time. In short, it is portraying God's character and His life to a dying world.

Just Charge It!

Credit card usage is one of the most dangerous temptations to people who have a hard time controlling their spending in the first place. First, credit cards facilitate impulse spending. Second, as we said before, studies show that people spend an average of 34 percent more when using a credit card, even if they pay it off every month. Third, and most important, unless we pay the balances in full every month, credit card usage compounds our debt.

Consider this example: Charging a $20 dinner on your credit card could cost you more than $50! How? If you routinely make the minimum required payment, that meal will eventually cost you $30.66 in interest, plus the principal of $20.00, for a total of $50.66.[5]

If you currently have $2,000 in debt on one of your credit cards and routinely send in only the minimum required payment, you will be paying that $2,000 for the next seventeen years! Your final cost will be $5,065.51, which is $3,065.51 in interest plus the $2,000 principal, assuming a 16.8 percent interest rate on your credit card.

Credit cards are properly used only when you are going to spend the money anyway and you pay off the balance within thirty days regardless. If you have credit card debt, either destroy your cards or at least put them away where you will not use them until you have completely eliminated that debt. Under no condition should you continue charging on your cards if you owe a balance on them because the principle of compounding is working against you. The money you spend today will consume part of your income for years to come if you continue to pay interest on what you are consuming today.

Credit cards are often called revolving credit, which reminds us of a person stuck in a revolving door, going around and around and never getting out. This is what happens with revolving credit. While you are paying for prior purchases and the interest on them, you continue to add new charges, so you never get the debt repaid. You pay off a little, add a little, pay off a little, add a little, and never get anywhere. With credit cards you pay as much as 18 percent interest—far more than people earn on conservative investments. Our best advice: Get credit cards under control or destroy them!

The Origin of Debt Dependency

One of the biggest problems with all these enticements to spend is that they lead to a dependency on debt, which is a relatively new phenomenon in our culture. Installment debt originated right after World War I and prior to the Great Depression of the 1930s. With the advent of the assembly line made famous by Henry Ford, American manufacturers began to produce more than consumers could buy—if they paid cash for everything. So manufacturers invented a system to enable the American public to buy as many goods as industry could produce. They began using heavy advertising and promoted consumer debt, which allowed people to make a small down payment and pay the balance over time.

A positive viewpoint toward debt was promoted by an economist named John Maynard Keynes. Keynes, a Fabian socialist in England in the 1920s, wrote the book *The General Theory of Money and Credit,* in which he revolutionized people's thinking concerning debt and economics. Keynes was a humanist and an atheist who believed all of the world's problems would ultimately be solved by a one-world socialistic government. Prior to Keynes, our economic structure was Bible oriented, stressing little or no debt. But since the advent of Keynes' philosophy, Americans have become perpetual debtors, which is certainly not leading us into prosperity. Nor should we expect a theory developed from such a mind-set to be in line with God's Word, the source of all eternal truth.

The Problem with Debt

The natural result of this type of thinking is a society that is increasingly short-term oriented and that cannot exist without massive amounts of debt. The economy becomes consumer driven and consumption based, with the view that prosperity equals high consumption levels with the trappings of wealth. We consider expensive cars, luxurious houses, jewelry, and big-screen televisions as part and parcel of the deal. Advertising tells us that we can't be happy without these things, so we bite and constantly strive for more. The result is far from fruitfulness and happiness. The long-term result is financial lack and an overwhelming emptiness. Using debt to acquire goods, happiness, and success is like using gasoline to put out a fire. It simply will not work in the long run.

In reality, this philosophy creates bondage. Lacking self-control, most people habitually consume more than they make and end up deeply in debt. Some people—many more than you would imagine—are actually addicted to spending. While most Christians abhor the thought of drug or alcohol addiction, many are lured into an addiction to spending and end up in a type of debtor's prison in which their souls, minds, and emotions are in bondage, with the prison bars being stress, anxiety, and a lack of money.

The Bible's View of Debt

While debt is not prohibited in the Bible, it is certainly discouraged. This is verified throughout the Word of God, in both the Old and New Testaments. In biblical times, a debtor was akin to a social outcast, in a position of servitude or slavery. Proverbs 22:7 states, "The rich rules over the poor, and the borrower becomes the lender's slave" (NASB). The Hebrew word for *slave* in this verse is *eved*, the same word used in Exodus 21 where God lays out the principles for taking care of a Hebrew servant or slave. The implication is clear. Just as the poor often come under the dominion of the rich, borrowers become slaves to the lenders. When we become debtors to other people, a company, or a credit card, we have become their slaves. Now we are working for them. Yet Paul teaches that since we "were bought with a price," we are not to "become slaves of men."[6]

In Deuteronomy 28 the Lord describes what will happen to the people of Israel if they obey His commands. They will have a surplus from which they can lend to others. They will be the head, and not the tail, among the other nations. However, if they disobey, they won't have enough food, and they will have to borrow from other nations. As the United States has moved away from the paths of God over the last thirty years, we have seen a similar pattern. It has gone from being the largest creditor nation in the world to the largest debtor. In 1980, the United States had eight of the top ten banks in the world; in 1990, we had only one bank in the top twenty-five. We are now the ones dependent on other nations to help us finance our massive budget deficit, which today runs around $400 billion a year.

Perhaps we would take debt more seriously if we were to look more closely at its root meaning. The largest debt most people owe is on their houses—their mortgage. The word *mortgage* is from the Latin word *mortuus,* meaning "death," and is the basis of our words *mortician, mortality,* and *mortuary.* And the root of the biblical word for *interest—usury*—literally means the "bite of the serpent."

In Romans 13:8, we are encouraged to pay all of our obligations and not let any debt remain outstanding. As it says in the Amplified Bible, "Keep out of debt and owe no man anything, except to love one another." We have the ongoing obligation to love one another, but we are not to have other ongoing obligations. The Bible views debt as unnecessary and sometimes evil. If debt itself is not good, then those things we acquire through debt cannot be good either. The end does not justify the means. Debt is simply not God's way.

What's the Real Problem?

Most people think, "If I just had a little bit more money, everything would be all right." But money isn't the problem. Over the years that we've examined the finances and budgets of hundreds of people in an effort to help them get out of debt, we have found that rarely is the issue how much they make. People can make $100,000 a year and still overspend their income. The issue is what they do with what they make. In 99.9 percent of the cases we see, the problem is not too little money; it's too little stewardship. And it will remain this way unless people make a diligent effort to become better stewards over their money and begin saving and paying off their debts.

God has told us repeatedly that His ways are higher than our ways. What we think is wisdom, God knows is foolishness. We need to understand this when God shows us that materialism does not work. If materialism worked, the happiest people in the world would be the richest people in the world, and we all know that is far from the truth. Despite the fact that the lifestyles of the Hollywood stars are the envy of most Americans, the stars themselves seem to constantly search for the grail of self-fulfillment and yet have more pain and turmoil than most of us will ever know. Indeed, the richest man in the Bible, and perhaps the richest man who ever lived, Solomon, had something to say about this. In Ecclesiastes 5:10-12, he said, "Whoever loves money never has money enough; whoever loves wealth is never satisfied with his income. This too is meaningless. As goods increase, so do those who consume them. And what benefit are they to the owner except to feast his eyes on them? The sleep of a laborer is sweet, whether he eats little or much, but the abundance of a rich man permits him no sleep."

Before we go to the next chapter, let's stop and take inventory. Have we been wasting the precious resources that God has entrusted to us? Have we been guilty of striving after material goods? Have we become workaholics? Have we decided we can't be happy or fulfilled unless we have the best of everything? If so, we need to change our ways, not simply ask forgiveness.

If the Holy Spirit is pricking your conscience, sit down with pen and paper and ask God to reveal to you any area where you have been out of His will. If you are married, sit down individually with pen and paper and ask the Lord to reveal any area where you have allowed our culture or worldly values to affect your value system, or behavior, or actions. Then as a couple, compare notes and pray together. If we want to experience God's blessings in life, we have to live His way. Then our lives will testify to the world what great things God's principles will accomplish.

CHAPTER NINE

Gaining God's Perspective

*"For my thoughts are not your thoughts, neither are
your ways my ways,' declares the LORD. 'As the heavens
are higher than the earth, so are my ways higher than
your ways and my thoughts than your thoughts.'"*

ISAIAH 55:8-9

Imagine for a moment, if you can, the perspective of God. His Word states
that:

He created the heavens and the earth.

He raises up rulers and pulls them down.

He judges nations, declaring their beginning and end.

He rules over all; He is King of kings and Lord of lords.

Consider the vast expanse of the heavenlies, the stars, the galaxies, the
tremendous universe beyond. God created all of it—not just the earth but
the animals on the earth and the creatures in the sea. He formed people
from the breath of His nostrils, creating the force that gives us life. God is
the creator of all and owner of all.

Land, houses, money, televisions, cars—they are given to us on a tem-
porary basis. When we die, we will give all of it away. Psalm 39:4-6 says,
"Show me, O LORD, my life's end and the number of my days; let me know

how fleeting is my life. You have made my days a mere handbreadth; the span of my years is as nothing before you. Each man's life is but a breath. Man is a mere phantom as he goes to and fro: He bustles about, but only in vain; he heaps up wealth, not knowing who will get it."

Imagine what will happen to your possessions in the next hundred years, if the Lord doesn't return first. Which of the items you own will still be in existence—your house? your cars? your clothing and jewelry? The odds are high that the majority of the material things we spend so much of our time scurrying for, worrying about, and trying to accumulate will not be around anymore. And what is left may not even be owned by our ancestors. Land changes hands. Farmland that has been in a family for generations can be lost to the bank because of imprudent decisions. For this reason, it makes little sense literally to sell our lives and our souls in pursuit of material gain.

As Christians, that's one reason we should not try to build our kingdoms here on earth—everything on earth will eventually pass away. We are to store up treasures in heaven as Jesus said in Matthew 6. This doesn't mean we shouldn't save or invest for the future. The question is, what are our heart motives? Why are we doing this? Our purpose is to use our resources according to God's will for us with the aim of advancing His kingdom on earth. In other words, God is the general, we are the foot soldiers, and our objective should be to do what He wants and says.

God has called us to be salt and light to our society. We should be a preservative. We should illumine God's true character and the meaning of life to the world around us. Yet even in the church we have such a poor understanding of God's perspective on money that we constantly battle financial problems. We are battered by unemployment, lay-offs, and serious debt. If we are not experiencing God's blessing in the financial realm, maybe we are not conducting our lives according to His way. If we are going to demonstrate God's wisdom to the world, we must first be certain we are living according to His wisdom.

God's Principles

1. Work as unto the Lord. Our duty is to do the job we have been given here on earth—our physical, temporal job—as if we were working directly for God. Colossians 3:23-24 says, "Whatever you do, work at it with all your heart, as working for the Lord, not for men, since you know that you will receive an inheritance from the Lord as a reward. It is the Lord Christ you are serving." Regardless of whether we have a Christian or secular employer, we should do the very best job we can as a testimony to the character of Christian workers. Doing our best in everything we do is proper stewardship of our time.

Ironically, cholerics and melancholies may have their own difficulty learning to work as unto the Lord. Because cholerics usually work harder than anyone else, and melancholies are self-sacrificing, they may allow work to have too much prominence in their lives. They may lose all balance, getting burned out or sacrificing relationships. Stay balanced in your work.

2. Be diligent in our work. Proverbs says, "Lazy hands make a man poor, but diligent hands bring wealth"[1] and "The plans of the diligent lead to profit as surely as haste leads to poverty."[2] Diligence in our work will tend to push us toward advancement.

Since phlegmatics have a tendency to be lazy and sometimes slow, they really have to work at being diligent as a good testimony to those around them. Sanguines may also have trouble in being diligent because they love people and may spend too much time in the workplace socializing, thereby robbing their employers of time they are paid to work.

3. Don't strive. Although we need to be diligent in our work, we don't need to be constantly striving after material gain. Proverbs 10:22 says, "The blessing of the Lord—it makes [truly] rich, and He adds no sorrow with it, [neither does toiling increase it]" (AMP).

If we sacrifice our lives to the pursuit of worldly wealth, we will accumulate sorrow along with the wealth. But God says that His blessing makes us truly rich, without sorrow, and that toiling will not increase His blessings. If God desires to give us wealth, He does so, including spiritual richness, without having to sacrifice our families and relationships. The issue is balance, keeping God's perspective on money and stewardship, which is difficult for cholerics.

4. Don't store up for ourselves. We should save and invest money, but we must not do it with ungodly motives and a desire to hoard it for ourselves.

Melancholies may be prompted by fear to store up for the future, but they will give to others if they are convinced of the need. The stingy phlegmatics may tend to hoard for themselves out of fear also. Sanguines, on the other hand, will be generous and may not save at all but may instead rely entirely on the Lord to take care of the future. For them, balance is a key. Cholerics need to hold their finances with an open hand and not get too preoccupied with their own goals.

5. Be generous. Many passages speak of the blessings of generosity. Proverbs 11:25 says, "A generous man will prosper; he who refreshes others will himself be refreshed." And 2 Corinthians 9:6,11 reminds us of the true value of generosity: "Whoever sows sparingly will also reap sparingly, and whoever sows generously will also reap generously.... You will be made rich in every way so that you can be generous on every occasion, and through us your generosity will result in thanksgiving to God."

Phlegmatics and cholerics need to learn to be more generous with their time and money, while melancholies and particularly sanguines need to learn not to go overboard and give everything away.

6. Support the Lord's work. Again, one of our primary objectives as Christians is to spread the gospel to every living creature, which requires money. So tithing and giving should be a major part of our financial planning in order to further His work. We do this for several reasons: We do it in obedience to God because He says to give and tithe. We do it in faith because God promises that if we give and tithe, over the long run our assets actually will grow, not shrink. We will be like the widow of Zarephath whose oil was continually replaced. We also give because we recognize that everything is His and we are returning a part of what He already owns to support His work.

7. Learn to be patient and wait on the Lord. The world constantly promotes impulsive spending and the desire to have everything now. However, if we learn to wait on the Lord to provide what we truly need, we will be better stewards in the long run.

Patience is especially difficult for both sanguines and cholerics. Since melancholies and phlegmatics are not high stress personalities, patience will come easier for them. In fact, they can be too patient and not take action when it is appropriate.

8. Learn to serve others. As Jesus said in Matthew 23:11, the one who is "the greatest among you will be your servant." If we take the attitude of a servant in our work, in fulfilling others' needs, we will be most fulfilled and the most rewarded. This will be a more difficult lesson for cholerics to learn since they are used to taking the lead. Sanguines may also struggle with this more as they are more self-focused.

9. Be content. Hebrews 13:5 says, "Keep your lives free from the love of money and be content with what you have, because God has said, 'Never will I leave you; never will I forsake you.'" While we "work as unto the Lord," which oftentimes will allow us to advance to higher positions or to earn more, we need to be content with where God places us in life. Contentment can only be found in the absence of striving. Again, the key word is balance.

Contentment is most elusive for cholerics, who are always driving to the next goal. Sanguines also may desire many things and thereby become discontent.

God's Warnings

While the Scriptures are clear regarding what our attitudes are to be toward money and possessions, they are equally clear about attitudes that are not godly.

1. Do not act selfishly. By nature, phlegmatics may truly struggle with being stingy, and cholerics may be selfish as they tend to run over anything that gets in the way of their goals.

2. Do not be greedy. Proverbs 15:27 says, "A greedy man brings trouble to his family." Whenever we are operating out of greed, we make poor financial decisions, whether it is getting into debt to try a get-rich-quick scheme, overspending our income, or buying a bigger house than we really need. As Paul told Timothy, "But those who crave to be rich fall into temptation and a snare, and into many foolish (useless, godless) and hurtful desires that plunge men into ruin *and* destruction and miserable perishing."[3] Again, the cholerics' goals may make them most susceptible to greed.

3. Do not be fearful. Second Timothy 1:7 says, "God has not given us a spirit of timidity." Instead, "perfect love drives out fear."[4] We need to trust God to provide for us and not operate out of fear. Melancholies, by far, will struggle most with being fearful; they can be frozen by it. Phlegmatics also have a tendency to be fearful.

4. Do not love the world. First John 2:15-17 says, "Do not love the world or anything in the world. If anyone loves the world, the love of the Father is not in him. For everything in the world—the cravings of sinful man, the lust of his eyes and the boasting of what he has and does—comes not from the Father but from the world. The world and its desires pass away, but the man who does the will of God lives forever." We continually are to set our mind on eternal things and not love the things of this world. Loving the world is a temptation for the sanguines, in particular. They will conform to the will of others in order to be approved by them. Cholerics, with their strength, will conform only if it allows them to get to their destination earlier. Phlegmatics will conform to avoid conflict.

5. Do not trust money or goods. "Command those who are rich in this present world not to be arrogant nor to put their hope in wealth, which is so uncertain, but to put their hope in God, who richly provides us with everything for our enjoyment."[5] Phlegmatics and melancholies may be prone to put their security in money because they are more fearful.

Jesus' View of Material Possessions

To get a better understanding of God's perspective on money and material things, look at Jesus' life and teachings. He had no place to lay His head. He never built a home. He didn't accumulate wealth or worldly goods. He didn't try to build His own kingdom on this earth. He knew that

His home was in the next life. And when He taught about material possessions, His primary focus was our hearts' relationship to goods.

In Matthew 6 Jesus teaches us what our attitudes are to be:

> Do not store up for yourselves treasures on earth, where moth and rust destroy, and where thieves break in and steal. But store up for yourselves treasures in heaven, where moth and rust do not destroy, and where thieves do not break in and steal. For where your treasure is, there your heart will be also.... Therefore I tell you, do not worry about your life, what you will eat or drink; or about your body, what you will wear. Is not life more important than food, and the body more important than clothes? Look at the birds of the air; they do not sow or reap or store away in barns, and yet your heavenly Father feeds them. Are you not much more valuable than they? Who of you by worrying can add a single hour to his life?
>
> And why do you worry about clothes? See how the lilies of the field grow. They do not labor or spin. Yet I tell you that not even Solomon in all his splendor was dressed like one of these. If that is how God clothes the grass of the field, which is here today and tomorrow is thrown into the fire, will he not much more clothe you, O you of little faith? So do not worry, saying, 'What shall we eat?' or 'What shall we drink?' or 'What shall we wear?' For the pagans run after all these things, and your heavenly Father knows that you need them. But seek first his kingdom and his righteousness, and all these things will be given to you as well. Therefore do not worry about tomorrow, for tomorrow will worry about itself. Each day has enough trouble of its own.[6]

There are several overriding principles in this scripture:

1. We are to invest in the eternal, not the temporal. And those things in which we invest our time and money indicate our true values and commitments in life.

2. We are not to worry about financial affairs or material goods or how

God will provide for us in the future. Worrying is a useless attempt to try to carry tomorrow's burdens today. Studies have shown that 95 percent of the things we worry about never come to pass. As we face burdens in the future, God will give us the grace we need to bear them at that time. This is especially hard for melancholies and phlegmatics who are naturally given to worry.

3. *We are not to be like non-Christians.* Jesus says in verse 32 that "the pagans run after all these things." Here, the word run translates the Greek word *epitezeo,* which comes from the root word *zeteo,* meaning "to search, inquire for with intense demand, to crave, desire, inquire, seek after and for." Jesus is telling us not to seek or to crave the things in the material world, and certainly not to be devoted to them with the type of devotion we would give to God. Although non-Christians often have this intense allegiance to seeking these things, Christians should not. And if we have fallen prey to this, we need to repent, change our ways, and give everything we own to God.

4. *Keep the teaching in context.* Some people combine these principles with Jesus' teaching in Matthew 19:16-30, where He is talking to the rich, young ruler. When the man asked Jesus, "Teacher, what good thing must I do to get eternal life?" Jesus responded that he should obey the commandments. The man replied that he had kept these commandments and asked what else he lacked. Jesus answered, "If you want to be perfect, go, sell your possessions and give to the poor, and you will have treasure in heaven. Then come, follow me."

Some people conclude that in order to inherit the kingdom of God we must give away all of our material possessions and never accumulate anything. That misrepresents the passage's intent. Jesus didn't tell everyone to sell all they possessed and give it to the poor. He told the rich, young ruler to do that. Why? Because Jesus saw the man's heart. He knew that the man was trusting in his wealth and this was inhibiting his ability to enter into the kingdom of God. He knew that this young man would be drawn away by concerns over worldly wealth and would not be able to give his full heart and life to following Jesus. So Jesus told him to get rid of those things that would hinder him and to follow Him because eternal life is much more important than temporal wealth. Although providing for the poor is certainly a scriptural imperative, that was not Jesus' purpose in this passage. Jesus was telling this man what barriers stood in the way of his being perfect in God's sight.

By contrast, when Nicodemus came to Jesus in John 3:2, Jesus did not tell Nicodemus to sell everything he owned and give it to the poor. Nicodemus was also a wealthy man—a trader and a merchant—but Jesus told him to be born again. Jesus told each man what he lacked, what barriers he would have to overcome, and what he had to do.

If we as a church would really learn to implement God's principles concerning these things, then perhaps God would fulfill the promise contained in Proverbs 13:22: "the wealth of the sinner is stored up for the righteous" (NASB). God would love to be able to fulfill this verse. But if He were to put wealth into our hands when our hearts aren't right, we would misuse it, consuming it with our own desires as opposed to funding the things He would want us to fund. And God, being a wise heavenly Father, will not give something to His children that would be wasteful or spiritually harmful.

Remember, We're Just Passing Through

We need to remember where we're headed, that our citizenship really is in heaven and not here on earth. As Paul says in Colossians 3:1, "If ye then be risen with Christ, seek those things which are above, where Christ sitteth on the right hand of God. Set your affection on things above, not on things on the earth" (KJV). If we will fix our minds on these things and seek first His kingdom and His righteousness, then our perspectives will be clear and our priorities will automatically be in order.

Psalm 37:4 says to "delight yourself in the LORD and he will give you the desires of your heart." This scripture does not teach that God will give us whatever we want if we are Christians. It teaches that if we delight ourselves in the Lord, if we spend time in His presence and in His Word every day, if we submit our desires, our wills, and our ways to Him, then He will give us the desires of our hearts. Why? Because He will birth His desires in our hearts.

Let's take another look at the words of a wise, old man. By the time Solomon wrote these words, he had already lived life to the fullest. God had given him unparalleled wisdom. Solomon had built great projects, amassed tremendous holdings of silver, gold, and slaves, and had seven hundred wives and three hundred concubines. He had spared himself nothing. And as he wrote the book of Ecclesiastes, he reflected back over his extraordinary life.

> I thought in my heart, "Come now, I will test you with pleasure to find out what is good." But that also proved to be meaningless. "Laughter," I said, "is foolish. And what does pleasure accomplish?" I tried cheering myself with wine, and embracing folly—my mind still guiding me with wisdom. I wanted to see what was worthwhile for men to do under heaven during the few days of their lives.

> I undertook great projects: I built houses for myself and planted vineyards. I made gardens and parks and planted all kinds of fruit trees in them. I made reservoirs to water groves of flourishing trees. I bought male and female slaves and had other slaves who were born in my house. I also owned more herds and flocks than anyone in Jerusalem before me. I amassed silver and gold for myself, and the treasure of kings and provinces. I acquired men and women singers, and a harem as well—the delights of the heart of man. I became greater by far than anyone in Jerusalem before me. In all this my wisdom stayed with me.

> I denied myself nothing my eyes desired; I refused my heart no pleasure. My heart took delight in all my work, and this was the reward for all my labor. Yet when I surveyed all that my hands had done and what I had toiled to achieve, everything was mean nothing was gained under the sun.[7]

What greater illustration could there be that achieving worldly success and accumulating material goods will not fulfill us in the long run? Just like a father watching his children fighting over their toys, the Lord sees us devoting our lives to acquiring our own toys instead of seeking His will and His righteousness. The only thing that gives lasting fulfillment is accomplishing the will of God in our lives. All else is meaningless. When we do His will, we find that the things which fulfill us are added to our lives.

God's Word simply works.

CHAPTER TEN

He Owns It All

*"But when the time had fully come, God sent his Son,
born of a woman, born under law,
to redeem those under law, that we might receive
the full rights of sons."*
GALATIANS 4:4-5

Imagine a dark, dank dungeon. Inside, you lie beaten and chained to the wall. Your master, an evil, hateful man, has had you imprisoned for crimes too numerous to count. Your sentence is death, and you wait in agony for the date of your execution.

There is a rustling sound at your cell door, and it swings open. Your whole body tenses, expecting the black mask of the executioner. Instead, a well-dressed nobleman appears before you. Ignoring the grime and filth, he kneels down beside your quaking body. In his hands, he hold the keys to the shackles that bind you.

"I've come to release you," he whispers as he unfastens the locks.

You try to say, "I don't understand," but nothing comes out. Who is this man? What would someone of his obvious stature have to do with a commoner like you...especially one condemned to die? How did he get permission for your release? Your crimes are worthy of death, and that is the only payment that will suffice.

"You've been released into my care," he says in soothing tones, melting away your fear. His face all but demands trust. As he reaches out to help you stand, he says, "Come with me."

He leads you out of the dungeon, past the cells of hundreds of prisoners. Their cries fill your ears, but you do not hear them. Your mind is still reeling with the thought of freedom.

Down the long, musty corridors you walk until you push aside a massive wooden door and find yourself in a large courtyard. The sun is blinding, yet wonderful.

Suddenly, the nobleman stops. His eyes focus on something across the courtyard. Strangely, the eyes that were filled with such compassion now exude pain.

You follow his gaze to a young man. His clothing bears the same richness as those of the gentleman who now clutches your hand. His bearing is just as regal. The similarities between the two leave no doubt. They are related... perhaps father and son.

As you watch, the executioner appears. In his hand, he holds the ax that was to end your life. In a blur, he smashes the hilt of the ax into the young man's stomach, causing him to double over in excruciating pain. With a snarl the executioner seizes the young man's arms, and before he can recover, hauls him away.

You try to pull free to somehow help him, but the older man's grip is too tight. After the two disappear within the confines of the dungeon, you cease struggling. Why didn't the young man try to escape, or even fight back? As you look back at the nobleman, wondering why he wouldn't let you help his son, you hear the dull thunk of the ax. The man beside you lowers his head. Tears form in his eyes and splash freely to the ground.

After a long moment, the executioner reappears and yells at you from across the courtyard, "The debt has been paid. You are free to go!" The gentleman nods slightly to him and leads you to a carriage waiting outside the prison walls. He orders the coachman to take you to his manor. During the ride, questions crash within your head. Why did he rescue you? Why did he allow his son to die in your place? Your thoughts are cut short as the carriage rocks to a halt before the most beautiful estate you have ever seen.

You open your mouth; whether out of surprise or in an attempt to speak, you're not sure.

A hand squeezes your shoulder, and you turn to face the gentleman who saved your life. For reasons you can't explain, the pain that clouded his eyes is gone. In its place is a warm glow. "Welcome home...my son," he says.

Your stomach drops and tightens at his words. You feel your mouth go slack once again, and your palms are suddenly sweaty.

The nobleman continues, "From now on, you will no longer be looked upon as a slave, but today you have become one of my family. The debt you owed was paid by my son. Now, all I have is yours. You will lack for nothing. Come, let's begin your new life together."

We Are Not Our Own

We must recognize who owns us. If we are Christians, the Lord owns us—all of us. As Paul wrote in 1 Corinthians 6:19-20, "Or do you not know that your body is a temple of the Holy Spirit who is in you, whom you have from God, and that you are not your own? For you have been bought with a price: therefore glorify God in your body" (NASB).

We were bought by the blood of Jesus and His substitutional death on the cross. The word *bought* is a translation of the Greek word *agorazo*, which comes from *agora*, meaning a marketplace. The symbolism is that we were purchased as slaves on the auction block. God, as our new master, purchased us with the precious blood of His son, who was executed in our place. We were literally redeemed from Satan's kingdom of darkness and brought into God's kingdom of light.

Not only were we delivered into the kingdom of God, but God also set his Holy Spirit in our hearts as a seal of ownership and a deposit on our future inheritance. As 2 Corinthians 1:21 says, "Now it is God who makes both us and you stand firm in Christ. He anointed us, set his seal of ownership on us, and put his Spirit in our hearts as a deposit, guaranteeing what is to come."

The first step, then, in making godly financial decisions is to realize that God doesn't own just 10 percent but everything—100 percent of our paychecks, our homes, our household goods, our cars, our jobs, our retirement plans, our mates, and even our kids. And since He owns everything and we are His property, our job is to be caretakers or stewards over His property. When we begin to understand and apply this principle, we will then be able to overcome some of the weaknesses of our temperament.

What Is a Steward?

Funk and Wagnall's dictionary defines a steward as one "entrusted with the management of property, finances, or other affairs not his own." The key phrase is "not his own." So many times we Christians act as if our possessions and money are ours to deal with as we wish. But God in essence said, "You are my property. I purchased you with the blood of my Son, Jesus Christ. Therefore, I own everything that you are. I am charging you with the responsibility of stewardship over this property. Your job is to care for it in a manner that brings glory to me."

Because we are not our own, then anything we "have" is also not our own; it belongs to God. We simply take care of it for Him while we are here on earth. Once we allow this concept fully to penetrate our hearts and minds, it will revolutionize our financial behavior.

How Does a Steward Handle Money?

1. A steward does not covet. God, in His ultimate wisdom, knew the human tendency toward selfishness. That's why the tenth commandment is "You shall not covet."[1] God could have said, "You shall not be bitter," or "You shall not be angry," or any one of a hundred other sins, but He didn't. He said, "You shall not covet" because He knew this would be an especially difficult temptation for us. Coveting is not limited to what belongs to someone else. Coveting can be desiring something with all our heart and soul. When making financial decisions, one of the keys is to lay our desires on God's altar and allow Him to give us what we truly need, not necessarily what we want. When we learn this attitude, we will be much more fulfilled and satisfied.

2. A steward has an open hand. We should constantly evaluate the control we exercise over finances and material goods to ensure we are following God's will, not our own. Under Old Testament law, the Israelites were commanded to give 10 percent of their earnings to the Lord. While the New Testament reinforces this in Matthew 23:23, Jesus' teachings go a step further and remind us that everything we own belongs to God, not just the tithe, and should be held with an open hand. Here, and throughout the New Testament, the emphasis is on the attitudes behind the actions, and often a higher level of accountability is demanded than in the Old Testament.

Consider the law against adultery. The Old Testament states, "You shall not commit adultery."[2] In the New Testament, Jesus said you have already done the deed in your heart if you look at a person lustfully. Jesus was revealing the root of the problem. It's almost impossible to fall into adultery without first fantasizing about it. First we allow the temptation to enter our minds, and then we entertain the thought of it. If we don't deal with the temptation here, we're headed for trouble. But when we immediately surrender that thought or temptation to the Lord, we refuse to allow the seeds of sin to take root and grow. If we consistently deal with the source of potential problems, then we will not have to deal with their consequences later on. In the same way, if we maintain an attitude of stewardship, then we will not be stingy or legalistic in our handling of money and goods.

3. A steward doesn't desire to hoard wealth for himself. Some Christians take an extreme view of Jesus' statement "Do not store up for yourselves treasures on earth."[3] They believe people should not save or invest money but give everything to the kingdom of God. However, this is not an accurate interpretation of the scripture. In the Greek, the word *not* is a qualified negative, not an absolute negative. It does not mean "you may not ever, under any circumstances, store up." Rather, it is a qualified statement, meaning there are some conditions which would make it permissible and other conditions which would make it wrong.

Again, Jesus was dealing with the root of the matter: selfishness. The key word in this scripture is *yourselves*. God is not opposed to His children having material goods as long as their hearts are focused on Him and His commands.

This concept is exemplified in Luke 12:16-21 in Jesus' parable of the rich fool. This rich man has such a large crop that he decides to tear down his barns and build bigger ones to store all of his grain. But the man's attitude is revealed in verse 19: "'I'll say to myself, "You have plenty of good things laid up for many years. Take life easy; eat, drink and be merry."' But God said to him, 'You fool! This very night your life will be demanded from you. Then who will get what you have prepared for yourself?' This is how it will be with anyone who stores up things for himself but is not rich toward God." The Amplified Bible perhaps states verse 21 best—"So it is with the one who continues to lay up and hoard possessions for himself and is not rich [in his relation] to God [this is how he fares]."

This text and many others make it clear: We are not forbidden worldly possessions or saving and investing money; the qualifier is "where is our heart?"

Owners Have Rights; Stewards Have Responsibilities

Stewardship and ownership are entirely different things. As stewards, we do not have rights. God has rights. We have responsibilities—responsibilities to take care of things in the best way possible. And although we may realize that we are to be stewards, in reality, we frequently act like owners.

How can we recognize when we are not functioning as stewards? Stewards are characterized by love, joy, peace, generosity, contentment, fulfillment, and sharing. Each of these qualities indicates that God, not materialism, controls our hearts. On the other hand, owners may exhibit anger, anxiety, bitterness, envy, fear, irritation, worry, frustration, preoccupation, covetousness, and striving.

When we exhibit the characteristics of stewardship, which flow from our relationship with God, we are portraying the qualities that Jesus taught.

But when we exhibit the symptoms of ownership typical of most Americans, we are behaving like the rest of our culture. How can we effectively witness to non-Christians if they see no difference between our lives and theirs? If they don't see peace, freedom, love, and joy in our lives, what will draw them to Jesus?

Whenever we catch ourselves becoming angry, frustrated, worried, or fearful, we should realize that God may be pricking our hearts. He may be saying, "Remember child, this is mine and not yours. You don't own it. I own you, and I own everything that is yours. Surrender this thing back to me." We need to respond first by stopping and praying, thanking the Lord that we are His. Second, we need to surrender the problem to God and place it on His altar.

What Is Promised to Stewards?

To gain a better understanding of what it means to be God's stewards, look at the parable of the talents in Matthew 25:14-30. Verse 15 says that the master gave three servants a different number of talents to manage, "each according to his ability." This parable indicates that God gives each person opportunities and responsibility commensurate with his abilities. Those to whom much has been given, much will be required. We should consider that the resources which God has made available to us must be used wisely or they can be lost. We may discover that in managing money the closer our attitudes and actions conform to the will of God, the more responsibility we will likely receive in the future.

Secondly, this parable implies that our faithfulness with the things God has placed in our care may have redeeming value in the hereafter. In verse 23, the Amplified Bible states: "His master said to him, Well done, you upright (honorable, admirable) and faithful servant! You have been faithful *and* trustworthy over a little; I will put you in charge of much. Enter into *and* share the joy (the delight, the blessedness) which your master enjoys." When we are faithful stewards over what God has entrusted to us, including our finances, our families, and our time, we will experience His joy, His delight, and His blessedness, but only if we are faithful to the One who has given us the talents in the first place.

Before going any further, we encourage you to make a covenant with God that you will acknowledge His ownership of everything you have. As a sign of your commitment to a lifestyle of stewardship, each member of the family should sign it. This can be a wonderful object lesson to teach your children more about how Christians should treat their money and their possessions.

If we are faithful stewards of what God has entrusted to us, we will find our Master quick to say, "Well done, good and faithful servant! You have been faithful with a few things; I will put you in charge of many things. Come and share your master's happiness!"[4]

CHAPTER ELEVEN

Receiving God's Wisdom

"My son, if you accept my words and store up my commands within you, turning your ear to wisdom and applying your heart to understanding, and if you call out for insight and cry aloud for understanding, and if you look for it as for silver and search for it as for hidden treasure, then you will understand the fear of the LORD and find the knowledge of God."

PROVERBS 2:1-5

Back in the early eighties, we were investing in silver—remember it was the *early* eighties. One evening after work I had an unusual feeling of foreboding that wouldn't go away. As I prayed about it, the thought came to mind that this foreboding might be related to our silver investments.

The next morning after a restless night's sleep Mona and I arose early to spend time with the Lord. Then I left for the office.

After a few moments, Mona called to read me an obscure scripture she had come across that morning in her Bible study time. She had been studying the minor prophets when this scripture in Zephaniah seemed literally to jump off the page: "'On that day,' declares the LORD, 'a cry will go up from the Fish Gate, wailing from the New Quarter, and a loud crash from the hills. Wail, you who live in the market district; all your merchants will be wiped out, all who trade with silver will be ruined.'"[1]

My mouth fell open in amazement. Could this be a warning from the Lord, a confirmation of our uneasy feeling the evening before? A crash, in silver? We prayed about it some more and decided this was too big a coincidence to be ignored. So as soon as the markets opened, we called our brokers and told them to sell our clients' and our own silver positions immediately. At the time, the price had been rising gradually so our traders wanted to know why we decided to sell. When I told them what had happened, they were pretty amazed themselves. Although they may have thought we had lost our marbles, they responded with, "Well, who are we to argue with God?" So they sold our positions at a slight profit early that day.

But what happened next really blew their minds. Unbeknownst to us or anyone else at the time, just the night before, the head of one of the largest gold and silver companies in the country had committed suicide. His company had gotten into financial difficulty, and he had been secretly borrowing from the till to meet ongoing bills, all the while speculating in the market to try to make it up. When his efforts to right the company failed, he gave it all up.

At the same time, one of the largest brokerage firms in the United States was left holding a tremendous number of silver contracts which were owned by this particular company. When they got word of the suicide after that morning and realized the apparent worthlessness of the company's collateral backing these positions, this brokerage firm sold all of the contracts, dumping a monstrous amount of gold and silver into the market all at one time. That drove the price of silver from over twelve dollars an ounce to under nine within minutes.

It turned out that the failed company had only about five million dollars' worth of metals on hand to cover the hundred million dollars of clients' accounts. Their bankruptcy forced millions of other investors into large losses, even though they had no personal connection to that firm.

We got out just in time!

What is the message of this story? Did God lead Mona to that scripture? At the time we weren't certain, but since then we have come to believe that God was indeed directing our path. No one is perfect at discerning the leading of the Lord. But we do know that He promises to meet our needs.

He promises to give us wisdom. He promises to direct us, and He can direct us in any way He chooses. And we believe God keeps His word.

Some people may be skeptical. Some may question if God would lead us in these types of things, even in investments. We believe He does. Does He always rescue us from circumstances and our mistakes? Certainly not, for our own good. But with all our hearts we believe that seeking the Lord's wisdom and His leading, especially in our financial dealings, is an important aspect of our walk with Jesus.

Are you facing a quandary, not knowing what to do about a major financial decision? Perhaps you're trying to decide between staying at your present job or branching out in a business venture of your own. Or perhaps you believe that your children need more time with Mom, but if she quits her job, it will cause a financial earthquake in your household. Be it a major, life-changing decision or something simple and everyday, like what the food budget should be, in all our financial decisions, we need wisdom!

God's Wisdom or Ours?

Suppose for a moment that you hold two blank books in your hands. One of the books, though not brand new, appears to have been rarely opened. The binding is tight, the cover is clean, and few pages bear any sign of writing.

The other book is vastly different. It is worn, the binding is stretched and cracked, and its pages are cluttered with thousands of scrawled notes and entries. It's on the verge of falling apart in your hands.

Both of these books are your life's story. God is the author of the book that is in good condition. You rarely give him the opportunity to make entries, so its pages are seldom touched. Instead you prefer to write your own destiny, and as a result you now hold a book that could come apart at any moment, scattering the pages of your life...into eternity.

The question you must ask yourself is, which author would you prefer to write the book of your life? God, on the one hand, is omniscient; He sees all things and knows all things. He's all powerful, and His wisdom and knowledge far surpass our finite capability to comprehend. He not only knows your past and your present but sees exactly what each turn of the page will bring, all the way to the book's end. You, as the other author, can see only one line of a page at a time. When all is considered, who would you prefer to chronicle your life? Will you give the pen of your destiny to the author and finisher of your faith, producing a bestseller, or will you, with your limited understanding of the incredible enormity of life, choose to take the pen?

God will allow us to operate according to our own wisdom if we so choose, but He holds out a promise to those who desire His higher ways. The promise is that we can gain His wisdom and not be forced to rely on our own flawed reasoning. As we learn how to receive God's wisdom, we must first distinguish between our wisdom and His. God's wisdom is unlike that of the world's. As it is written in 1 Corinthians, "For the wisdom of this world is foolishness in God's sight."[2]

God's Promise of Wisdom

One of the keys to overcoming weaknesses in our temperament and to experiencing God's blessing in our finances is to understand that only by seeking God and His wisdom will we obtain the best in life. To obtain godly wisdom, we must go to the source of all wisdom. God promises, "If any of you lacks wisdom, he should ask God, who gives generously to all without finding fault, and it will be given to him. But when he asks, he must believe and not doubt, because he who doubts is like a wave of the sea, blown and tossed by the wind."[3]

The Greek word for *wisdom* in this passage implies being skillful, as an expert, operating sensibly or prudently. In other words, wisdom is knowing the sensible, the right thing, to do. The Greek word for *ask* means "to request" or "to beg," as a subordinate seeks an answer from a superior. As soldiers in God's army, we ask the Lord, our commander, what to do next. God does not get upset when we ask for His wisdom; He prefers that we ask for it rather than operate independently of Him.

The context of this verse is a discussion of trials. Trials—financial or otherwise—test our faith and develop perseverance in our walks with the

Lord. As we face seemingly insurmountable obstacles, God promises that if we need wisdom or understanding all we have to do is ask for His guidance and He will bestow it liberally.

But, as with most promises of God, there are conditions. The first condition is that we *ask* God for His wisdom and not be self-reliant, presuming that we already have what we need. While we certainly need to train and strengthen our minds, we must learn to submit our thoughts to God's wisdom. Read the following verse slowly and don't pass over the power of its promise: "Lean on, trust in, *and* be confident in the Lord with all your heart *and* mind and do not rely on your own insight *or* understanding. In all your ways know, recognize, *and* acknowledge Him, and He will direct *and* make straight *and* plain your paths."[4]

We must be willing to seek God's will and to submit to it once it has been revealed to us, not only when we're going through trials but continually. God is even interested in what we may consider insignificant decisions, because He desires a relationship with us.

The second condition is that when we ask, we must ask in faith. James 1:6 in the Amplified Bible says, "Only it must be in faith that he asks with no wavering (no hesitating, no doubting). For the one who wavers (hesitates, doubts) is like the billowing surge out at sea that is blown hither *and* thither and tossed by the wind." If we don't believe that God will give us wisdom, then, as verse 7 says, we will not receive anything from the Lord.

The King James Version translates verses 6 through 8 "But let him ask in faith, nothing wavering. For he that wavereth is like a wave of the sea driven with the wind and tossed. For let not that man think that he shall receive any thing of the Lord. A double minded man is unstable in all his ways." The word *wavering* in the Greek *(diakrino)* literally means to be divided in one's mind, implying two minds never in harmony with one another. The Greek word for *double minded* is *dipsuchos* from *dis,* meaning "twice," and *psuche,* meaning "souled" or "minded." Picture a person split in half—one side saying yes, the other side saying no—in a constant state of confusion.

When we ask for wisdom without having faith, we are unable to receive anything from God. Our doubts and unbelief keep us in constant confusion and turmoil, not knowing which way to turn.

What's the Source of the Wisdom?

How do we know the wisdom we're receiving is from God and is not our own understanding? One way to determine our source of wisdom is to look at those things that accompany God's wisdom, which are not necessarily a part of human wisdom.

One of the first things that accompanies God's wisdom is humility. James 3:13 states, "Who is wise and understanding among you? Let him show it by his good life, by deeds done in the humility that comes from wisdom." Humility and wisdom go hand-in-hand. When we are truly wise, we realize just how insignificant our worldly wisdom is, compared to God's. Furthermore, God's wisdom cannot be received unless we are walking in humility, because "God opposes the proud but gives grace to the humble."[5] When we are walking in pride, we can be sure that we will not receive God's wisdom.

Jesus is our prime example here. Jesus, the author and finisher of our faith, the creator of the universe, the one and only Lamb of God, "did not consider equality with God something to be grasped, but made himself nothing....he humbled himself and became obedient to death—even death on a cross!"[6] Just think of it. If anyone had the right to be proud about His status, His position, or His knowledge, it was Jesus. Yet He was completely humble and obedient to the wishes of His Father. Because of His humility and His obedience, He received all wisdom.

We must test the wisdom we are receiving to see if it is prompted by envy, selfish ambition, self-exaltation, or ungodly desires or motivations. If so, that wisdom is definitely not from God. James continues in verse 17 of chapter 3, "But the wisdom that comes from heaven is first of all pure; then peace-loving, considerate, submissive, full of mercy and good fruit, impartial and sincere." That's how we can know the source of the wisdom.

How Do We Receive God's Wisdom?

The Wisdom in the Word

The first way to get God's wisdom is through His Word. Psalm 119:105 says, "Your word is a lamp to my feet and a light for my path." In our journey along rocky or unfamiliar paths, the lamp of God's Word illumines our path, shows us where to go next, and reveals dangers which lurk just beyond in the darkness. Without it, we would be lost, stumbling about in futility and injuring ourselves.

However, we must become diligent seekers, not just casual inquirers. A sleepy-eyed nod to God early in the morning will not allow us to learn the ways of God. Second Timothy 2:15 in the Amplified Bible states: "Study *and* be eager *and* do your utmost to present yourself to God approved (tested by trial), a workman who has no cause to be ashamed, correctly analyzing *and* accurately dividing—[rightly handling and skillfully teaching] the Word of Truth."

The word *study* in the Greek is *spoudazo,* which means "to give diligence, be diligent, endeavor, labor, study." We study so that our lives may be transformed from the ways of the world and conformed to the ways of God. Our goal is to hide the Word in our hearts to such a degree that it sets the parameters for how we think and react to any circumstance. The Word of God should dwell in us until it literally controls us, becoming an internal guidance system that checks against worldly wisdom and improper financial motives.

God Can Lead Us Through Prayer

The second way God can lead us and give us wisdom is through prayer. Praying makes us aware of how much God really cares for us. When we pray specific, direct prayers and God faithfully answers them, our trust in Him builds and our relationship with Him increases.

Our children, who are now young adults, pray about everything that concerns their lives because they know from experience that God answers prayers. They have seen it in their own and their parents' lives. Hannah, our daughter, at the age of eleven wanted some new clothes. We told her to pray for them because we wanted God to teach her at an early age that He cared enough for her to answer a prayer for the littlest detail of her life. So this young child purposely prayed to God daily for some new clothes. To her amazement, she was given three bags full of clothing by a woman in our church. This woman, before she got pregnant, was exactly the size of our daughter. As a legal secretary, she had some of the finest clothes our daughter had ever seen. Being a melancholy, Hannah was thrilled to have the beautiful, fine quality clothing we would never have provided for her at that age. Her prayers were answered far beyond what she had asked.

As a child, our son continually lost his wallet. It was amazing to watch him repeatedly sit down in absolute exasperation and cry out to God, "Oh, God, You are the omnipotent one. You know everything and You definitely know where my wallet is. Will you please show me? Will you please have it turn up?" To this day, our son has always found his missing wallet.

Our children saw us pray over every area of our lives. If we had a need, they were included in our time of prayer, and they watched God provide on a daily basis in our business, our home life, and our marriage. Not only did we receive the benefit of God's faithfully answering our prayers and meeting all of our needs, but this precious time with God had a tremendous impact on the spiritual lives of our children. Now, as young adults, they have no doubt that God will provide for their needs just as He provided for their parents' needs. Hannah says, "As I have prayed over the little things throughout my life, I have learned to trust God. Now that I am older, I am having to trust Him for bigger things, like who is going to be my mate and what is the call that God has for my life. Because I have a track record of God's answering my prayers, it is much easier for me to believe that He will answer these prayers also."

When we first began really walking with the Lord, we wondered why a person would pray. We thought, "If God knows what we need before we ever ask, why pray?" One of the things that convinced us of the need for prayer was the important role it played in Jesus' life. If the very Son of God, who was the embodiment of wisdom and truth itself, needed to go away and spend extended time in prayer, how much more do we mortals need to do so?

In 1 Thessalonians 5:17, Paul exhorts us to "pray continually." Obviously we cannot stop and go to the prayer closet every time something comes up. We believe the Lord was saying through Paul to be in a constant state of prayer. If we are walking with the Lord continually, we will not only want to have good quiet times in prayer, but we will also want to continue praying about decisions we should make, how we should react, and what we should do throughout the day. Our constant asking for God's wisdom makes us far more receptive to continually receiving His wisdom than our having a quiet time in the morning and doing our own thing the rest of the day. As one man explained it to his Bible study group, "My wife can be in the kitchen cooking, setting the table, or doing the dishes while she is talking on the phone. She is going about her daily activities, but she is communicating the whole time. Continual prayer is much the same."

God desires the same kind of relationship with us as He had with Adam and Eve in the garden. The Lord walked with them and communed with them and talked with them. Because of Adam's sin, people were unable to continue that same relationship with God, but because of Jesus' obedience, we again have the ability to commune directly with God.

So often Paul begins his letters by saying he prays for the people constantly. For too long the weapon of prayer has lain dormant in the church of America. It's time to take up that sword again. As the Amplified Bible says, "The earnest (heartfelt, continued) prayer of a righteous man makes tremendous power available [dynamic in its working]."[7]

He Can Direct Us by His Spirit

The third way God can direct us is by His Spirit. In John 14, Jesus told the disciples that He was about to be crucified and return to His Father. But He said in verses 16 and 17, "And I will ask the Father, and he will give you

SMART MONEY

another Counselor to be with you forever—the Spirit of truth." Jesus had promised the disciples that He would not abandon them. Remember, they were accustomed to going to Him anytime they needed help. If they needed to know how to cast out a demon or how to feed a hungry crowd, Jesus directed them every time. And Jesus is reassuring them that they will continue to be guided, now through the Holy Spirit.

Christians today also need to learn to be sensitive to and yielded to the Holy Spirit. Paul assures us that our minds can be controlled by the Spirit: "Those who live according to the sinful nature have their minds set on what that nature desires; but those who live in accordance with the Spirit have their minds set on what the Spirit desires. The mind of sinful man is death, but the mind controlled by the Spirit is life and peace."[8] So how do we learn to live controlled by the Spirit?

The first step to making Spirit-controlled decisions is to realize that our flesh, our human nature, will not guide us into God's will. Our flesh will oppose God's spirit. Paul speaks for all of us when he says, "For what I do is not the good I want to do; no, the evil I do not want to do—this I keep on doing."[9]

The story of Abraham and Sarah is one of the Bible's great examples of being led by our flesh rather than by God's Spirit. Abraham had received God's promise to make him the father of many nations, with offspring which would outnumber the stars in the sky. Since receiving this promise years earlier, he and Sarah had diligently waited for God to provide the miracle son through which their descendants would come. Finally, after years of waiting, Sarah and Abraham became impatient. In an attempt to fulfill God's promise themselves, Sarah told Abraham to have a child by her maidservant Hagar. As a result, Ishmael was born and the conflict began between Ishmael and his descendants, the modern Arab nations, and the descendants of Isaac, the child who would later be born to fulfill God's promise to Abraham. We, like Abraham and Sarah, are tempted to follow the desires of our flesh, rather than waiting to be led and directed by God's Holy Spirit. When we follow our own desires or get too impatient, we create a work of our flesh—an Ishmael—which will never be God's best for us.

154

Yet the Lord promises to guide us and direct us into all truth, if we will abide in Him. "He that abideth in me, and I in him, the same bringeth forth much fruit: for without me ye can do nothing.... If ye abide in me, and my words abide in you, ye shall ask what ye will, and it shall be done unto you."[10] *Abide* comes from the Greek word *meno,* meaning "to remain, to dwell, to abide, endure, to last, persevere, to stand firm or steadfast." We are to remain in Him, and in return, He will dwell within us. As He dwells in us, He gives us abundant life.

Abiding only occurs when we have an intimate, ongoing relationship with the Holy Spirit, not just an intellectual Christianity. It means daily fellowship with God. Abiding is the key to all of life, including our finances.

As fathers, when we abide in Him, we will not abandon our responsibilities toward our wives and children. We will not let the bills slip by unpaid or declare, "Nobody is going to tell me what to do with my money."

As mothers, we will not nag our husbands or demand they give in to our ways. As daughters of Abraham, we will declare that we will not give way to fear.

As abiding people, we will bear much fruit. Abiding in God is what enables us to overcome the weaknesses of our temperaments. Sanguines will be able to wait on the Lord and not act impulsively. Melancholies will have joy instead of fear and will learn to be content with what God gives them. Phlegmatics will be given a sense of destiny and purpose which will motivate them out of their passiveness. And cholerics will learn to love others and to acknowledge their utter dependence on God.

Being led by the Spirit is so crucial in the major decisions of life that we are going to share our own pilgrimage in the next chapter. At the risk of being a bit redundant, we want you to see why we believe this is the most essential step toward finding financial freedom.

Five Steps to Discerning the Will of God

1. Keep the Lord in mind as you make decisions during the day, and ask for His wisdom on a continual basis. Before making major decisions such as accepting a new job or buying a house or a car, spend extended time studying His Word, praying, and praising Him. By spending time in daily fellowship with God, you become more attuned to His wavelength so that you are more open to His guidance. That's the secret of abiding. Be open to the Lord any way He should choose to lead, even if it doesn't fit your previously conceived ideas. Don't put God in a box.

2. Study and thoroughly research your options using all available resources. That includes soliciting the advice of godly men and women who are trained in the field. While excellent advice can be gained from non-Christians, assess their wisdom in light of God's principles. Be open to listening to people with differing viewpoints.

3. Become emotionally neutral about the outcome. Whenever our emotions are tied up in an issue, it becomes more difficult to discern God's direction. Too often we make our decisions independent of God and then ask Him to bless them. Prayerfully submit all circumstances to God and become content to accept His decisions. Put your own will and desires on the altar. Just as Paul was content in humble means or prosperity, so should we be. When we put ourselves in neutral, then God can more easily move us whichever direction He desires.

4. Take time to be still, quiet, and focused on God. Remember Elijah did not hear God in the noise. He heard God in the silence.

5. Wait for the peace of God. Wait for the timing of God. Don't rush. God has plenty of time. He knows our future before we do and can easily guide us into the proper actions in plenty of time. God will give us His peace when He is confirming the direction we are to go. As Proverbs 3:5-6 promises, "Trust in the LORD with all your heart and lean not on your own understanding; in all your ways acknowledge him, and he will make your paths straight."

Result of God's Wisdom

Jesus said in Matthew 11:28-30: "Come to me, all you who are weary and burdened, and I will give you rest. Take my yoke upon you and learn from me, for I am gentle and humble in heart, and you will find rest for your souls. For my yoke is easy and my burden is light." Since Jesus, the Father, and the Holy Spirit are one, we receive God's rest when we are led by His Spirit, study His Word, and abide in His presence.

As we look at Jesus' words, two pictures come to mind. First, we see the results of not following His leading—we are overburdened. The image is that of a pack animal trying to carry a load that is too heavy and too large.

But as we yoke ourselves with Jesus, submitting our cares and burdens to Him and following His leading by the Spirit, we receive His rest. We're joined together with Him and as a result, He helps us carry our burdens. Together we accomplish our ends.

A further benefit of being yoked to the Lord is balance. In the Greek, the word *yoke* not only depicts a joining together for a common purpose or a yoke of servitude with Jesus as our master, it also can literally be translated "the connecting of the scales." In other words, it is the point at which the scale balances. Although we will always have times of stress and turmoil, when we are following God's direction for our lives, we have balance in our lives. We won't take on more than we can handle and burn out.

As we learn to make the right choices, we receive God's peace, His direction, His rest. And the result is a life that is balanced, fruitful, and fulfilled.

CHAPTER TWELVE

Finding the Spirit's Direction

"'No eye has seen, no ear has heard, no mind has conceived what God has prepared for those who love him'—but God has revealed it to us by his Spirit. The Spirit searches all things, even the deep things of God."

1 CORINTHIANS 2:9-10

Have you ever wondered what it would have been like to be on earth while Jesus was here, to walk beside the Lord and watch Him walk on water, heal the sick, and give sight to blind eyes? Although it would have been marvelous to witness those things, God has a different plan for our lives. Maybe in facing a financial decision you have thought, "It sure would be nice to have the Lord here to tell me what to do. 'Move here and take this job offer.' 'Be sure you buy this car.' 'Don't worry about the mortgage payment. I'm going to provide.'" But the reality is, God is with us; He abides within us in the person of the Holy Spirit. Our problem is that we need to learn how to be led by God, to obey the prompting of the Holy Spirit.

How can we tell the difference between being led by the Spirit and being led by our own desires in making decisions? How does God use our temperament strengths while compensating for our weaknesses? How do we function so that the power of the Holy Spirit directs our lives and finances?

Let us tell you about our pilgrimage to discover the answers.

The Tale of Two Houses

Early in our marriage we bought the world's lie of bigger, better, best—the large house, the fancy car, the images of success. Fresh out of college, I [Jerry] went to work for a financial planning company. Within three years, our income had shot up beyond our wildest dreams. We were working with high rollers who had sailed through the seventies with the Midas touch. Surrounded by their opulent lifestyles, we were confident that our own success was not only going to last but increase. I was driving a new Riviera provided by the company and had become a local radio station personality. Being new to the business world, I believed that my boss and other successful, Christian, financial advisors knew what they were doing, so I followed right along. I invested my personal money heavily in tax shelters, as they had done for years, and presumed it would continue to work. (The IRS soon would have a different idea.)

Mona, in the meantime, was staying at home with our two kids who were quickly outgrowing their rooms. Our modest house was definitely getting too small. Besides, there was not enough room to host Bible studies. So the hunt for a bigger house began.

Using sound financial principles, we came across a house in a development that had gone bankrupt. It was a terrific buy. It was in a good neighborhood. It was a great tax shelter, since we had been renting until now. The house fulfilled every desire of our hearts, down to the large room for Bible studies. My boss said we shouldn't pass up such a good deal. So we were hooked. We bought the house and filled it with brand-new furniture, including custom built sofas that were Scotch-guarded for life.

What's Wrong with This Picture?

By this point in our young married life, we had violated at least six basic biblical principles of finance.

1. We bought into the lie of our culture that we had to look successful, especially since I was a financial consultant. Plus, we thought we were being rewarded for our godliness—oh, the pride.

2. At what we later recognized was the pinnacle of success in our early years, we bought the big house and incurred a huge debt.

3. Mona became discontent with what God had provided for us and desired something "better."

4. We spiritualized our fleshly desires by rationalizing that we would use the house to be "missionaries to the rich."

5. We prayed and asked God to bless our plans—after we made them.

6. We presumed that the blessings were going to continue.

The Doubt Begins

Christmas came nine months later. The opportunity for ministry was at hand. We reached out to our church and invited a group over for a fellowship. The house was beautiful, but the guests were uncomfortable with the discrepancy in our income levels. One couple we had been ministering to during a family crisis was visibly distant. Never again did they invite us to their home. Mona recognized that the very purpose for which we had supposedly bought the house had been negated. The words of her brother Tom, who was a missionary to the poor, rang in her ears: "Mona, you don't own things. Things own you."

God didn't write on the walls, but His message came through with equal clarity. One morning as Mona was reading her Bible, a passage from Haggai hit her with full force: "Is it a time for you yourselves to be living in your paneled houses, while this house remains a ruin?... Give careful thought to your ways. You have planted much, but have harvested little.... You earn wages, only to put them in a purse with holes in it."[1]

Yes, we had paneled walls, walls so nice they intimidated our friends. We earned much, but kept little. Our house payment was certainly large enough to put a few holes in our purse. We had expected the money to continue on the upswing, and yet it was going out just as fast as it came in. We were tithing and thought we were following God's will for our finances, but we had not yet learned how to discern between the desires of our flesh and the leading of the Spirit. We had subtly bought into our flesh's desires, focusing on its values and not God's. Conviction about how the world's viewpoint had affected our lifestyle weighed heavily upon us, and in obedience to what we felt was God's leading, we put our "dream" house on the market.

Thus began our pilgrimage from wanting God to bless our decisions to becoming open to His will for everything, including our financial resources. We realized we could get there only by learning to discern God's ways and the Spirit's leading in our lives. It was then that we really began to understand the difference between the ways of the flesh and the ways of God.

The Flesh Versus the Spirit

The first step to making Spirit-controlled decisions is to realize that our flesh will not move us in the right direction. Our flesh will oppose God's Spirit, therefore we must learn to recognize when our flesh is in operation. In the Greek the word *flesh* includes the corrupt nature of humanity subject to its appetites and its passions. If we choose to allow our flesh rather than God's Spirit to determine our choices, then our corrupt nature is making our decisions, and we can't possibly expect those decisions to be blessed by God. "For the mind set on the flesh is death, but the mind set on the Spirit is life and peace, because the mind set on the flesh is hostile toward God; for it does not subject itself to the law of God, for it is not even able to do so; and those who are in the flesh cannot please God."[2]

Our decision about the house had been heavily influenced by the works of our flesh—selfishness, ego, envy, pride—and we had entered a battle for control. Since we already had to fight the influences of our culture, the last thing we needed was another, ongoing battle within ourselves. Paul described his inner battle in Romans 7:19: "For the good that I wish, I do not do; but I practice the very evil that I do not wish" (NASB). In Galatians 5:16-17 he identified the battle as a war between the flesh and Spirit: "But I say, walk by the Spirit, and you will not carry out the desire of the flesh. For the flesh sets its desire against the Spirit, and the Spirit against the flesh; for these are in opposition to one another" (NASB).

When we operate according to the dictates of our flesh, we're separated from God's influence. But when our spiritual life consists of constant communion with God, He promises to guide us and direct us into all truth. He tells us that the Spirit searches out and knows all things. If these things are true, we will make much better financial decisions when we are led and controlled by His Spirit rather than when we succumb to the dictates of our flesh.

We were beginning to understand how our flesh had directed us toward decisions that were out of line with God's will.

Our Next Move

We would love to say that we had learned our lesson at that point and that we found the will of God and moved on in perfect bliss. Wrong. We still had more steps—uphill ones—to take in our pilgrimage. We had sold our thirty-five hundred square foot house in the city and moved to the country, where we looked for a place to build. In the meantime we rented a small house, which Mona loved because she was no longer a slave to cleaning. Our focus was no longer the house but rather the relationships with people in our church and the people we could minister to.

However, I was still struggling with the image. After all, I was supposed to be a financial expert. How could I be that if I was living in a small house in a small town? I had enjoyed the large house and the status it indicated. My pride and ego had to die before I would be open to the Spirit's leading.

Over the next seven years, God would deal a death blow to our flesh in this area. The tax shelters we had invested in heavily in the early eighties had been disallowed by the government. We now had to repay the government the taxes, as well as interest and penalties. By the time the bill became due, the interest and penalties exceeded the initial tax obligation.

The night we sat down together and laid out all our debts and the inevitable consequences of the tax shelters we hit bottom. I felt like a failure and even considered going into a new field to try to dig our way out. Our life was in ashes, but we held on to the hope found in Isaiah 42:3, "A bruised reed he will not break, and a smoldering wick he will not snuff out." As our pain was crucifying our fleshly desires, I sought God in a new way. And He began to deliver us, but not without pain or consequences.

What Did We Learn?

By Him taking us to the edge, where we had nothing left of our personal finances except His provision, we came to understand how absolutely essential it is to kill our fleshly desires and become totally committed to His will. We came fully to the point where we could truly say, "Not my will but Thy will be done."

All the financial principles we have come to believe and teach were learned at the hands of God during these years. Mona began to shop smarter. I began using the seven steps to financial freedom and applying the domino theory to our debts. We quit using our credit cards and went to a Spartan lifestyle. And we taught our children what we learned.

We learned to rest within God's sovereignty, that He would provide another house when He had accomplished what He had begun in our lives and hearts.

We learned not to presume the future concerning our level of income and debt.

We learned to be content with God's parameters for our lives and to wait until He directs us to move.

We learned to distinguish between being driven by the desires of our flesh versus being gently led by the sweet Spirit of God.

We learned to distinguish between the world's principles of finance versus God's principles.

Materialism was ground out of our lives and was replaced by God's values. We discovered that what was important to people was not always important to God.

Later, we studied the temperaments and applied them to our relationships and our finances. As a result we began working better together, implementing biblical principles for the husband's and wife's roles within the family.

The principles of God were being burned into us like a brand. And we began to be transformed.

Living in a Glass House Isn't All Bad

After several difficult years we were totally out of debt, as God blessed these principles. We even built up a significant surplus by tenaciously following the principles. Eventually we felt it was time to start looking to buy a home rather than continuing to rent, but we were determined not to repeat our past mistakes. We were committed to making ourselves totally neutral in the decision and to praying and asking God where He wanted us to go. And we were determined to be content wherever He led us.

We laid out our desires, and then we laid them down. After looking for months, we chose a particular area about which we had a sense of peace and direction. We wanted a place where we could impact our neighbors and the community and where we could be a part of a local church. We were seeking relationships, not status or comfort. The house we found was smaller than we would have chosen earlier, but we sensed a strong peace about the neighborhood, the house, and the area.

The house sits up on a slight rise and is glassed in across the back, facing our neighbors. It has become a symbol of what we desire our lives to be—transparent before others. Consequently, others have become a greater part of our lives. Within three streets of our house a network of Christian friends has developed and sustained us. One of our neighbors does all our typesetting for our newsletter. The lady across the street has a prayer closet that we can see from our front door, and she goes in that prayer closet daily to pray for us. The pastor in our local church has not only fed us from the pulpit but has become an advisor to us in this project as well. Another lady has become Mona's Barnabas, keeping her many projects ordered and timely and offering her encouragement. Two streets over another friend has proofread and edited and meticulously checked every word we have written for our many projects. They have not only blessed our lives, but they have found new outlets for using their gifts to build up the body of Christ. We are functioning as the body of Christ together, each uniquely gifted, each dependent on the other, and most importantly walking together to follow the Lord more closely.

This process was an incredible pilgrimage, but it represents like no other events in our lives how dangerous it is to follow the desires of our flesh and how bountifully God blesses us when we follow the leading of His Spirit.

Tools for Being Led By the Spirit

There's an old saying that "God gives His best to those who leave the choice to Him." As we walk by the Spirit and not by the flesh, we are participating in God's life, His best and highest blessing. While that doesn't mean we'll have a stress free life, it does mean we'll have His peace, His rest, and spiritual renewal.

Over the years of our pilgrimage we have learned and developed some principles we believe are crucial in learning to follow God's leading and not our flesh. They are not a pat formula but follow as a natural outflow of our relationship with God.

1. When considering different alternatives, become completely neutral about the outcome. Our own desires will get in the way if we let them. We must ask for God's will, not our own.

2. Beware of fleshly motivation. Ego, pride, envy, or impatience are dead giveaways that our motives are based on our flesh. Anger, pride, fear, worry, presumption, or self-sufficiency will short-circuit the process, grieving the Spirit and causing us to be shut off from His leading. We must be humble and dependent on the Lord to receive His leading and wisdom. The pride and anger that are characteristic of cholerics and sanguines will tend to be obstacles in their following God's leading. The fear and worry which characterize melancholies and phlegmatics will do the same.

3. Continually ask and expect to receive God's will, while at the same time keeping your own will on the altar. Like learning to walk, this is a process. At first, we stumble but gradually God confirms His way to us and we become more certain of following His leading (or direction). When we are fully submitted to the Lord and His Spirit, these characteristics will be smoothed out and we will flow in God's direction.

4. Look for the peace of God. Where His Spirit is, there is peace. When we're led by the Holy Spirit, we will not experience confusion, turmoil, or anxiety. Although we may have doubts at times, wait until the haze clears and continue praying and expecting Him to answer. Look for peace to confirm decisions or direction.

In learning to follow the Spirit keep in mind the words of Galatians 5:16-25, but don't let the familiarity of the verses rob you of their power, especially the power of these last two sentences: "But I say, walk by the Spirit, and you will not carry out the desire of the flesh. For the flesh sets its desire against the Spirit, and the Spirit against the flesh; for these are in opposition to one another.... But the fruit of the Spirit is love, joy, peace, patience, kindness, goodness, faithfulness, gentleness, self-control; against such things there is no law. *Now those who belong to Christ Jesus have crucified the flesh with its passions and desires. If we live by the Spirit, let us also walk by the Spirit* (NASB; emphasis added).

CHAPTER THIRTEEN

God's Principles of Money Management

*"Go to the ant, you sluggard; consider its ways
and be wise!"*

PROVERBS 6:6

Remember Aesop's fable of the grasshopper and the ant? While the ant was diligently harvesting and storing up provisions during the summer, the grasshopper was content to play. Then when winter came, the grasshopper had nothing to fall back on and was forced to rely upon the charity of the ant.

I believe America has become a nation of grasshoppers, content to live in the now. Most people function as if our economy is invincible and therefore save virtually nothing for tomorrow. And not only do they not save, they compound the problem by borrowing heavily.

Someday our country will face an economic winter—not just another recession, but something much worse. At that time, only those who have prepared like the ant will be able to meet their own needs and have a surplus to meet the needs of others.

As Christians, we are to be good stewards of our time, our talents, and our money. But in order to do that, we must understand God's principles for saving and investing, and then we must faithfully apply those principles.

The Bucket Principle

The first subject we need to grasp, in order to gain God's blessing financially, is the Law of Compound Growth. To make our money grow, we have to begin putting money into savings or investments. As we discussed earlier, Christians are not forbidden to save or invest money. In fact, it is one of the keys to proper stewardship, as long as we remember whose money it really is.

The law of compounding is best illustrated by what we call "the bucket principle." If you place a bucket under a leaky faucet, dripping a drop at a time, the bucket eventually fills up. A person who saves a little at a time will eventually see his money grow. As Proverbs 13:11 says, "Wealth hastily gotten will dwindle, but he who gathers little by little will increase it" (RSV). God usually does things exactly opposite of the way the world does. While the world is always trying to find some new scheme to strike it rich quick, God's way is to increase little by little.

There are three primary ingredients which determine how fast your money grows:
- the amount of time your investment is allowed to grow,
- the rate of return you earn on your money,
- and the amount of money you invest.

If you don't have much money to invest, then you need either a lot of time or a high rate of return. If you don't have much time to get ready for retirement, then you need a lot of money or a high rate of return. If you get a low rate of return on your money, then you need a lot of time or a lot of money. All three work together, producing your long-term return.

Just $1.74 a Day

Almost anyone can save a small amount of money every day just by changing his spending habits a little. Just eliminating a Coke and a candy bar could save as much as $1.74 a day. And if you took the $1.74 you saved each day and invested it, which is $52 per month, at a 10 percent growth rate, your money would grow to $1,375 in two years' time. While this is not an impressive amount, over time it can become significant. If you continue to allow this money to grow year after year, and add to it little by little, in five years it will grow to $4,027. In ten years, it will be $10,652; in fifteen years, $21,552. At the end of twenty years, you would have accumulated $39,487. (See Table A.) And if you had invested only $52 per month for forty years, you would accumulate over $328,000.

TABLE A
Investing just $1.74 per day (about $52 per month) at a growth rate of 10%, your money would grow as follows:

2 years	$ 1,375
5 years	4,027
10 years	10,652
15 years	21,552
20 years	39,487
30 years	117,545
40 years	328,852

That's not a bad sum. Plus it doesn't take into account that if you are able to save $52 per month in the beginning, you should be able to save more per month ten, fifteen, or twenty years later. Obviously, the more you increase the amount you save each month, the faster your savings accumulate. The bucket principle works. You don't have to make a lot of money in order to accumulate a lot by retirement. You just have to get started as soon as possible and save "little by little." The vast majority of clients I've seen over the years have accumulated their funds precisely this way, saving little by little over a long period. Often the biggest challenge is just getting started.

The $600,000 Estate

To prove the point, let's look at another example. Assume that you have a goal of saving $600,000 by retirement age. While this may sound like a lot of money today, it is not a tremendous amount when you consider the impact of inflation over many years. We will assume a rate of return of 12 percent per year, which is not improbable for a long-term investment. As shown in Table B, if you wait until you are fifty-five to start saving, you have to save $2,608 per month to accumulate $600,000 by age sixty-five. However, if you start saving at forty-five, you only have to save $606 per month. If you begin saving and investing at age thirty-five, you only have to save $171 per month to hit the goal. And if you start even earlier, at age twenty-five, you only have to save $51 per month to reach a goal of $600,000 at retirement.

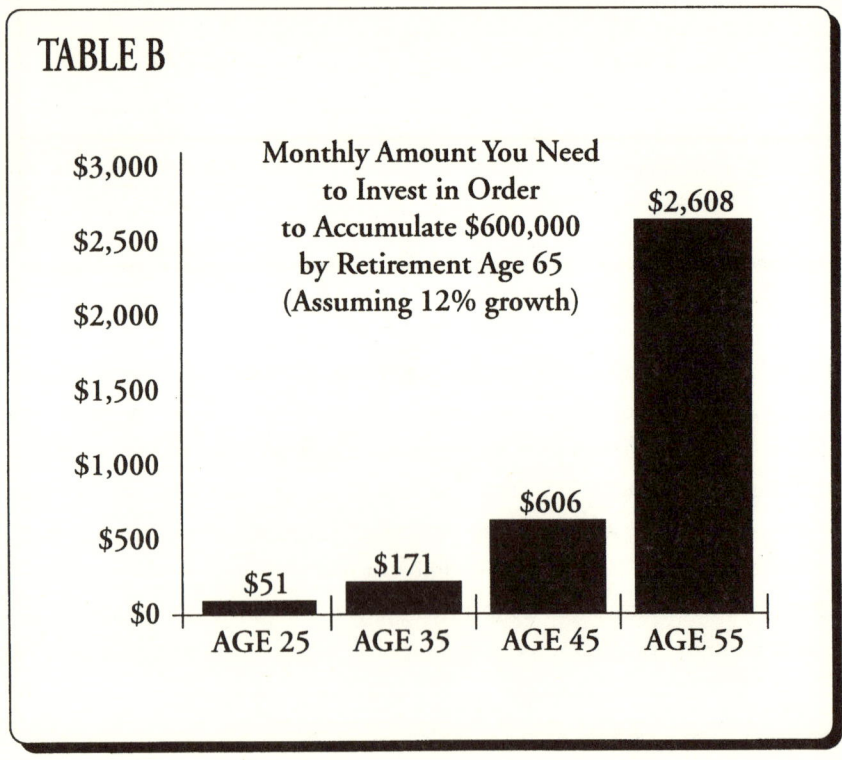

TABLE B

Monthly Amount You Need to Invest in Order to Accumulate $600,000 by Retirement Age 65 (Assuming 12% growth)

Remember, the three ingredients of compound growth are length of time to invest, rate of return, and amount of money. For the purpose of this illustration, we held the rate of return constant at 12 percent and varied the length of time of investments. If you compare the two examples, you will see that over a long period of time just a 2 percent difference in the rate of return has a huge impact on your money. In the first illustration, you invested $52 a month for forty years and earned 10 percent return per year, yielding $328,000. In the second illustration, we assumed a 12 percent rate of return on $51 a month for forty years, realizing a total of $600,000, which is almost twice as much as the same amount invested at only 10 percent.

The Difference 2 Percent Makes

Let's look at another example of various rates of return. Table C shows

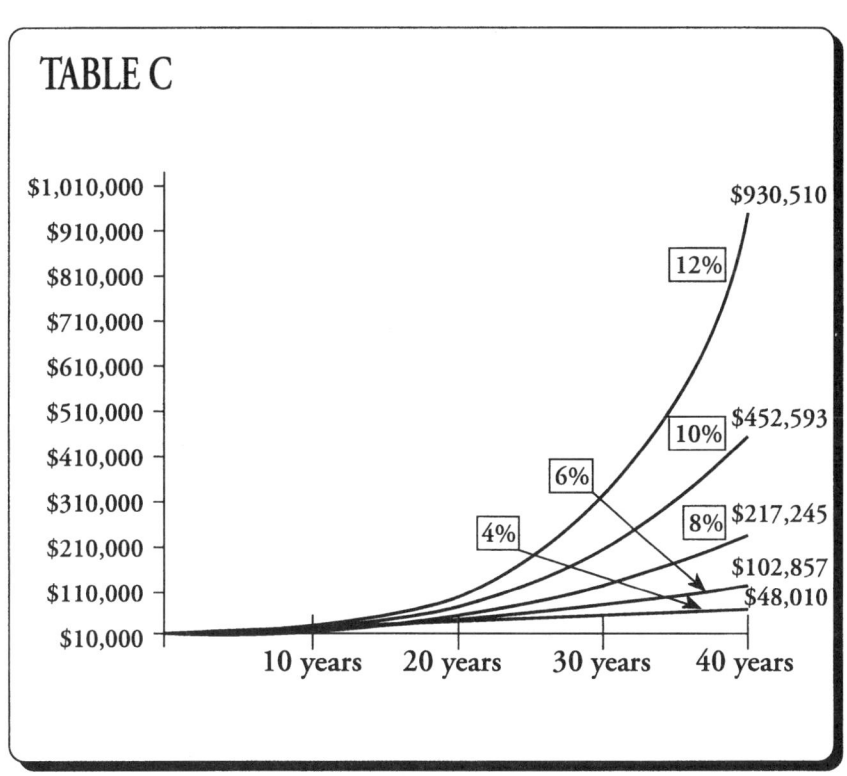

$10,000 invested at various rates of return. As you can see, a 4 percent return makes the investment grow steadily. By the end of the tenth year, it reaches $14,802, by twenty years it reaches $21,911, by thirty years it's at $32,434, and after forty years, it has risen to $48,010. This is steady, year -by-year growth. The problem is, after paying taxes it won't keep pace with inflation.

If you invested $10,000	# of years			
	10	20	30	40
at 4%	$14,802	$21,911	$32,434	$48,010
at 6%	17,908	32,071	57,435	102,857
at 8%	21,589	46,610	100,627	299,599
at 10%	25,937	67,275	174,494	452,593
at 12%	31,058	96,463	299,599	930,510

On the other hand, through patience and tolerance of principal fluctuation, we can often achieve a much higher rate of return. At 12 percent per year, the $10,000 investment produces substantially more money. At ten years, it would yield $31,058, over twice the amount generated by a 4 percent return. At thirty years, it would be worth just under $300,000, almost ten times as much. At forty years, it would be worth twenty-four times as much—over $930,000 compared to $48,000. Over many years, a few percentage points in the rate of return make a tremendous difference.

To be good stewards of the money God has entrusted to us, we need to put the law of compounding to work.

Saving and Investing Principles

Some people believe saving and investing for the future show a lack of faith in God's ability to provide. To the contrary, saving and investing are scriptural principles. Not saving or investing is presumption—presuming upon God to provide for us in the future. While God promises that He will not leave or forsake us, He has also told us to be wise and save for the future. Summer and winter exist in the economy as in nature. If we devour all that we have when times are good, we'll have nothing to fall back on when times get hard. Proverbs 21:20 says, "The wise man saves for the future, but the foolish man spends whatever he gets" (TLB). Over a long period of time, we will experience bad times as well as good, and we should save for the hard times.

The temperament least likely to save or invest is the sanguine. Because of their eternally optimistic nature, sanguines rarely worry about the future and consequently do little planning for it. Although sanguines frequently make more money throughout their lifetime than the other temperaments, they often have very little at the end to show for it, unless their spouse, education, or training has helped them to save consistently.

Diligence

Proverbs 27:23-24 says, "Be sure you know the condition of your flocks, give careful attention to your herds; for riches do not endure forever, and a crown is not secure for all generations." When the Bible was written, society was primarily agricultural, and these illustrations related to what people understood best. But these illustrations are not directed only toward farmers; they demonstrate scriptural principles for everyone. Just as the farmer was to be diligent and watch over his flocks, we are to be diligent over our sources of income, over those things which God has given us stewardship. We can't just presume that everything will always be fine.

Melancholies have the easiest time being diligent about their finances because they plan for the future. In fact, melancholies tend to overemphasize diligence so that this strength becomes a weakness that causes them to worry excessively about the future. At the other extreme, sanguines and cholerics, who have little interest in details, need to work in conjunction with their spouses or friends who are melancholy or phlegmatic for help in being diligent.

Diversification

Ecclesiastes 11:2,6 says: "Give portions to seven, yes to eight, for you do not know what disaster may come upon the land.... For you do not know which will succeed, whether this or that, or whether both will do equally well." The implication is that since we don't know the future, we should divide our investments into several different areas—as many as seven or eight—because we don't know which will do the best. The Amplified Bible says, "Give a portion to seven, yes, even [divide it] to eight," encouraging us to divide our investments into different areas for greater safety and for better use of our money.

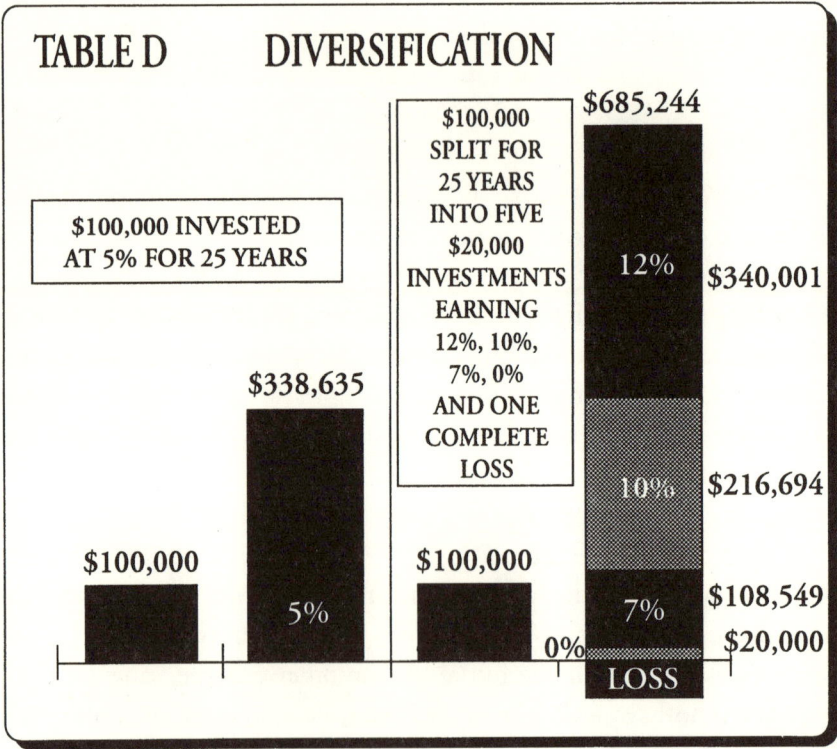

Table D illustrates the diversification principle. Investor 1 takes $100,000 and buys only long-term CDs, earning 5 percent a year for twenty-five years. Investor 2 takes the $100,000 and splits it into five different investments of $20,000 each. He makes a very bad choice on his first investment and loses the entire $20,000. His second investment is also a poor choice, and he merely breaks even over the twenty-five years, earning a 0 percent rate of return. His third investment gives him a modest return of 7 percent per year, while his fourth and fifth investments perform relatively well, earning 10 percent and 12 percent respectively. As you can see, over the entire period of time the diversified investor, in spite of making two bad investments, ends up with over twice as much money as the person who chose only guaranteed investments. Long-term diversification and compounding can make quite a difference.

Cholerics sometimes have trouble practicing diversification. Once cholerics make a decision, they rarely expect anything to go wrong. Since they are also natural risk takers, they may put everything in one, high-risk investment. This can set them back irreversibly if they haven't diversified and then suffer substantial losses in their investment.

Taking Risks

Excessive risk taking is usually motivated by greed or the desire to get rich quick, neither of which is godly. First Timothy 6:9 says, "But those who crave to be rich fall into temptation and a snare and into many foolish (useless, godless) and hurtful desires that plunge men into ruin *and* destruction and miserable perishing" (AMP). The Greek word for *snare* means "a trick or strategy." When we are greedy, we will almost surely fall prey to a trap or a strategy that will take our money.

Investments are relative; the higher the potential reward, the greater the risk. While there is nothing wrong with putting some money into aggressive investments, we first of all need to examine our motives. Then we need to carefully and prayerfully evaluate the risk, realizing that if an investment appears to be too good to be true, it usually is.

Although we advise against taking excessive risks, we do advocate taking prudent risks. Again, balance is the key. The scriptural basis for risk taking is found in Ecclesiastes 11:4: "He who observes the wind [and waits for all conditions to be favorable] will not sow, and he who regards the clouds will not reap" (AMP). If we wait for everything to be perfect, we won't ever take a chance. In the long run, some risk must be taken in order to earn a rate of return. In the parable of the talents, if the servants had not taken any risk at all, they could not have doubled the master's money over the period of time they were allowed to manage it. We also are expected to take risks, prudent risks, in managing God's money.

Sanguines sometimes overextend themselves with excessive risks since they are impulsive and may trust someone else's word for the soundness of the investment. Their egos can be manipulated into a position where they will take too much risk or put their money into investments which are not prudent.

The flip side of the issue is being too fearful of taking risks. Melancholies and phlegmatics, being more fearful in temperament, are the least likely to take risks. In spite of the fact that they may not need their money for years to come, many melancholies invest far too conservatively simply because they can't stand any fluctuation of principal. Opportunities may be missed for fear of making a wrong decision or taking any risk. When an investment drops a little bit in value, fear can prevent them from making the right decision for the long run. Fear can become a debilitating disease when it comes to investments, preventing melancholies and phlegmatics from making the right decision for the long term. The ideal is not to fall prey to either extreme—greed or fear, but to seek the Lord, make a decision, and then act on it.

Patience

Another principle of investing is patience. James 1:4 says, "But let patience have her perfect work, that ye may be perfect and entire, wanting nothing" (KJV). We must have patience if our investments experience short-term declines. We can't allow panic or fear to control our investment decisions. The higher the potential rate of return, the greater its potential for volatility. If we are going to be successful investors, we can't be like the farmer who pulled up his carrots to see how well they were growing. At times we must be willing to leave our investments untouched, even though things don't go our way in the short run. Patience is a virtue in all things, including investments.

Cholerics are the most impatient of the temperaments, and if an investment doesn't immediately perform the way they expect, they may change investments within a matter of months or even weeks. Since investments go through up and down cycles, oftentimes cholerics will jump from investment to investment and get in and out at the wrong time.

Sanguines may be more willing to ride through downturns in their investments, but their impulsive nature works against the necessary endurance in investments, and all areas of life.

Scriptural Motives for Investing

What are the scriptural reasons for investing?

Providing for Family

First Timothy 5:8 commands us to provide for our immediate family: "If anyone does not provide for his relatives, and especially for his immediate family, he has denied the faith and is worse than an unbeliever." We have occasionally seen a person become a Christian and then decide he is no longer responsible to provide for his family because God has promised He will provide and never forsake us. In essence, he uses his Christian faith as an excuse to jettison the responsibility of caring for his family. While God does promise to provide and take care of us in the long run, it remains our responsibility to provide for our family's daily needs. We still have the responsibility to do what is right, but we don't have to carry a burden of worry because God has promised never to forsake us. When a person uses his faith in God as an excuse to avoid these earthly matters, he is unbalanced in his approach.

In this verse the word *provide* comes from the Greek word *pronoeo,* which comes from *pro,* meaning "before," and *noeo,* meaning "to think or comprehend." In other words, it means to think or to comprehend beforehand. This means we need to plan carefully how we are going to provide for our families in the future, including retirement, disability, or death. The responsibility of provision does not end with our death.

A sanguine evangelist was convinced that the rapture was going to take place before he died. Because of this, he didn't save or invest and he charged his credit cards to their maximum. Then he died of a heart attack, leaving his widow with only a ten thousand dollar life insurance policy. After burial costs of six thousand dollars, the remaining four thousand dollars didn't come close to covering his credit card debt. This sanguine, like many others, was guilty of presuming the future. While they are wonderfully optimistic about the future and trust God, they often take their responsibility to provide for their family too lightly, assuming the Lord will provide. God will provide for our families even if we are irresponsible, but we cause them unnecessary suffering if we fail to plan for their needs.

Using Money as a Witness

We believe one of the reasons God gives us money on this earth is so we can practice Christian virtues and demonstrate them to the non-Christians in the world. With the wealth the Lord has given us, we can show God's character to those around us by giving gifts, taking care of our neighbors, or helping those who are having hard times. Luke 16:9 says, "I tell you, use worldly wealth to gain friends for yourselves, so that when it is gone, you will be welcomed into eternal dwellings." If we can use money to help someone and influence them toward the kingdom of God, we could not find a better use for that money.

Leaving an Inheritance

Proverbs 13:22 says, "A good man leaves an inheritance for his children's children." While it is not wise to leave a large inheritance to children, especially if they're young, parents and grandparents can leave an inheritance behind to help their children, but it requires prudent planning and execution.

Many people we know are giving their children their inheritance a little bit at a time to see if they will be diligent in managing it. When the children are twenty-five years old, the parents give them a little sum of money. If they waste the money on excessive living, then they don't give them anymore for the time being. Oftentimes, a small failure in these early years will teach the children to make wiser decisions in later years. If we are going to leave an inheritance for our children's children, then we must train our children to be wise in managing their money.

We also recommend that grandparents set up education funds for their grandchildren to help with those expenses. But the greatest inheritance a parent or grandparent can leave behind is that of a godly character.

Providing for Others' Needs

A godly believer allows the Lord to use him as a conduit of blessings for others in need. If we're acting as stewards, then we realize everything we own belongs to God. And since He is the true owner of all we have, He has the right to redirect those savings or investments to meet the needs of other people. As 2 Corinthians 8:14 admonishes, "Your plenty will supply what they need, so that in turn their plenty will supply what you need."

Even as Christians, too often we find ourselves focusing on our own goals, our own plans for life. Reality is that we need to submit our goals and plans to God to see if they are the same as His goals for our lives. If we become too preoccupied with having a certain amount for retirement, we may find ourselves missing the mark. As stewards, we need to be open to God's changing the course of our investments and redirecting them toward the needs of other people.

In fact, God may desire to use some people in Joseph's capacity, accumulating money now so that it can be used to help other people during hard times. We believe in the next fifteen years that our nation is going to enter a period of extreme economic difficulty. During this time, we will need many Josephs to help provide for the needs of Christians and non-Christians alike by using the resources that God has entrusted to them.

Investing can show our support of the gospel. Throughout the Bible, both Old and New Testaments, God commands us to support His people. Some people may decide to invest part of their money now so they will have more money to give to God's kingdom later. Both giving and saving should be a part of the Christian's life so that neither is out of balance. Like a farmer with seed corn, we can't eat all of the seeds now and have a crop to harvest later. By wise investing, we can give some now and have some of the harvest later also.

Assume you have built up the $600,000 estate we discussed earlier in the chapter. Six hundred thousand dollars invested at 8 percent will generate $48,000 a year. This income could supplement your retirement, be given to children or grandchildren, be given to charities, or be used for the Lord's work in your latter years. In other words, we are simply planting some money so we will be able to give to God's kingdom at a later date also.

However, we must apply wisdom with this principle as with all of them. Sanguines especially may tend to neglect their own family's needs in order to provide for others. One sanguine we interviewed had given away his last quarter to a needy person, leaving his family with nothing. Everything must be balanced.

Other Money Management Principles

Tithing

No book on Christian financial planning would be complete without discussing the tithe. In both the Old and New Testaments, God's Word endorses tithing as a method of supporting the church and its work.[1] By giving to God's work, we acknowledge that He is in control and that our money is His. In faith, we trust God to provide for our needs, even though we have less money after tithing to support ourselves. Tithing is a demonstration of God's ownership of us and our money, and it is a step of faith.

We are often asked if a person should continue to tithe while trying to get out of debt. Our answer is yes. If God's Word has convicted a person to eliminate all debt, he or she can't deny God's Word in one area and obey it in another. We recommend people continue to tithe as they commit their debts to the Lord and ask for His help. We believe that, by continuing to obey God's Word in this area, people will get out of debt quicker than if they did not tithe.

While tithing is certainly important, it is only a fraction of what God's Word says about money. At times, we've seen Christians who tithe and yet are sometimes frustrated because they haven't experienced God's blessing to the degree they would like. Their attitude seems to be, "God, I've tithed in obedience to your Word, but it doesn't seem that you're holding up your end of the bargain."

While we don't want to generalize too much, because each case is different, we believe the answer lies in the fact that so few Christians really understand what God's Word says about money and stewardship. Yes, tithing is a part of the answer, but only a part. Generosity, avoiding debt, work, saving, and investing—there are so many other areas of stewardship that God's people fail to practice. To receive God's full blessing, we must practice all of what God's Word says, not just part of it.

Demonstrating Godly Character

Even when we make a mistake which sets us back financially, it is important to maintain our testimony, pay what we owe, and fulfill our commitments to other people. Psalm 15:4 talks about a person who keeps his oath even when he swears to his own hurt. As Christians, we must maintain a good testimony of doing what is right and what we promised to do. When we uphold the Word of God, we never know what it will accomplish for His kingdom.

A Final Word

In summary, if we Christians will learn to apply God's principles of money management to our finances, we will move toward having a surplus of money. God created the universe and knows exactly how everything should function. He knows what works and doesn't. He knows what is best for us, and He knows best how to grow money. It is a sad testimony that the people of this world are often much better at managing money than we Christians are, despite our access to the wisdom of the universe through the Bible. This is a testimony that we need to change.

As we begin practicing what God's Word says about money and investments, we must understand that God is not worried about just the temporal. He is concerned about developing godly character, and He will use money as a tool to accomplish His goals.

■

Your Family and Your Money

CHAPTER FOURTEEN

Seven Steps to Financial Freedom

"He who gathers money little by little makes it grow."
PROVERBS 13:11

According to the most recent statistics, the average American family today has over 85 percent of its disposable income spent before they ever see it! This means that after deducting taxes, 85 percent of what remains goes to paying off debts, including mortgages. Is it any wonder we're experiencing record bankruptcies in this country?

It's a tragedy that a person can graduate from high school, get a college degree and then a master's, and never have a course in basic financial planning. You can graduate from some of the best schools in the country and yet not know how to balance your checkbook, much less understand the principles for long-term financial success. Our lack of financial knowledge and our dependence upon debt have created a crisis.

In this chapter we're going to give you seven steps to financial freedom, which if practiced will lead you into the surplus God intends. While testing and trials will always be a part of our lives on earth, if we will line up our financial affairs with God's eternal Word, we will be able to experience the best He has for us in this life.

Step One: Take Inventory

Have you ever been driving in a strange city and gotten lost? To find your way out, you first had to know where you were, then you could determine your course for reaching your destination. The same thing is true in reaching financial freedom. You must first find out where you are in order to figure out how to get where you want to go. That's why the first step to achieving financial freedom is taking inventory.

Begin by reviewing the last three months and recording your expenses. If the last three months are not typical of your year—if your expenses were unusually high or low—then use the three prior months to determine a typical spending pattern. Examine your checkbook and record the various expenses by category, using the Household Expense Worksheet in the Appendix. If you aren't certain what was spent in a particular area, make an educated guess and add it to the worksheet.

After you've done this, you will probably discover a couple of things. First, if you're like most people, you'll find out that you're not at all sure where a lot of your money goes. In order to more accurately determine this, stop spending cash. For the next three months, write a check for every expense, and record the category for the expense on the memo portion of each check. Once you have identified by category all your expenses, you will have a pretty accurate picture of where your money is going. Then look at the percentages on the left of the Household Expense Worksheet, which will show you the approximate recommended amounts that should be spent in each category.

Most people don't blow their budget in every area but in just one or two, and these areas are frequently related to their temperament. For example, sanguines may blow it on eating out too much or on entertainment or gifts. The melancholies' weakness may be gift giving or merchandise that is too expensive. Cholerics may overspend on too big a house or expensive cars.

Sanguines usually have the hardest time figuring out where their money went, so if you're a sanguine, we recommend you get a melancholy spouse or accountant to help you. They should also be able to help you set up a system you can follow.

Phlegmatics may have a hard time getting started, since they are often unmotivated. Here, a choleric partner can be helpful in pushing them to get started.

Once you see where your money is going, begin cutting back in every area possible. Make a commitment to the Lord, and to your spouse if you are married, that you'll eliminate all nonessentials in spending until you are completely free of consumer debt.

Remember the old saying that "a penny saved is a penny earned"? Today, with inflation, we probably should say "a dollar saved is a dollar earned." But reality is, a dollar saved is actually much more than a dollar earned. Let me give you an example. Let's say that you analyze your expenses and by cutting out all nonessentials, you can reduce your spending by $100 a month. That $100 is really worth a lot more. Why? Because after deducting taxes and social security, you actually have to earn $135 a month in order to net $100, assuming you are like most people and are in the 28 percent tax bracket.

Think of it this way: Saving money earns you a guaranteed 35 percent tax free rate of return—instantly! Any financial counselor who could guarantee a 35 percent return in one month with no risk, tax free, would have people lined up around the globe to buy his investment. Yet this is exactly your rate of return when you cut out nonessential spending. Follow this principle over the long run, and you'll eventually enter a position of surplus.

Step Two: Buy Adequate Life Insurance

The second major step toward financial freedom involves life insurance. First Timothy 5:8 says, "If anyone does not provide for his relatives, and especially for his immediate family, he has denied the faith and is worse than an unbeliever." Nothing in this scripture implies that our responsibility to provide for our families ends upon our death. Yet, we find that too often young families have inadequate life insurance to cover them if the primary breadwinner dies prematurely.

If both spouses are working and intend to continue working, they should consider getting equal life insurance coverage. However, since circumstances can change, we still recommend getting adequate insurance on the husband as the first priority. If the husband is completely irresponsible and cannot be trusted to take care of his family so that the wife becomes the primary breadwinner, then she should have the most coverage.

A good rule of thumb for a young family with children at home is to buy life insurance on the husband equal to ten times his earnings. For example, if the husband earns $35,000 a year, he should have $350,000 worth of life insurance. Why? Because the objective is to replace the income which is lost to the family in case he dies.

Most experts agree that a family should be able to live on approximately 80 percent of their present income if the husband is not present to add to the household expenses. So in order to maintain the family's present standard of living, you need to replace 80 percent of the husband's $35,000 income, which is $28,000 a year If you buy insurance equal to ten times his yearly income—in this case $350,000 of coverage—and he dies, you have a lump sum of money which can be invested to replace that income.

If you can achieve an 8 percent annual return on investment, then the $350,000 of life insurance will generate $28,000 a year, which covers the necessary expenses to keep the household going. Even though this is a somewhat simplistic approach, it is a good rule of thumb to use.

How can you afford that much coverage? Simple. Most people should have the majority of their coverage, especially when they are young, in inexpensive term insurance, which provides no savings or investment feature. During the early years when the family budget is stretched to the limit, term insurance is the least expensive way to go. A male, aged thirty-five, who is in good health and could qualify for preferred rates can buy $350,000 worth of term coverage for about $35 a month with one of the largest companies in the country, and the rate would be fixed for fifteen years. That's about the same cost as cable television, something many families have. With such a low cost, buying an adequate amount of term life insurance is not only affordable, it is a necessity for the family's protection in the future.

Universal life, whole life, and other variations of these policies have advantages, but they are much more expensive. We won't get into a discussion of those other forms of insurance here since the primary concern in this chapter is how to get out of debt. Of utmost importance is ensuring there is sufficient coverage on the primary breadwinner, which in the early years necessitates the use of term insurance. Later on, when a couple is out of debt and has money for savings, they can consider other types of life insurance. (For more information on the different types of life insurance and what is best for you, see the Appendix.)

We must not be guilty of presuming upon the future and assume that we are not going to die prematurely or that we'll be raptured. Sanguines often have the hardest time with this. They are eternal optimists and don't want to think about dying.

Cholerics are so ambitious and confident that many prefer to place their money in an investment or a business venture rather than buy an insurance policy.

Again, phlegmatics may not be motivated to get around to it.

Since melancholies are the most conscientious and tend to be planners and worriers, they are the most like to follow step two.

Part of the job of a good financial planner is to help a family see any area where they would be vulnerable to a catastrophic, irreversible loss. Only life insurance creates a large estate instantly at very little cost. No investment can provide that. Be sure you don't let your temperament deter you from protecting your family.

Step Three: Pay Off All Consumer Debts

If you have gotten your budget under control so you are saving every month, and you have made sure you have adequate life insurance, your next step is to work toward paying off all consumer debts. This includes credit cards and finance companies—anything beyond your automobile and home. These consumer debts are the worst form of debt since they primarily represent consumption and not investment, and they have the highest rate of interest. So they are the ones we should attack first.

If you look at Table E, you will see an example of a typical consumer who has accumulated almost $10,000 worth of credit card debt, with a little charge here and a little charge there, here a charge, there a charge, every where a charge charge. This couple did what most young couples do when they get out of school. Enticed by all the friendly credit card companies who are eager to extend them credit, they decided to try them out. And the cards actually worked! The couple could buy things without having to pay for them in advance. Over three or four years, they charged everything from wedding rings to furniture and even took out a bill consolidation loan. At first, it seemed like a wonderful invention, but before long they realized that they were trapped. Not only did they owe almost $10,000, but they could barely make the minimum payments. At the rate they were going it would take years to get out of debt. (That, of course, was before they met us.)

Let's apply the domino theory, a theory we have personally found to be the quickest way to get out of debt. The key to the domino theory is to eliminate excess spending of any type, which should enable you to save at least $100 to $200 a month that can be immediately applied to your debts.

To determine what can be eliminated, first surrender all your desires to God and be content to live within the parameters He sets for you. By doing so, you will rarely overspend your income or have financial difficulties. Second, divide your spending into three categories: needs, wants, and desires. Needs are the minimums required to get the job done. You may need a car for basic transportation. That need could be fulfilled by a reliable used car. Your want might be a new Oldsmobile, and your desire, a new Mercedes. Let's not confuse facts. God promises to supply all of our needs, not our wants or desires. Pare your spending back to just your needs.

In this case we've listed the couple's debts from largest at the top to smallest at the bottom, which is the way we recommend you do it. In the next column, we have listed the monthly minimums they are supposed to pay on each credit card. In the next column is the amount they have available to pay on that monthly minimum.

TABLE E CREDITOR/ACCOUNT	PAY OFF	MONTHLY PAYMENT (MINIMUM)	AVAIL. PAYMENT	PMTS. LEFT	DUE DATE	% OF DEBT
MasterCard	$4,000	$100	$100	--	15th	42
Visa	$1,800	$50	$50	--	8th	19
Mont. Wards	$1,650	$45	$45	--	10th	17
Commercial Credit	$1,500	$35	$35	48	21st	16
Sears	$450	$25	$25	22	20th	5
J.C. Penney	$225	$20	$20	14	15th	2
TOTALS	$9,625	$275	$275			

In some cases, people have gotten so far in debt they can't make all the monthly minimums. If you're in this situation, you need extra help. We recommend our *Mastering Your Personal Finances* tape series which you can order from Cornerstone for $25. But for this illustration we're going to assume they have just enough money to make the minimum monthly payments. Next we'll assume they can save $80 in their budget by cutting out unnecessary spending. (We believe most people can actually find a lot more than that.)

Step number one in the domino theory is to apply everything you can toward the smallest debt first. While some people presume they should apply the money to the largest debt first, beginning with the smallest is by far the better approach. If you apply the money to the largest debt first, you barely make a dent in it, and soon you get discouraged and give up because you don't appear to be making progress. By beginning with the smallest debt, you make almost instant headway. Then, like a long line of dominoes stacked next to each other, the debts are knocked off, one right after the other.

The key to making the domino theory work is that you make an absolute commitment not to use your credit cards no matter what happens. While this may be scary at first, it actually puts you in a tremendous position. The reason is that now, instead of trusting your credit card if something goes wrong, you are forced to trust the Lord, which will build your faith in His ability to provide for your needs. That, in turn, will develop in you a greater degree of stewardship.

One of the chief problems with credit is that it doesn't give God a chance to say no. We can function on our own, whether it is God's will or not, by simply whipping out the plastic. Credit also doesn't give God the chance to solve our problems and meet our needs His way. Over the years we have received many testimonies from people who, when they made an absolute commitment not to go deeper into debt, have received God's blessing as He met their needs. Debt is not God's way to financial prosperity, and He will honor our commitment to follow His principles and depend on Him for supplying our necessities.

Back to our couple. The first thing to do is to attack the Penneys debt, since it is the smallest. Take the $80 a month that they saved in their budget for debt reduction, and add it to the $20 already allocated to pay Penneys. That gives them $100 a month for Penneys so that by the third month they have only $25 left to pay, not counting interest (for the sake of simplicity here).

In the third month, they will completely pay off Penneys. Take the $100 now available for debt reduction, subtract the $25 left on the Penneys card, and pay the remaining $75 to Sears. Two significant things have just happened: They have retired one of their debts, going from six debts to five. And they have achieved something. They now have a sense of accomplishment. Instead of owing six companies and having six payments each month, they now have only five. In addition to providing a sense of accomplishment, their money begins to compound in their favor, and the dominoes start to fall.

Next we work to pay off Sears. In the third month of using the domino principle, they have $75 to go toward debt reduction after paying off their Penneys bill, plus the $25 monthly payment they had already allocated for Sears. So in the third month they have $100 to apply to the Sears bill. During the previous two months, they've paid $25 a month, reducing their $450 bill to approximately $400, not counting interest. Applying another $100 in the third month reduces it to $300.

In the fourth month, they have the $80 that they freed up from the budget, the $20 they were paying Penneys, and the $25 they had already allocated for Sears. Since the Penneys bill is paid off, they now have $125 to apply to the Sears account. The balance by this time would be down to about $300, so they can make a significant dent in that debt. At $125 a month, they can pay Sears off in just over two months. They will have gone from six debts to only four.

The principle is clear. Each month you apply to the smallest remaining debt the money you freed up from your budget by eliminating all nonessential spending. Every time you pay off a debt you take the monthly payment you had been making and use those additional funds exclusively for further debt reduction on the next highest debt. Going back to this couple, we find that once Sears and Penneys have been paid off, the couple now has $45 from the minimum payments they were making to them, plus $80 they had allocated from the budget for debt reduction, for a total of $125 extra they can now apply on their Commercial Credit bill. That, added to the $35 minimum payment they were already making, gives them $160 monthly for the debt.

Depending on how much debt you have, it may take you several years to get out of debt, but this is definitely the best and quickest way we have found. Staying out of consumer debt will be one of the most critical things you can do to remain financially free in the future.

Before proceeding to step four, let's look at two more quick examples to emphasize the importance of getting out of consumer debt. If you charge a $50 dress or pair of slacks and make only the minimum payment on your credit card each month, that item could end up costing you as much as $147. How? Assume you have a $4,000 balance on your credit card at an interest of 16.8 percent. If you make only the minimum payment each month and don't add to the debt, it will take you twenty-six years, or over three hundred months, to pay off the credit card. This would result in $7,731.16 of interest on a principal of $4,000 for a total cash outlay of $11,731.61. And the $50 charge will end up costing $147 after paying interest.

Even if the $50 pair of slacks or dress was on sale, it was no bargain. If it had been a $100 item marked down by 50 percent, you ended up paying $147 for it because of interest. Plus, you would actually have to earn at least $198 in order to have $147 left over after paying income tax and social security on your earnings. In essence, you would pay $200 for a $50 item.

Having to earn $198 in order to pay for a $50 item is very sobering, but the laws of compounding have never changed. How do you think the rich of the world got that way? They put the laws of compounding to work for them. Our objective is not to become rich, but good stewardship requires that we not violate the law of compounding.

Consider another illustration. If you have $4,000 worth of credit card debt and are paying a high interest rate of 18 percent, you are actually wasting $720 a year in interest. Imagine going to the bank and getting seven $100 bills and a $20 out of your bank account, then building a roaring fire, and tossing the money into the fireplace. That is exactly what you are doing every year if you have $4,000 worth of credit card debt. But that is not the end of the story.

Remember that the laws of compounding are at work here. If you were to take that same $720 a year that you are now burning up, and invested it at a rate of return of 10 percent, in thirty-five years you would have $195,198. That is how much you are wasting with a $4,000 credit card debt. You are not wasting just the $720 per year but over $195,000. Now imagine going to the bank and getting a loan from your friendly banker for $195,198. (Surely that wouldn't be a problem!) Then go to your fireplace and take that bushel basket of $100 bills and start throwing them into the fireplace. Isn't consumer credit wonderful? Great way to the good life, right?

If you are a young and better investor, the picture is even more extreme. At 12 percent interest over forty years, you would have $552,306 from the $720 a year that is being burned. What an amazing amount can be accumulated using the principle of Proverbs 13:11: "He who gathers money little by little makes it grow," and what an amazing amount is lost when we violate it.

We recommend that if you've had trouble with consumer debts in the past, cut up your credit cards so that you are not tempted to use them. This is especially true if you are a sanguine who spends a lot and spends impulsively or if you are a melancholy with expensive taste. Phlegmatics and cholerics don't have as big a problem with this. Phlegmatics are unmotivated, and they don't usually spend a lot anyway. Once they are committed to getting out of debt, they are pretty steady. Cholerics, once they grab the vision of getting out of debt, will be adamant.

The biggest problem most people have with consumer debt is that they never really tackle it. They say, "Oh well, I owe $4,000 on my Visa card, so what's another $25?" They end up going in circles, paying in $40 or $50 and then charging $40 to $50 more next month. The only way to be free of consumer debt is to commit to getting out and staying out, using the principles we outlined here.

Step Four: Start an Emergency Reserve

A common saying prior to the sixties was "put some money away for a rainy day." We don't know about you, but we haven't heard that saying in years. Yet the principle is biblical. Since we don't know what the future holds, we should put some resources in an emergency reserve. It's the principle Joseph used to save the entire nation of Egypt.

Recently a *Wall Street Journal* article cited how experts are amazed at the number of well-educated, yuppie couples who are going bankrupt. In many cases both had master's degrees and were earning $75,000 to $125,000 a year, but because they lacked basic financial training, especially from a biblical perspective, they went broke. What happened? They violated James 4. They assumed they were going to continue to make the same kind of income all the time, and they set up their payment schedules and debt based on this assumption. In other words, they didn't put any money away for a rainy day, and they presumed on the future.

When one of them lost a job, got laid off, or was disabled and out of work for a few months, they had nothing to fall back on. They fell two or three months behind on their house payments. Creditors began to call as bills went unpaid. They borrowed on their credit cards to put food on the table and gasoline in the car. Finally things snowballed until they were bankrupt. As we proceed for the next ten to fifteen years, there are likely to be an increasing number of bankruptcies unless we get back to biblical principles of finance.

We advise that you set aside two to three months' living expenses—the bare bones amount on which you could live—in an emergency reserve fund. This could be a bank account, an interest-bearing money market fund, or something similar. Although it won't make much interest, it gives you the security of knowing you wouldn't have to resort to charging on your credit cards in order to make it in an emergency. You have a cushion.

Ideally, we recommend that people build up at least three to six months' income in conservative, liquid accounts of some type, not in retirement accounts. This could include conservative mutual funds or interest bearing accounts, but with today's low paying interest rates we don't recommend that you put your entire amount in them. Having several months' income in something conservative could save you from having to disturb your retirement accounts or more volatile growth oriented accounts.

Step Five: Begin a Long-Term Savings Plan

Once you are out of debt and have at least three months' reserve set aside, begin putting money into long-term savings or investment plans. One of the best choices is a mutual fund, especially an internationally diversified fund. By using a proven mutual fund, you can achieve diversification, giving you more safety in your investments, and professional management. Plus it allows you to have a diversified portfolio of investments with just a small amount of money. Mutual funds are great for small investors and large investors as well.

Again, you are using the Proverbs 13:11 principle of growing little by little. Start saving money in long-term savings accounts—not just retirement accounts—as soon as you are out of consumer debt and you have your liquid reserve set up.

Let's update the old fable of the tortoise and the hare in terms of modern investors—Robert Rabbit and Ted Tortoise. Rob is one of those guys who gets off to a quick start. He's impulsive, and once he gets sold on a good idea, he doesn't have to waste time thinking about it. (Rob is probably a sanguine.) His financial planner told him he ought to start contributing early to an IRA, so when he graduated from college at age twenty-two, he began putting $2,000 a year into a retirement account which would grow, tax-deferred. (Let's assume a 10 percent annual rate of return, which is quite achievable with a long-term perspective.) Being a sanguine, he started out fast, and after ten years he had quite a bit in his IRA. But he got bored with it and decided that he wanted to spend his money on other things, like buying a giant screen TV, a VCR, and expensive musical equipment. Plus he bought a house and needed extra money for the house payment. He figured that he could start another IRA later on, but never got around to it.

So Robert made a $2,000 a year contribution to his IRA for ten years, from age twenty-two to thirty-one. Then he stopped putting money into savings for retirement. He made no payments for the rest of his life, investing a total of $20,000. Not being a detail-minded person, he simply forgot about the account. Even though he continued to get statements, he just threw them in a pile and ignored them, figuring that over the long run they would probably be worth something.

On the other hand, Ted Tortoise is steady, consistent, and careful—a true phlegmatic/melancholy. Teddy first learned about an IRA when he got out of college, but he just never got around to making a contribution. He wanted to study his options before starting. By the time he finally got started, he was thirty-two. He began putting $2,000 a year into an IRA, earning the same return that Rob did—10 percent. From age thirty-two to age sixty-five, he contributed $2,000 a year, every year, for twenty-three years. True to his phlegmatic nature, he was reliable and stable once he got off dead center.

Rob started well but didn't finish, only contributing $20,000. Ted studied it for a long time before he decided to act, but he contributed for twenty-three years, putting a total of $46,000 in his retirement plan. At the end of the race, who had the most money?

Surprise! Robert Rabbit actually won the race this time! Despite the fact that he contributed less and was not nearly as diligent as Teddy Tortoise, he still won. Why? Because of the laws of compounding. Rob had something Teddy didn't—an extra ten years to let his money compound. So even though he made no contributions after he turned thirty-two, the compounding he gained during the first ten years was such a big head start that Ted could never catch up. What a lesson there is to be learned here. So many people wait to start planning for their retirement until it's almost too late. It reminds me of the saying, "Procrastination is such a sin. It brings me constant sorrow. I really shouldn't practice it. Perhaps I'll stop—tomorrow!"

Most of us procrastinate on starting our long-term savings plans because we have other priorities. But when we procrastinate, our lack of discipline ends up costing us hundreds of thousands of dollars. Since we know that the formula for long-term growth is the amount of money, times the rate of return, times the amount of time we have, we need not forget that time is one of the most valuable of all commodities. We need to start saving while we are young.

Once you have begun your long-term savings plan and have started putting aside $25, $50, $100, $250—whatever you can afford—each month into a long-term vehicle, then you need to begin attacking the rest of your debts. As we have stressed throughout the book, remember that balance is the key. You don't want to put all of your money, especially your liquid money into retirement accounts, because you would have no funds to fall back on in case of an emergency. By the same token, once you've paid off your consumer debt, you don't want to put 100 percent of your money toward paying off your home or cars, because again you would have no liquidity, and you would lose the compounding on your investment that is so important in your early years.

PLANNING FOR YOUR RETIREMENT? DON'T PROCRASTINATE... IT COULD COST THOUSANDS

Compare these two retirement plan contributions (assume 10% annual rate of return).
Robert Rabbit: Starting at age 22, contributing $2,000 annually for only 10 years.
Ted Tortoise: Starting at age 32, contributing $2,000 annually for 34 years (to retirement age 65).

Robert Rabbit			Ted Tortoise		
Age	Payment	Accumulation	Age	Payment	Accumulation
22	$2,000	$2,200	22	$0	$0
23	2,000	4,620	23	0	0
24	2,000	7,282	24	0	0
25	2,000	10,210	25	0	0
26	2,000	13,431	26	0	0
27	2,000	16,974	27	0	0
28	2,000	20,872	28	0	0
29	2,000	25,159	29	0	0
30	2,000	29,875	30	0	0
31	2,000	35,062	31	0	0
35	0	51,334	35	$2,000	10,210
40	0	82,674	40	$2,000	29,875
45	0	133,148	45	$2,000	61,545
50	0	214,436	50	$2,000	112,550
55	0	345,351	55	$2,000	194,694
60	0	556,192	60	$2,000	326,988
65	0	895,752	65	$2,000	540,049
TOTAL	$20,000	$895,752	TOTAL	$46,000	$540,049

Step Six: Pay Off Your Automobiles

Once you have started your long-term savings plan, then try to accelerate paying off your automobiles. While it is hard for some people to believe, many people will actually spend more in their lifetime for automobiles than for a house.

Financially, your best bet is to buy a reliable automobile and drive it as long as possible. Certainly there are other considerations also, especially if you are a single woman or if you need reliable transportation and know nothing about cars. But purely from a financial standpoint, we recommend you drive your car as long as it runs. If the car is still reliable, paying for minor repairs is much better than making $250, $350, or $400 monthly car payments on a depreciating item. Although there is a point of no return when cars require more to repair them than they are worth, keep in mind that cars are not a good investment. They are guaranteed to go down in value every year, and we need to spend the least amount possible on them. So the first and best rule of thumb is to buy used cars, service them, and keep them as long as possible.

The second alternative is to buy an inexpensive new car, service it well, changing the oil regularly, and keep it for a long, long time, up to 100,000 or 200,000 miles. Our secretary has a car with 255,000 miles on it, and although it is on its second engine, this car has been tremendously reliable transportation for her most of the time. Constantly trading for new cars, buying one every two or three years, is financially disastrous since a car devalues most during the first three years you own it. Conversely, the best car to buy is one that is two or three years old and has been maintained well. Go to any large book store, and in the auto section you will find helpful books on how to buy wisely. Reports can tell you not only what new cars cost the dealer, but they will also make recommendations on used cars. Other sources can tell you how to find one that is in good repair. (See the Appendix for more information.) Above all, do your research, but also pray over the decision, asking the Lord to guide your path.

It's easy to justify overspending on an automobile by saying we have to look successful or people won't do business with us. In my opinion, this is one of the biggest fallacies that has been fed to American businessmen. It doesn't exhibit faith that God will send business our way and will provide for us. For instance, a real estate agent may feel the pressure to have a nice car in which to drive clients around. For people who feel they must have a nicer car, we would at least recommend buying a car that is two or three years old.

Cholerics and sanguines will probably have the toughest time with this, but we recommend that you stay conservative in your choice of automobiles. They are functional, not indicators of our worth.

Step Seven: Prepay on Your Home

Once your cars are paid for and you are adding to your investments, begin prepaying on your home. While prepaying on your home is one of the most important things you can do, the sequence is very important. Steps one through four are basically sequential and should be completed in that order. However, steps five, six, and seven can be done simultaneously; you could begin prepaying on your home as you're paying off the cars and adding to long-term savings.

Prepaying a home can save thousands and even hundreds of thousands of dollars, regardless of whether you have a fixed or variable mortgage. Although it works if you're going to live in a home for only a few years, it works best if you're going to live there for the long run. But even if you move after a few years, you carry your savings forward in the form of home equity for the next house that you buy.

Let's look at some information regarding mortgage prepayment taken from our good friend Marc Eisenson, author of *A Banker's Secret*. (See Appendix for more information.)

We are going to consider three different homes, one selling for $75,000, one for $100,000, and one for $200,000. In each case, we'll assume an 8 percent loan. In Table G the first column shows loans of $75,000, $100,000, and $200,000, and it shows the number of years of the loans and how much you would have to pay. So if you had a $75,000 loan and you were only going to pay on it for three years, you could pay $2,350.23 a month and pay off the $75,000 loan in just three years. On the other hand, if you have a fifteen-year loan, your payments would be only $716.74. (None of these figures include homeowners' insurance, or taxes, which will add to the amount of your monthly mortgage payment.)

TABLE G	Monthly Loan Payment Table Dollars Required to Amortize Loan				
Loan Amount	Term of Loan in Years				
	3	5	15	20	30
$75,000	2,350.23	1,520.73	716.74	627.34	550.33
$100,000	3,133.64	2,027.64	955.66	836.45	733.77
$200,000	6,267.28	4,055.28	1,911.31	1,672.89	1,467.53

Most people take the maximum amount of money they can afford to spend on a home and buy the largest home they can. It would be much smarter to buy a smaller home, and to live below our means, and to pay if off quickly. As you can see, the longer you stretch out the loan, the smaller your monthly payment is but the more you pay in total. If you pay the $75,000 loan out over only three years, your total of all payments will be $84,608.28 ($2,350.23 x 36 months). But if you pay it out over fifteen years, you will pay a total of $129,013 ($716.74 x 180 months). If you pay it out over thirty years, you will pay a total of $198,119 ($553.33 X 360 months).

One of the first things we can learn here is the difference in how these loans work. Typically, in the first few years of thirty-year home loans, almost 100 percent of the mortgage payment is going for interest, and the more years you take to pay out the loan, the more interest you are going to pay. For example, in the illustration of the $75,000 loan above, it only cost an extra $166.41 a month to pay off the mortgage in fifteen years rather than thirty years. By paying a little more each month, you can cut in half the total amount you will pay on the loan, because of the nature of amortization loans.

Table H shows the same loans, $75,000, $100,000 and $200,000, at 8 percent, with a little bit of prepaying every month. For this first illustration, let's stick with the $75,000 loan. In this case, paying an extra $25 a month saves $22,073 over the course of the loan, which is equal to fifty-four months of payments. Why? Because 100 percent of every dollar you put into prepayment of your mortgage goes to the principal.

TABLE H	Pre-payment Savings Table for a 30-year 8% Loan		
Loan Amount	Pre-pmt	Dollars Saved	Months
$75,000	$25	$22,073	54
	50	36,473	90
	100	54,758	139
	200	74,148	194
$100,000	25	23,337	42
	50	39,906	73
	100	62,456	118
	200	88,260	171
$200,000	25	25,579	23
	50	46,677	42
	100	79,817	73
	200	124,920	118

Since during the early years of your mortgage virtually none of your payment is going toward the principal, you can chop your loan down dramatically by prepaying a little each month. In this case, a person who prepays $200 a month can save $74,148 in interest charges. That would cut 194 months (a little over sixteen years) off the mortgage, reducing a thirty-year mortgage to fourteen years. So if this person would pay $750.33 instead of the scheduled payment of $550.33 (again, not counting real estate taxes and insurance), he would save almost $75,000 in interest.

The principle holds true for every loan; the numbers are just bigger for larger loans. Suppose a person with a $200,000 mortgage makes $1,467.53 monthly payments. If he can add just $200 a month, making the payment $1,667.53 before insurance and taxes, he would save $124,920, or 118 payments. And the thirty-year loan becomes a twenty-year loan approximately. Unless they are completely strapped, most people who can afford a $1,500 monthly house payment could also find an extra $200 each month, saving a tremendous amount of money in the long run.

Table I shows basically the same information from a different perspective. With the same 8 percent mortgage, it shows how to reduce a thirty-year mortgage to twenty-five years, twenty years, or fifteen years, respectively. Assume you have a $100,000 loan. To reduce it to twenty-five years, you would have to pay $38.05 extra a month on your present payment, chopping five years off your mortgage and saving you $32, 607. Paying an extra $221.89 a month would reduce a thirty-year loan to fifteen, saving $92,133 over the course of the mortgage.

TABLE I	Debt Reduction Table To Reduce a 30-Year Loan to:					
Loan	25 years		20 years		15 years	
Amount	Pre-Pay	Save	Pre-Pay	Save	Pre-Pay	Save
$75,000	28.54	24,456	77.01	47,554	166.42	69,067
$100,000	38.05	32,607	102.68	63,407	221.89	92,133
$200,000	76.11	65,225	205.36	126,822	443.78	184,276

Prepaying your mortgage is vital, and it works best in the early years. Once you have paid several years on the mortgage, prepayments have less effect. But everything you can do will help. The more you prepay, the more you will save in the long run.

There you have it. Seven steps to financial freedom. If you will use these seven steps, we strongly believe you can go from a position of debt to a position of surplus within a few years. With a national debt that is currently over $4.5 trillion and growing exponentially, we believe our nation is headed for a financial crisis, which requires more than ever that we get our own homes in financial order, and as quickly as possible.

One final thing, we recommend that you consistently attempt to live below your means. Adopt the 80/20 rule. Live off of 80 percent of your disposable income after taxes. Put the remaining 20 percent to work. Pay 10 percent as a tithe, and put another 10 percent into long-term investments, using these seven steps. Don't procrastinate. As the tortoise and hare principle shows, the one who starts earlier has the greatest advantage.

Remember the words of Jesus in Matthew 7:24-27. He said the person who hears His words and puts them into practice is like the man who built his house on the rock. Even when storms came, the man's house was secure because it had a solid foundation. The foolish person who ignores the commandments of the Lord is like a man who built his house on sand. And when the winds came, it was blown away. We believe these seven principles will protect your house because the foundation is biblical and therefore solid.

Questions and Answers

1. Should I take out a variable mortgage or a fixed-rate mortgage?

When interest rates are low, we definitely recommend a fixed-rate mortgage unless you plan to move within five years. Over the long run we are quite likely to have much higher interest rates than we currently have, so a fixed-rate mortgage would be better.

2. Should I keep tithing while I am attempting to get out of debt?

We believe you should. Since you are attempting to get your financial affairs in order according to God's way, we believe you should follow His teachings in this area as in others.

3. What about other types of life insurance such as universal life, variable life, or whole life?

Those life insurance products have particular uses for certain types of individuals, and many do have advantages, some of which are significant. However, you should not consider them until you are completely out of consumer debt and beginning your long-term savings plans. Once you are at step five—you have gotten your budget under control, you have adequate term insurance, you have paid off all of your consumer debt, and you have an emergency reserve—then other types of insurance make sense.

A couple of words of advice. Make sure the company you are dealing with has a strong rating. We recommend looking at Moody's Standard and Poor, or Weiss, to find out which companies are the strongest. (See Appendix.) A good Christian financial professional should be able to help you with this. Of these types of insurance, we believe that the best type typically is a good universal life policy, although we would recommend the other types under some circumstances.

4. Should I start a long-term savings plan before my house and car are paid off?

Yes, because of the additional compounding that you will experience by starting early. Get started even if it's just a small amount per month. A second benefit to starting your long-term savings plan while you are paying off your house and car is that it gives you other incentives. Besides just working on debt retirement, you are now beginning to build equity for your future, and some people are more motivated by seeing their money accumulate for their future than just concentrating on debt retirement. It also provides an opportunity to learn about investing, starting on a small scale. We recommend that you do all of them.

5. What about a biweekly mortgage?

Biweekly mortgages are fine if you take one out in the beginning. But normally we do not recommend pseudo biweekly mortgages, which involve a third party taking your money and making payments every two weeks for you. In this case, you are trusting someone else to make your payments. Most banks don't accept biweekly mortgages, and you can accomplish the exact same thing by prepaying. For more information see Marc Eisenson's book *A Banker's Secret.*

6. Should a wife have life insurance?

As we stated before, the primary purpose of life insurance is to make sure there is adequate coverage on the primary breadwinner, and we assume that in most cases the primary breadwinner is the husband. We do not believe financially that the wife should be the primary breadwinner unless something unusual has happened in the family such as a death, divorce, or disability. If after covering the primary breadwinner you have enough disposable income, we recommend a term policy for her of approximately $100,000. The cost on this for a female, aged thirty-five, in good health (preferred rate) for a fifteen-year level term policy would only be about $15 a month. If the wife were to die, this would allow the husband to provide his children with child care, extra expenses for eating out, and other additional services.

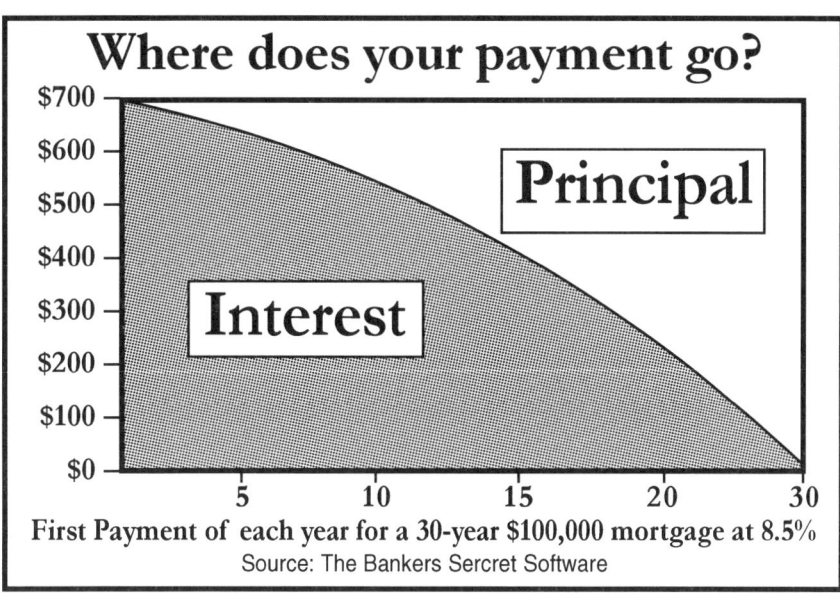

Where does your payment go?

First Payment of each year for a 30-year $100,000 mortgage at 8.5%
Source: The Bankers Sercret Software

Above you see the normal curve for a typical mortgage. As you can see, your payment goes mostly toward interest, very little toward principal. Thus, if you're staying in a house for the long run, prepaying a little principal will go a long way. Note that changes in interest rates should have no affect on principal payoff.

CHAPTER FIFTEEN

Advice for Family Finances

"Husbands, in the same way be considerate as you live with your wives."

1 PETER 3:7

S tatistics indicate that 70 to 80 percent of all marriage failures are caused at least in part by financial difficulties. Everything costs money—your job, your children's educations, your clothes, your car—all of this and more. Couples struggle daily with financial decisions. Combine this with the fact that opposite temperaments, which have different ways of handling money, attract each other, and the result is a powder keg. We should know. Because of what we went through in our personal finances, we have come to believe that a couple's understanding of these principles can strengthen not only their finances, but their marriages.

According to Dr. Tim LaHaye's book *I Love You, But Why Are We So Different?* there are several common temperament blends:

Sanguine/Choleric attracts Melancholy/Phlegmatic
Sanguine/Melancholy attracts Melancholy/Sanguine

Sanguine/Phlegmatic attracts Melancholy/Choleric

Choleric/Sanguine attracts Phlegmatic/Melancholy

Choleric/Melancholy attracts Phlegmatic/Sanguine

Choleric/Phlegmatic attracts Phlegmatic/Choleric

There are no right or wrong temperament combinations, but each combination has its unique problems. For example, a phlegmatic will most likely marry a choleric. A strong-willed, opinionated choleric man knows where he is going and what he wants to do. On the other hand, a phlegmatic woman prefers not to make decisions, likes the security of having someone else in control, and likes to follow rather than lead. While it may be an ideal combination in the courtship phase, once they are married, the combination can lead to tremendous conflict, particularly in the area of finances.

A choleric husband leads his phlegmatic wife to the razor's edge of life because his quick, intuitive, risky decisions make her quake inside with fear. The melancholy/choleric woman who marries the phlegmatic man finds her stomach continually in knots as she wonders when or if he will ever pay the bills. To her utter despair, she finds that he doesn't even remember what bills have to be paid, nor does he care. His attitude is rather laissez-faire because he believes it will all work out somehow.

We counseled with a sanguine/choleric man married to a melancholy/phlegmatic woman. The husband nearly destroyed their business with his impulsive decisions. Like most sanguines, he had made a lot of money, and his choleric drive and sanguine impulsiveness had caused him also to spend a lot of money. Since he never considered the checkbook balance, he frequently overspent. Tragically, he would then blame his wife for running out of money. The battle raged. Not only did they lose their business, they almost lost their marriage as well.

A phlegmatic/sanguine wife we interviewed had a real problem with anger, as sanguines often do. Combining the sanguine impulsiveness with the phlegmatic "I don't care" attitude, she nearly drove her melancholy/phlegmatic husband into the insane asylum. Every time they had an argument, she would get even with him by going to the store and buying anything she saw, whether or not the money was in the bank.

Fortunately, not all financial fights are tragic. To outsiders, some are pretty humorous. Take the melancholy/choleric husband married to a phlegmatic/sanguine wife. Their on-going fight was over the wife's inability to remember to record her checks. Getting her to balance the checkbook became absolutely out of the question. The melancholy, detail-oriented husband decided to strike a compromise. He would be satisfied if his wife would at least record the check number and the amount. After several arguments, she finally agreed. She would, at all costs, record every check.

One day as she was outside talking to a neighbor, the UPS man and the paperboy came at the same time. She recorded the checks as directed, writing down the check numbers and the amounts. Several days later, when her husband was balancing the checkbook, he asked her for the amounts for checks 5459 and 5458. She assured him she had written them down somewhere. She was certain she had kept her promise. Finally, she remembered. To the husband's dismay, he had to crawl on his back on the garage floor to retrieve the figures from the bottom of the Ping-Pong table. When she had written the checks, she had seen a piece of plywood leaning against the garage wall and recorded her transactions there, not remembering that it was the Ping-Pong table. Her husband was not amused.

If We're Different, Are We Doomed?

How do we solve this dilemma? Although God gave each of us a different temperament, he also gave us the ability to communicate with each other in order to bring harmony into marriage. His ways do not depend upon our temperaments but only upon our willingness to obey His principles. Regardless of the temperaments involved, the rules are the same. All the temperaments must discover their weaknesses and decide to follow God's perfect plan. When a marriage operates in God's perfect order, there will be peace and harmony in every area, including financial decision making.

It begins with understanding the roles the man and woman are designed to fulfill within their home. The first issue is that of headship. Who should make the final decisions within each family? If each person is trying to make the final decisions, chaos results. God has a chain of command. Headship is not a male/female issue. It began with God and the Trinity. You have God the Father, God the Son, and God the Holy Spirit. Each is absolutely important, each is absolutely individual, and each fulfills a distinct role. God the Father is the head. The Holy Spirit is the Comforter and the Director. And Jesus is the Suffering Servant, who was willing to yield His rights in order to save humanity. Where would we be if He hadn't?

The Trinity is our example for families. God is the head of our household, then the man, then the woman. Just as God sanctioned the family, He also sanctioned the chain of command. We must accept and implement His design for headship in the family to bring order to our finances.

The Husband's Responsibilities

What is the husband's role? According to Ephesians 5:25, the husband is to love his wife as Christ loves the church. In verse 28, he is commanded to love his wife as he loves his own body. Men are very conscious of what they think, feel, and desire. They love what they think, their opinions, their perspective. They love their desires. Christ is saying to love *her* desires with the same intensity. Love what *she* thinks. Love *her*. When you love someone, you know that person.

Adam knew Eve; Abraham knew Sarah; Isaac knew Rebekah. The word *know* does not mean just a physical knowing. The Hebrew word is *yada*, which means "to ascertain by seeing, observation; care; recognition; acknowledge; advise; answer; appoint; to be aware of; comprehend; consider; discern; discover; to be a familiar friend; to have regard; respect; to teach; to tell; to understand"—all that from one little word. If a man loves his wife as much as he loves himself, he will listen to her. That is the very essence of the two becoming one. For a man to fulfill his headship role, he must not be selfish. Quite the contrary, God designed headship as an absolutely unselfish position.

First Peter 3:7 gives the husband his marching orders for his relationship with his wife, and they carry with them the caveat that if he doesn't follow those orders, his prayers will be hindered: "You married men, in the same way, must live with your wives in an intelligent consideration of them. You must show them deference too as the weaker sex as they share with you the gracious gift of life so that your prayers may not be hindered" (Williams).

Here the man is given three directives. He is to have an attitude of gratitude toward his wife. He should also maintain an attitude of deference toward her as the weaker sex, which in no way implies inferiority. Finally, he is also to intelligently consider her.

Just what does all that mean? As Proverbs 31:11 declares, "The heart of her husband trusts in her confidently *and* relies on and believes in her securely, so that he has no lack of [honest] gain or need of [dishonest] spoil" (AMP). The Hebrew word for *trust* is *batach*, which means "to trust, to be confident, to take refuge, to be sure, and to be boldly secure." If a man is boldly secure in what his wife says, it means that he is not only listening to what she says but he is intelligently considering what she has to say.

The choleric man, especially the choleric/melancholy man, will probably have the most difficulty accepting this principle. He is extremely goal-oriented and detail-minded. He possesses a quick, analytical mind, is decisive, thorough, and a strong leader. You can always count on him to do an extraordinary job. He is an excellent debater. By combining verbal aggressiveness with attention to detail, he can make mincemeat of a phlegmatic woman. Since he is extremely competitive in all that he does, his battle plan will always be the same: "Nothing can stop me now." He can easily become a dictator. That man, and other temperaments like him, should realize that God may be resisting his prayers.

Often he will be so caught up in his own destiny that he will consider his wife's feelings and desires inconsequential. After years of marriage, the wife will likely be severely silenced and left totally unaware of their finances. The result is disastrous. Take, for example, the thirty-two-year-old melancholy woman whose choleric husband died suddenly after fourteen years of marriage. After he was gone, she discovered how poorly he had handled their finances. She found a credit card she didn't even know he had—with $10,000 charged on it. "I was left with enormous debts and no records or files to work with. If couples knew how important this is, it might help someone else." A widow left unprotected, uncovered, confused, and unaware of where she stands financially is totally dependent upon the advice of others.

Husbands should consider their wives. We have seen selfish men take the house payment and spend it on flying lessons. We have counseled choleric men who make their spouses accountable for even a pack of gum. Submit one to another and your prayers won't be hindered.

Men Are Visionaries

Regardless of the husband's or wife's temperaments, they will both experience a great release as they begin to understand how God made men and women different. Men tend to be visionaries, oriented to long-term goals. Women tend to see the here and now, focusing on the short-term. For example, the wife knows the rent is due next month and wants to put money aside for it. The husband thinks if he puts the rent money into restoring his beat-up jalopy, he could possibly sell it for a profit, producing this month's rent as well as next month's. The wife sees the possibility that nobody will buy the jalopy and that when the rent is due, there will be no money to pay it. She sees the right now; he often sees the "well maybes."

Without a vision, the people perish, and without a vision, the family perishes. Wives must recognize that the dreamers in their husbands are from God, and they must release their husbands to pursue their dreams. On the other hand, the husbands must listen to their wives' wisdom and find in them their chief counselors. As this balance enters a marriage, the outcome will be glorious.

Proverbs 31:23 declares when the woman fulfills her responsibilities toward her husband and her household, she can rest in the promise that her husband will be "respected at the city gate." When I [Mona] took this promise for my life thirteen years ago, I began applying biblical principles to my household, my family, and even my femininity. I stopped looking for my rights, my autonomy and position, and began to focus on Jerry's rights and his fulfilling his potential. As a result, Jerry has been released to his destiny, my children are grown and walking with God, and God is allowing me to be fulfilled by studying and teaching His Word. By losing my life, I found it.

The Wife's Responsibilities

The wife also has responsibilities. If her husband is going to trust in her, she must be trustworthy and committed to do him good. Proverbs 31:12 states, "She will do him good and not evil all the days of her life" (KJV).

The Hebrew word for *evil* is *rah*, meaning "to tear apart." The woman is not to tear apart or criticize her husband's financial decisions. The law of kindness is to be on her mouth. What a responsibility. Women are to be committed to do their husbands good and not evil all the days of their lives.

It is amazing what vindictive women can do to their family finances. One phlegmatic/sanguine would become frustrated with her husband for not helping around the house. To pay him back she would take the checkbook, go to the mall, and write checks to her heart's delight, even when there was no money in the account. Her melancholy husband was driven to distraction. He admitted that when she did this, it was hard for him to love her. Another woman, a choleric as you might guess, got so mad at her husband that she drove *his* car into their house.

If her husband is loving her as Christ loves the church, his decisions will not be selfish. Likewise, if she is committed to do him good all the time, her responses to him will not be selfish. As each considers the other, each spouse is protected, and neither will become self-protective.

We have received testimony after testimony declaring that these principles work. When a woman knows her husband is listening to her and considering her advice, she can more easily allow him to be the head of the house and to control the finances because she knows he is not making self-ish decisions. Even if he decides that her way is not the best way, she can be confident he will make a mature, well-informed decision concerning the security of their household. Rather than being like two rocks hitting each other, they will become like two cogs meshing together, each operating in harmony and support of the other.

The Woman Must Accept Her Biblical Role

Women must not follow in the footsteps of Eve and Jezebel who reversed the whole order of God regarding the man leading and the woman following.[1] The choleric Jezebel was married to the passive, phlegmatic Ahab. Ahab wanted Naboth's vineyards, but Naboth valued the land his father had given him more than money. Ahab sulked and pouted. He refused to eat. He quit being a husband and the king, went to bed, and turned his face to the wall.

Believe it or not, we have seen men in adverse financial situations react exactly the same way. A man invests in a business venture, but something happens and it goes sour. The man becomes sullen and gives up in despair. He fails to make decisions and stops carrying his load. We know one man who came in and told his wife of fifteen years, "I don't love you anymore." When we asked why, he admitted that he felt financially trapped. He was in debt beyond hope, and at fifty-two he saw no way out but to abandon his wife, leaving her to handle the problems thus making his life easier. Another man left his wife with three small children, one only a week old, not for another woman, but because he was so buried in financial difficulties that he had lost his vision.

Ahab's reaction caused Jezebel to assume control. In essence she said, "Why are you bellyaching? Get up! Aren't you the king? I'll get you your vineyard." So Jezebel wrote letters in Ahab's name and sealed them with his signet ring, the symbol of his authority. She took matters into her own hands.

In this country, we see wives reacting similarly when they sense their husbands have abandoned their responsibilities. They jump right in, declaring, "I'll get you the vineyard." And we have seen this emerge as a primary reason for marriages ending in divorce.

A modern-day Ahab gets fired from his job. For a few weeks, he looks for a new one. He comes home defeated. As the rent comes due, he becomes more depressed. Instead of facing his responsibilities, he begins to ignore the facts. If he is a sanguine, who needs his wife's approval, he might buy her a nice gift rather than saving the money for the rent. Of course, this blows up in his face. His wife sees his actions as ridiculous. Since he didn't earn her pleasure, he becomes further depressed. The ball keeps rolling, and the financial mess gets bigger. She gets tired of the creditors calling her. (Credit card companies know where the pressure point is in any marriage, so between 10:00 A.M. and 2:00 P.M. they purposely call the wife.) She begins to think about getting a job, and soon that thought becomes a reality. She assumes more and more of her husband's responsibilities, as she continues to perform her household duties. Pretty soon she decides she doesn't need this ball and chain and she can make it better without him.

One woman we interviewed described her fifteen-year struggle with this issue. Her manic depressive husband was repeatedly out of work. Although he would sob over the lack of money, he wouldn't try to find a job. Tiring of this, she got him a job by merely making a few calls to companies listed in the yellow pages. When he failed to stay on this job, she finally gave up and went to work herself rather than let her children starve. She had lost her strength to bail him out again and filed for separation. He then filed for divorce. Twelve years after the divorce, we asked her if she could have saved her marriage. She said, in retrospect, if she had been courageous enough not to bail him out, then perhaps he would have accepted his responsibility to provide for the family. If women are faced with this situation, they need to consider letting go and not trying to fix the problem themselves. When women release their husbands, the husbands may then assume their God-ordained responsibilities.

Some friends of ours proved the point. Being a phlegmatic, the husband repeatedly forgot to pay the electric bill. His wife, a choleric, had tried everything she knew to get him to carry out this responsibility. Finally she decided to test the principle of 1 Peter 3:4 that a woman should have a meek and gentle spirit. This time when the electric bill came due, she didn't nag him, and sure enough he forgot to pay it. The day the electricity was cut off she went to a neighbor's house and cooked dinner. That evening, when the husband came home from work, he found a candlelit table set with china. His wife was dressed up, and his favorite meal was waiting for him. He was delighted. They visited pleasantly over dinner, and when they had finished, as she began to clear the table, he flipped on the light switch. Nothing happened. Assuming it was a blown fuse, he went out to the fuse box. Nothing wrong. Returning to the kitchen, he asked his wife if she knew what the problem was. She calmly replied that the electricity had been cut off for nonpayment. That was several years ago, and he has never failed to pay an electric bill on time since.

The Woman Must Be Content

God gives every wife financial parameters through the family pay-check. With that in mind, it is the responsibility of the woman not to be discontent with what she has. In counseling families with severe debt, we can sometimes trace the root of the problem to the wife's being unable to live within the financial boundaries of her marriage. Because of her discontent, she manipulates her husband until finally he can stand no more. He capitulates, gives her what she wants, and the resulting debt buries them both. This particular problem can best be seen when the woman is choleric or melancholy and the man is phlegmatic or sanguine. A choleric woman may become discontent with her small house and begin to manipulate her husband into buying a bigger one. The sanguine man will so desire her approval that he will do anything in his power to please her. The phlegmatic husband doesn't want a conflict, or worse yet, fears losing his wife if he does not do as she wishes. So he concedes just to keep peace.

By contrast, one of the greatest biblical illustrations of a woman being content to follow her husband's vision and live willingly within his provision is that of Abraham and Sarah. Sarah was probably choleric and Abraham was probably phlegmatic. We realize how strong she was when we consider Peter's opinion of her: "You are her daughters if you do what is right and do not give way to fear."[2]

According to J.P. Free's book <u>Archaeology and Bible History</u>, archaeologists believe that Ur, Sarah's home, was a prosperous town. Sarah probably lived in regal comfort for her day. More than likely, her house had ten to twenty rooms with a lower floor for servants and an upper floor for her family, a guest chamber and a lavatory reserved for visitors, and probably a private chapel.

God came to Abraham and promised He would lead him to a new land and make him the father of many nations. God gave the man a great vision for the future, but sometimes a vision can reek havoc on a woman's security. When Sarah heard Abraham was going to be the father of many nations, she really heard one thing: She was going to have a baby. She had been barren for many years and greatly desired a child. Because Sarah saw the short-term reward, she was able to risk it all and go with Abraham and support his vision.

It takes great faith for a woman to believe in a man's dream. In some of the hardest times of a man's life, the dream will drive him forward, while the woman's fears will often try to quench that dream. But women can withstand the insecurity which comes with the vision by clinging to their short-term reality. Sarah clung to the fact that she was going to be a mother; therefore, she was able to follow Abraham. Interestingly, Sarah's name was changed. Her original name, Sarai, meant "general, dictator, ruler." That dictator produced an Ishmael, a work of the flesh. Not until her name was changed to "princess," and she became simply the wife of Abraham, did she produce Isaac.

Sarah forgave much. She had left her comfortable home for a tent. Twice her husband had relinquished her to another man, yet, unlike Jezebel, Sarah submitted even though Abraham was wrong. What courage! What tenacity! Even though they wandered, produced an Ishmael, and took some wrong turns, they held on to the vision, and ultimately God called them righteous and listed them in His Hall of Faith in Hebrews 11.

What does all this about Sarah and Abraham have to do with finances? Everything.

The word for the 1990s is *change*. More and more middle management jobs are being eliminated. Blue collar manufacturing jobs are being lost to other nations. Few men, whether blue-collar worker, white-collar worker, or executive, can expect to have one job for their entire lives. No longer will your job be your security. No longer will a person's identity be wrapped up in the position he holds. In a moment, without explanation, a man or woman with years of tenure can be on the street looking for a new job. More than ever, households are being shaken up. Some wives may be asked, like Sarah, to leave a grand house to live a simpler life. How will you cope? Will your heart fail with fear? Husbands, will you be like Ahab and lie down in defeat? Wives, will you be like Jezebel and take over your husbands' roles? What can we learn from these biblical examples that will help us in the midst of these economic changes?

Breaking the Cycle

How do we stop this cycle? The man must pick up the pieces of his life and begin rebuilding. The woman must allow the man to fail and must forgive him. What an act of faith on both sides. The man must trust God to bring his life and home in order as he begins to master his finances step by step. The woman must forgive her husband, release him to find God's plan for their family, and begin to trust him again. God didn't think too highly of the way Jezebel handled her family problems; the end result of her selfishness was a bloody death. God doesn't think too highly of us either when we mimic Jezebel and Ahab in our handling of money and family problems.

A Charge to Men

Men, rise up and be men. Fathers in this country are abandoning their families and their responsibilities by the droves. Winston Churchill said, "Never, never, never, never, never give up." Peter did not give up. Paul did not give up. Jesus did not give up. Not giving up is the sign of a true man. You may have to change course, but changing course is not throwing in the towel. Keep beating on the doors until one of them opens. Ask God to restore your vision. Ask Him to fan the flames of hope in your life. If you have failed financially, if you bought a franchise that is not working, if you are buried in debt, if you feel you have failed your wife, begin by asking her forgiveness. Then set a plan to get out of debt.

Men love your wives. Look over your years of marriage. Recognize how many times she was right and learn to honor your wife. In Jewish families, the husband brings in the Sabbath by reading Proverbs 31 to perpetuate honoring the woman before his family. As you lay down your selfish ambitions, your wife will trust you. You will take your place as head of the house, and she will willingly and thankfully trust your leadership.

Husbands, give your wife a short-term anchor to make her feel secure as you pursue the dream God has given you.

A Charge to Women

Wives, will you lay down your lives so that your husbands can reach their full potential? Will you commit to do your husband good and not evil all the days of your life? Will you have a meek and gentle spirit? If so, your husband will not resist your suggestions. He will find it easy to receive from you. He will not feel rejected and emasculated. He will more willingly assume the responsibilities of headship.

Do not become like Jezebel, rather become a daughter of Sarah. Do not take matters into your own hands. Place them in God's hands. Walk in faith. Be still. If you take over your husband's responsibility, it will break you and destroy your health. God gave a man broad shoulders to carry his load, so let him carry it. When Hannah committed Samuel to the house of Eli, she was not entrusting her beloved son into a man's hands; she was trusting God with her child. When women submit to their husbands, they are not trusting mere men; they are trusting God. It is the safest place of protection a woman will ever have.

The Hot Spots of Family Finances

Who Writes the Checks?

From counseling couples and talking about household finances everywhere we go, we have concluded that it is almost always better for the husband to handle the checkbook. We are not legalists. No scripture states, "Thou shalt let the husband handle the bills," but we believe it is consistent with biblical teachings.

To a large extent, you can tell where a man is spiritually by looking at his checkbook. Is he a tither, a generous man, a tightwad? In a similar way, how a man handles the checkbook indicates if he is the head of the household. If you are newly married or are facing financial difficulties, the husband absolutely should be in control of the checkbook. It will make him aware financially. Nothing is more devastating to a woman than to have her husband leave her in control of the checkbook and then demand, "Why don't we have any money? What are you doing with it?" As head of the household, the man has the responsibility to protect his family, and it is difficult for a husband to remain aware of the finances if the wife writes the checks. Sometimes this takes great faith on the part of the wife, particularly if she sees him as a financial failure. When wives forgive their husbands and trustingly turn over the checkbook, we have seen men emerge as knights in shining armor as God renews their vision.

But what about the temperaments that are just not good record keepers? Sanguines find it particularly difficult to keep good checkbook records because they are too impulsive and forgetful. Phlegmatics sometimes procrastinate until they forget to pay the bills. One woman said, "If my phleg-matic husband handled the bills, he would forget to pay them and they would be late, which would drive me crazy." In unusual cases, the wife may need to be responsible for the mechanics of taking care of bills and house-hold finances, but this should be the exception. Regardless of who main-tains the process, the responsibility must still be on the husband's shoul-ders.

In test after test, regardless of the temperament, women cried out for their husbands to take control. As one melancholy declared, "My phleg-matic husband takes no part in the finances. I don't mind writing out the bills. I just wish he would look over the checkbook and savings accounts to see where we are at any given time. I want him to share the burden. I worry a lot about it because I am so aware, and he doesn't worry at all."

The man is never to abdicate his responsibility simply because he wants to escape the problem, as phlegmatics and sanguines are prone to do. One melancholy wife went for years feeling insecure about their household finances. She never knew where they stood. Her soft-hearted, loving, phleg-matic/sanguine husband had been handling the checkbook. True to form, when she would ask him if she could buy something, he would immedi-ately say yes, without looking at their checkbook. Then the check would bounce. His reason? "The bottom line is, because of my temperament, I have a hard time denying her anything." After realizing the strengths and weaknesses of each other's temperament, they struck a solution. She would take care of the basic number crunching, yet he would remain aware of their overall financial condition. He would take care of their IRAs and other investments, while she would handle the day-to-day recordkeeping.

This type of situation works. This husband wasn't irresponsible; he was a loving family man who recognized that he was not good at handling the daily details. His wife, on the other hand, was. Order was restored to their household. It is important to emphasize that when the woman han-dles the household finances, it is not a matter of responsibility. The weight of the provision and protection of the family still remains on the shoulders of the man.

On the other extreme are choleric and melancholy men. Because they are so controlling, they have to learn to inform their wives concerning their finances. Consistently, a large portion of our financial clients are women who have been divorced or widowed or whose husbands have been disabled. We know firsthand their grief. We have dried their tears as we have helped them wade through their financial fog, not knowing where the insurance policies are located or what investments they have or what their total assets are, and for that matter, unable to balance a checkbook. Not only do they have to deal with their emotional loss, they must oftentimes bypass their own grief in order to handle the financial mess they have been left with. In our opinion this is just as irresponsible as a man who has no awareness of his financial position.

Mona's own father suddenly passed away at the age of forty-four. Her phlegmatic/melancholy mother had never written a check, driven a car, or gone to the grocery store by herself. When her mother was in her late fifties, Mona had to teach her how to use a drive-in teller window at her local bank! Mona well remembers the paralyzing fear her mother lived with while she struggled for years to learn basic financial survival. To her mother's credit, she ended her days absolutely out of debt—even her house was paid for—by carefully tending her "widow's mite." She also made sure her young daughter was not likewise ill equipped.

Should Wives Work?

Batten down the hatches, folks. It's all right for women to earn money. Notice we said *earn*. Our example is Proverbs 31. Proverbs 31:16 says, "She considers a field and buys it; out of her earnings she plants a vineyard." Verse 24 adds, "She makes linen garments and sells them, and supplies the merchants with sashes." She buys a field from her earnings. She has a cottage industry. She is creative. She has turned her craft into a business. The balance regarding a woman's work can be seen in Proverbs 31. The woman's priorities were set: She loved God, her husband was number one in her life, and her children were clothed and lacked nothing. In fact, her children thought so much of her they called her blessed. If you are successful in juggling all of these balls and earning money on the side, you are blessed!

However, there is a fine line. We do not believe that the *burden* of providing for the family should be on the wife's shoulders. The woman was created to be the helpmate to the man. If she can have a business that brings in money to help her husband without abandoning her responsibilities at home, that's great.

Christians must give each other room to seek God for each circumstance. Women who sacrifice and stay home with their children are doing what they believe God desires them to do. While Paul declares that women are to be "keepers of the home" and it is evident that this is the ultimate role of a woman, we must realize that other women feel they have no choice but to work. Although this is a very difficult issue, our opinion is that God will provide a way for the woman to remain home with her children, even if it is by giving her the creativity to start her own cottage industry.

While there are definite biblical principles to follow, each person must seek God's direction for his or her circumstances. We on the outside must release others to decide what is best for them, without devaluing them or their choices. One working woman declared through tears that she felt such guilt and pressure from the Christian community that she never felt proud of the important work she was doing.

With these factors in mind, before assuming that the best solution to a financial crisis is for the wife to work outside the home, consider all the facts. Look at the Myth of the Mother's Paycheck chart, and explore other creative options as well.

The Myth of the Mother's Paycheck

Salary amount:	$16,000	$24,000	$34,000
Expenses:			
Income tax	$2,400	$6,720	$9,520
Social Security	1,224	1,836	2,601
Child care	5,200	5,200	5,720
Clothing	500	700	1,000
Cleaning	200	300	400
Auto/commute	1,800	1,800	2,400
Eating out	1,560	1,800	2,400
Doctor's cost	300	300	300
Total expenses:	**$13,184**	**$18,656**	**$24,341**
Actual income	$2,816	$5,344	$9,659

(These costs are estimated by Roger Yancey and Jerry Tuma assume a 28 percent tax bracket.)

Decide Together

One hard and fast rule for all couples is to settle financial decisions together. Nothing exasperates a mate more than to find out what had been discussed and finalized is no longer true. You are one flesh. Making separate decisions destroys trust and oneness. Be accountable to each other even for small amounts of money.

One woman declared that ten years ago she spent a thousand dollars on two pieces of bedroom furniture without her husband's knowledge, and to this day she still hears about it. One man bought a bulldozer for six thousand dollars after he and his wife had agreed never to purchase anything over fifty dollars without discussing it with each other. She couldn't believe how much he had spent and that he had not kept his word. "I had a great loss of trust," she wrote, underlining *trust* three times.

A phlegmatic/sanguine discussed with his wife, in great detail, a particular car he wanted to buy. Together they decided to make do with their current one. At work the next day the car's owner offered to let the man just take over the payments. That sounded like a great deal, so he made the decision on the spot. As he sheepishly drove the new car up to the house, his wife was standing in the doorway. With typical sanguine charm, he looked up and said, "Can I keep it? It followed me home." He told us later, "She didn't just roll her eyes back. Her whole face rolled to the back of her head!"

But this is the ultimate: A man, without consulting his wife, traded in his perfectly running car for a van. Unfortunately, the van had absolutely no seats. He managed to find a pretty solid chair for the driver's side, but for the passenger's side he picked up an office chair—on casters! The poor person who carpooled with him had the ride of his life. As they sped down a major metropolitan freeway, with every stop and turn the passenger in the castered chair reeled from one end of the van to the other trying vainly to hold on. Though we laugh, his wife failed to see the humor.

From the outside the stories are often humorous, but such behaviors unravel the very fiber of trust within a marriage. The principles should be hard and fast. You discuss everything. You agree on a decision, and then no matter what the circumstances are, you stick with that decision unless you consult your spouse again and the two of you agree on a change.

Pray about Everything

In responding to our surveys, people listed the following trigger points for arguments over family finances. We've ranked them below in order of priority.

1. One partner's not being able to live on a budget.
2. Jobs—a change, career, investing in a partnership or franchises, and whether the wife should work.
3. Children—small children, college education, how much to bail out adult children.
4. Credit cards—whether or not to get out of debt.
5. Impulsive spending and not being able to account for money spent.

6. What size house to buy.
7. What kind of car to purchase.
8. Lending money to relatives and friends.
9. To tithe or not to tithe.
10. The amount of gift giving.

These primary areas of argument merely relate to the details of life. Scripture says to cast all our cares upon the Lord because He cares for us. We believe it is critical for couples to pray jointly over each issue, remembering the biblical principles: lay down your own desires, lay down your own will, and seek God's will in all things. You will find to your amazement that the decisions will become easier to make, and over the years you will become more like-minded as you seek unity in your financial decisions.

CHAPTER SIXTEEN

Smart Shopping

"The plans of the diligent lead to profit."
PROVERBS 21:5

Having learned painful lessons in our personal finances, by the time we began setting up our financial consulting business we were determined not to assume debt, for any reason. We have been repeatedly tested on this ever since—with amazing results—as when we went on a quest for an office copier.

For some time it had been a source of great frustration to the secretaries in the office. Eventually the copies became so poor that the secretaries gave up and then had to go down the hall to another office and pay to use their machine. After three weeks of this added frustration of running down the hall for each and every copy—it was tax season after all—one of the secretaries went into the copy room, laid the material on the copier, and tried to make a copy. Naturally, it refused. In frustration, she hit the machine, which shoved the movable top from one end of the base to the other. To her shock, it made a readable copy. When tight-fisted, phlegmatic Jerry heard what had happened, he exclaimed, "See, I told you we didn't need a copier yet!" But she was the only secretary in the office who could force the machine to work. So it became one of her jobs. And whenever a copy was needed, she would place the material on the machine, slam the top, and surprise...a copy!

Eventually, the copier rebelled against this treatment. It refused to make another copy, no matter how hard she slammed. Again, the need for a new copier became desperate.

So the search began. Over the next six weeks we tested several machines, but none met our specifications. However, a need was met. By testing the various copiers, we were able to keep making copies. This was not done dishonestly; we truly were testing to find the best machine to fill our needs.

One morning I [Mona] noticed an ad in the newspaper. An office of executive suites was going out of business and was selling twenty, used Xerox copiers, each worth between three thousand and eight thousand dollars. When we went to check it out, to our surprise, we found several copiers which would meet our needs perfectly. Because the man desperately needed an immediate sale, he offered to sell us a slightly used, eight thousand dollar machine for twenty-five hundred. To my shock, Jerry—remember he's phlegmatic—said he had to think about it.

I well understood the need within the office and, being choleric, wanted to get it done. But I also knew it was pointless to pressure Jerry. I know from personal experience that you cannot outwait a phlegmatic. So another week passed.

After Jerry's prayer time one morning, he told me to check on the availability of the copier. When I called, the man was exasperated. Although prior to that day people had come into the office in droves, virtually no one had looked at the copiers since we had been there the week before. I told him we were ready to buy and I wanted to know his bottom price. He asked, "Will you buy it today?" I said, "Yes, we can give you a cashier's check." He responded, "I have bills due today. If you can give me fifteen hundred dollars cash, I'll sell you the copier." He was thrilled to make the sale, and our office was thrilled to have a new copier, that afternoon, delivered free of charge.

While this instance had its humorous side, the real lesson of it for us was that, once again, God's principles worked. We believed God would meet our need when it became a true need, and He did, far beyond our expectations. We tried to be smart in our shopping so that we would be good stewards of His money and so that our lives would be less stressful financially. This has not been an easy lesson for me to learn. Remember, I am a choleric, and I shop fast. *Posthaste* is my favorite word. After recognizing that this attitude has cost me a lot of money, I took the challenge. I determined to never, ever, pay more than is absolutely necessary for anything. I have become a consumer advocate and a crusader. In fact, I carry the flag!

Beyond saving money, we have discovered there are additional, more significant, benefits to smart shopping. Our faith is continually reaffirmed by God's provision for our needs. Our lives are less stressful. And because our finances are in order, we often have the privilege of buying missionaries and needy families fashionable clothes for pennies on the dollar. We have decided to abide by the principle of "living simply so that others may simply live."

What are these principles of smart shopping? Here are some that we use to significantly impact our budget.

1. Decide together.

Although I am the primary shopper, Jerry is just as committed to the cause of smart shopping. Husbands and wives must have the same vision of creating a secure financial household, and they must determine to make buying decisions together. This alone can save you major money because it causes you to stop and think before you buy.

Together you need to:
• remember God owns it all,
• then define your needs, wants, and desires,
• and, as a result, determine to make any necessary lifestyle changes.

God promises to meet our needs, not necessarily our desires. Needs are food, clothing, job, home, medical care, and transportation. Wants involve the quality of those goods, as in choosing a new car over a used one. Desires are choices which are met with surplus funds according to God's will. It is not just money to burn. If you have a surplus, God has a reason for it. Save it until He shows you what to do with it.

2. Avoid status symbols.

The world declares we must look the part, but we must remember that God's ways are not necessarily man's ways. You can save as much as 50 percent by not buying name brands. Most designer labels have had minimal, if any, input from the designer whose name they sport. The trend is to farm out the entire line to a lesser known manufacturer who pays a royalty of 5 to 10 percent for the use of the name. Designer-named items are not necessarily quality items. Actually, the label is a joke among merchandisers, and unfortunately, the joke is on the consumer.[1]

Just recently a man called in to a local radio program to relate his experience with this. He had gone to New York City's garment district to have a suit custom made for him. When he went for the final fitting, the tailor took him to a wall of small boxes and asked whose label he would like to have sewn into the suit.

From suits to perfume to medicines, overspending on name-brand items can bust your budget. Many generic medicines are now produced by the very same company that manufactures the original product. For example, the manufacturers of a well known pain reliever, also make its generic equivalent. According to a pharmacist, they are exactly the same medicine produced by the same company, yet the generic brand costs $10 less.

Cosmetics can be another real jolt. A famous maker of a cosmetic that supposedly reduces wrinkles sells its product for $79 a bottle. A product with the exact same ingredients which claims to do the same thing can be purchased from a cosmetic company which sells door-to-door for approximately $13. We are going to get old, whether we pay $79 a bottle or $13 a bottle. No wrinkle cream will prevent us from ending up like the woman who was painstakingly applying her makeup as her young niece watched in fascination. Finally, the young girl chirped, "Auntie, are you filling in the cracks?"

Women are not the only ones who have to hold the line on falling for status symbols. Men also have a lot of pressure put on them to look the part. When Jerry determined early in his business that he was never going to try to look the part again, he decided to "prove" God by believing Zechariah 4:10: "Who despises the day of small things?" When he began his business, he showed me two ugly yellow chairs that had been given to him—leftovers from a hotel conference room. He declared that if God had designed for him to be in this business, he was going to do it without debt and by following the principles of God. He would test God by setting up an office in a small area with an inexpensive desk, an old brown, vinyl desk chair, and these two very ugly yellow chairs. In my opinion this was testing God to the limit! Under my breath, I scoffed, "Nobody is going to come into the office, look at these simple, small beginnings, and leave their money with us to invest for them." But to my amazement and the amazement of many others, clients came, and little by little the business increased.

Jerry dreamed of the big leather chair with the checkerboard cherry wood desk, the huge credenza, and well-furnished offices, but he was determined to let God grow us in His way, little by little. Over several years Jerry progressed from the yellow chairs, to a set of brown vinyl chairs, to a set of padded blue chairs, and finally, he "looks the part" with his cherry wood desk. Everything was purchased with cash as he waited for God to provide for him.

Walking through these humble beginnings, we have learned how to be content as Philippians 4:11-13 describes: "Not that I am implying that I was in any personal want, for I have learned how to be content (satisfied to the point where I am not disturbed or disquieted) in whatever state I am. I know how to be abased and live humbly in straitened circumstances, and I know also how to enjoy plenty and live in abundance" (AMP).

We believe that discontent is one of the primary financial craters into which many households fall. The speedy exhilaration allowed by credit cards and debt oftentimes does not allow God to teach the Christian principles about His character and how to live a godly life. As a result, we often bypass God's character training and miss maturing principles for our lives. We must be content in who we are. Contentment will not be found by wearing the right label or sitting in the best chair.

3. Avoid impulse buying.

Time is the key factor to finding bargains. This is particularly hard for the impulsive sanguine and the time-conscious choleric. Stretch your looking-around time. Wait at least thirty days, if possible, before making a major purchase. It may be reasonable to spend weeks waiting for that swimsuit to go on sale, months looking for a car, and years shopping for a home. Make it a creative challenge to wait for the best possible buy. Improvise until the need is met. Maybe you can rent that chain saw you will use only once a year. Could you barter for a service you need? Do anything to give an object a little longer life. The balance, however, is not to wait too long. Don't keep cars and major appliances until they cost more in repairs than they are worth.

4. Avoid fads.

A fad is a craze which you know will fade away with the next whim of the fashion industry. Clogs come and go every twenty years. Bell bottoms, which went out of style in the early seventies, are on the rise again. A wise person will dress practically. A man might have a navy suit with several different shirts and ties. A blazer paired with a black, red, or navy skirt, some different blouses, and a scarf can give a woman a new, chic look that won't fade away.

5. Avoid advertising gimmicks.

Such phrases as "a dream come true," "easy to buy," "just twelve easy payments," "no credit refused," "no payments until March" are all advertising appeals to the lust of the flesh. Develop sales resistance. Turn your back on the lure to be sexy, tasteful, beautiful, adventurous. Do a reality check on product claims to lose while you snooze, and to prevent balding, wrinkling, and lumping. As Ecclesiastes states, "Vanity of vanities, all is vanity."

Beware of ad slogans such as "emergency sale" and "going out of business." Mark the time and see how long a company can "go out of business." A furniture store in Dallas for months and months sported a sign declaring they were going out of business. Then they changed the sign to say, "Help us keep from going out of business." The Better Business Bureau got so many complaints that the company finally did go out of business.

Perhaps the most misused ad slogan is the phrase "Manufacturer's Suggested Retail Price" or "MSRP." We ask you, who suggests that manufacturer's retail price? Manufacturers can suggest anything. The issue is what is it worth? Do not accept the MSRP as indicating the value of the item. You have to decide if it really fits your budget, if it really is the quality advertised, and if you need it. Challenge the ads.

As I said before, I have become quite the consumer advocate. My determination to smart shop made me recently confront a local grocery store. They had a sign in their window declaring they had "certified lower prices" than all of the other grocery stores in the area. I decided to challenge the ad. First, I asked the store manager, "Who certified the prices?" He wouldn't give me an answer that appeased me. I then contacted the home office of a competing grocery store, and they sent me money to shop at the store with the "certified lower prices." I did what every woman wants to do. I had the shopping spree of my life. I went through the competitor's store filling my shopping cart and making a list of everything I bought. Then I went through the manager's check-out line and didn't have to pay a dime.

Next, I went to the store with the "certified lower prices" and purchased the exact same items with their competitor's money. They truly did have lower prices on national brands, but their store brand foods were nearly 20 percent higher than the competitor's. I confronted the management and showed them my two receipts. As a result of my challenging the ad, this nationwide chain quickly removed the signs from their windows.

Not only did the stores change their advertising, I had two shopping carts of groceries which had not cost me a penny. That gave me a surplus to share with a needy family.

6. Learn to bargain.

Talk is cheap and things get cheaper if you talk. Look for flaws that you can easily repair and ask for a discount. Patiently wait for that floor model to go on sale, then show the sales personnel the little nicks and scratches and get dollars off. Note, I did not say scratch it first and then try to get your money! But if there is a legitimate scratch or ink spot or tear or missing button, ask for a discount. We got $75 off the price of a cherry leather executive chair for Jerry's office by noticing a small scratch on the back of the leather, which no one else would even see.

However, not everything that is cheap is a bargain. A word about value is in order. Use wisdom in all things. Check everything out. Once, to save money, I used a coupon to get a permanent from a hairdresser I didn't know and for whom I had no recommendations. The results were disastrous. I lost nearly all my hair, and it took two years for it to be healthy again. Just because you have a coupon or something is on sale does not make a product a good deal.

7. Save your receipts.

You do not have to live with second-rate or faulty items. For that matter, if your guaranteed-to-live plant dies, take it back and get a refund. If you buy something of poor quality and it breaks before the end of its guarantee, return it to the store. Don't be obnoxious, but do make your point. If you buy an item at full price and you find it on sale within thirty days, take your receipt back to the store manager, show the difference in price, and request a refund of the difference. I bought a birdbath which cost $19.95. Three days later, I went back to the same store for another item and discovered the birdbath was on sale for $10 less. I showed my receipt to the manager and was immediately refunded the difference.

8. Learn to barter.

Trade services. Trade talents. Trade anything that you think the other person needs. One single mother had a $700 car repair bill that she could not afford, so she offered to clean their floors or wait on customers. The auto repairman didn't need those services. Finally, in desperation, she asked him, "Well, what do you hate to do?" He replied, "Collect money from customers." She felt she could do that. She earned credit of $2 per call and 10 percent of any money collected and soon telephoned her way out of debt. Again, be creative; improvise rather than pull out that credit card.

9. Shop around.

Prices vary from day to day and from store to store. We bought some dining room chairs from a major department store only to discover that another store in that chain was selling the same chairs at a lower price. When we told the manager of the first store that his prices were higher than their other store, he refunded the difference.

10. Shop seasonally.

By shopping seasonally you can save as much as 50 percent. The time to buy an air conditioner is not during July when it's used most. Follow the principle of supply and demand. When everyone wants one, the price will be higher. If you know your air conditioner is on its last legs, buy a new one when no one else is buying—during January. Conversely, if you have a heater which needs repair or replacing, make your purchase in August. Buy summer clothes in August or September for the next season. Buy winter coats in March, not September. By learning to plan ahead, you can purchase before the need is critical and save lots of money at the same time. By avoiding impulse buying, you can often save 75 percent to 95 percent on some items. I had been waiting all summer for a pair of blue sandals that sold for $35 in a major department store. When I finally bought them on sale, off-season, I paid $3.95. (See the Appendix for specific tips on shopping off-season.)

11. Shop outlet stores.

Almost all major department stores have outlets. Before purchasing a particular item, ask the store if they have an outlet. Everything from tennis shoes to sofas to eyeglasses can be found at great discounts at outlet malls. After shopping for my daughter's college clothes, I sat down and tallied the cost. At the outlet stores, I paid $169.92 for clothes which retailed in department stores for $313.00.

When shopping at outlet stores, make sure you have a quality item before you leave because few of these stores allow returns. Check the seams, check for missing buttons, make sure there is no irreparable damage to furniture. Be sure to check the item very carefully before taking it out of the store.

Visit outlet stores on a regular basis to get the best buys. Nothing is better than getting a sale at a sale store. It is not uncommon for these outlet stores to have clearance sales where you can save 75 percent off of an item that was already reduced by 75 percent. That is the true shoppers' delight. Shop at the end of the month when they are trying to clear out merchandise. Shop after major holidays. Shop after the regular retail stores have cleared out their post-season clothing. Less than 5 percent of the merchandise found in outlet stores is defective. Most items are simply surplus stock that the regular retail stores didn't sell. Every major retail store has an outlet store somewhere in the United States. If it is close to you, it may be worth investigating.

Jerry wanted a down-filled, hooded coat that was listed in a catalog for $145, but we decided that was too much. Later, in browsing at an outlet store, we discovered the same coat for $40. Jerry was thrilled. But it got better. As we were standing in line to check out, an announcement came over the intercom that they were having a blue light special and all coats were 50 percent off the sale price, making his $145 coat cost $20.

12. Shop resale.

Shop newspapers, Salvation Army, garage sales, craft malls, and bankruptcy sales for second-hand items. Garage sales in an upper middle income neighborhood will often yield great bargains on high quality merchandise. When we expanded our office a few years ago, Jerry decided it was time to get the desk and credenza he had always wanted. We had looked at new desks and found prices ranging from $2,500 to $4,000 for this particular desk. However, I found the exact desk and credenza Jerry wanted by looking in the paper for a bankruptcy sale. When I called the man who had placed the ad, I learned that he had overextended himself and was losing his business. He still owed $2,000 on his desk and only wanted us to pay him what he owed. We paid him cash for the desk and received not only the desk, but the credenza, several secretarial chairs, waste baskets, paper clips, pencils, copy paper, and almost an entire year's worth of office supplies for only $2,000.

13. Recycle.

In days gone by, our grandmothers had button boxes and saved tin foil until it fell apart. They washed out bread bags and made quilts from worn clothing. Although some people are still recyclers, it is a less and less practiced art.

My grandmother had a spool of thread in her apron. As she worked around the house, she would find bits and pieces of string. When I was a young child, I asked her why she saved all those little tiny pieces of string. To which she replied that if I had lived through the depression, I would save string, too. Recycling can challenge your creativity.

14. Learn how to grocery shop.

• Plan before you shop. Don't buy anything not on your shopping list.
• Don't count paper products, dish washing detergent, cleaning products, and other nonfood items as part of your food bill. Shop for food at

the grocery store. Explore discount stores and hardware stores for nonfood items where they are often less expensive.

• The most expensive food items are snacks, which can easily add 10 percent to your weekly food bill. Buy them after you have purchased the needed items. Snacks are wants, not needs.

Dr. James McKeever, a friend of ours who is an economic consultant, has created an excellent and quick way to determine just how much is spent on nonessential grocery items. When you shop, get two carts. In the first cart put everything that is essential—meat, poultry, vegetables, bread. In the second cart, put all the nonessentials—sweets, soft drinks, prepared foods, snacks. When you get to the check-out counter, have the checker ring each cart up separately to see exactly how much you are spending on nonessentials. As you're getting out of debt, we recommend you severely limit or even eliminate nonessentials.

• For a cheaper grocery bill and the healthiest foods, shop the outer walls of the store. Regardless of the store, produce is on one side, meats and cheeses are on the back wall, and milk, eggs, butter, and bakery items will be on the other side. By avoiding the middle, you can leave the store without succumbing to temptation.

• Look on the bottom shelves at the supermarket for cheap surprises. Retailers put expensive food at eye level because middle shelves are easier to reach. Top and bottom shelves contain lower-priced items. Bypass the end racks. Anything within easy reach is there to tempt you to impulse buy. They are almost always more expensive.

• Use a hand calculator. Today many grocery stores attach them to the shopping carts. By being more aware of how much you're spending, you will be less likely to overspend.

• If you're married, leave your husband at home. Husbands are notorious impulse buyers when it comes to groceries. They will wreck the budget, unless you are married to a man as committed to the budget as you are. Leave children home with Dad, too. They will distract you from your main goal.

• Do not shop on an empty stomach. If you shop when you're hungry, everything looks good to you. Impulse purchases will jump off the shelves into your shopping cart.

• Shop specials.

• Clip coupons. By using coupons, the average family can expect to save approximately $16 a week on their grocery bill. Over a year, that could amount to $832. By investing the $832 a year at 12 percent in a good, long-term investment, in 35 years you could have $359,144 in savings. Remember the bucket principle.

• Learn how to bulk shop. Look carefully at the unit price. Look at all labels and take nothing for granted. Larger sizes are not necessarily a better buy.

• Compare forms of food—frozen, dried, fresh, canned—before you buy. Is an item cheaper fresh, canned, or frozen? Even this will depend on the seasons. Fresh fruit is cheaper in the summer. Don't shop first crops. Prices go down as supply increases. Steak prices go up in the summer for cookouts. Pot roasts go up in the winter because more people cook them then. This is one advantage of a home freezer.

• When an item says "4 for $1," you may be able to get the $.25 unit cost without buying four.

• Buy store brands and save big dollars. Many companies pay the wholesale food suppliers to put the store label on their items, so you can get the same quality but at a cheaper price.

GROCERY SHOPPING

ITEM	NAME BRAND	STORE BRAND
Chicken broth	.75	.41
Corn	.51	.47
Apple Juice	2.09	1.59
Baking soda	.69	.49
Coffee (Gourmet)	3.39	2.79
Green beans	.75	.55
Pears	1.09	.99
Coffee creamer	2.67	1.89
TOTALS	$11.94	$9.18
SAVINGS		**$2.76**

You save 23 percent by buying the store brand. If you normally spend $100 per week on groceries, this means an average savings of $23 per week, or $100 per month, or $1,196 per year. A hundred dollars per month invested at 8 percent for ten years becomes $18,295. In thirty years, it becomes $149,036. A hundred dollars per month invested at 12 percent for ten years becomes $23,204. In thirty years, it becomes $349,496. That's money that can be saved or applied to credit card debt.

15. Plan your gift giving.

Regardless of your financial status, in debt or otherwise, plan before buying. Determine to bring gift-giving under control. Here are a few hints to help you:

• Keep an event calendar. Plan ahead for the gifts. Buy on sale. Shop for birthdays and anniversaries ahead of time so you don't have to buy quickly. If you know a wedding is coming in June, buy the gift at a January white sale.

• Initiate some family fun and make some of the gifts you need. Making gifts will help bring your family together and will allow you to save money. Plus these gifts often mean more to the recipient.

• Draw names for selected gifts rather than giving each family member something.

• Don't buy gifts on credit. Creating debt for your family is not an act of love. It would be much better to make something with your own hands rather than borrow money for the gift.

16. Do not ignore recreation.

Your family needs the fellowship. Even though you may have decided to live on a strict budget to get your household finances in order, remember that family time is important. Find inexpensive ways to celebrate. Some video stores rent family movies for as little as $.49 a night. Play games. Go on picnics. Go camping. It is wonderful fun and the least expensive way to vacation. Of course, buy all your camping gear at garage sales and thrift stores. The best memories will be from all the things that can go wrong. Sometimes you can even save money by vacationing during the off-season. In February, you can stay in a beautiful condo on the sea for as little as $45 per night. This same condo would cost $150 per night during the peak season.

17. Plan your burial expenses.

When your emotions are overwhelmed is not the time to be making major financial decisions. Avoid the emotion. Check into a good pre-funeral plan.

18. Beware of some shopping clubs.

One of the worst opportunities for shopping addiction is the home shopping club. People sit glued to their television sets, listening to a salesperson proclaim the great price. These bored people get hooked into a credit card downspin. Also, watch out for other kinds of shopping clubs. If you have to pay a monthly fee to be a member, question the true value of their product. They can tell you anything, but the true test is "Can I get it cheaper by smart shopping?" I have yet to see a shopping club that can beat smart shopping talent.

What is the bottom line of smart shopping? Awareness. Be aware of the scams, the sales techniques, your budget, and how to dig for bargains. Make these a natural part of your shopping.

19. Eliminate costly habits.

THE HIGH COST OF SMOKING

A cigarette smoker who smokes one carton of cigarettes per week with a cost of $2 per package, is spending $20 per week, $80 per month, and $1,040 per year just on cigarettes.

If a smoker were to quit smoking and invest the money at 8%, the following amounts would be available at retirement age 65.

Quitting Age	Amount at retirement
25	$305,140
35	$130,037
45	$51,310

CHAPTER SEVENTEEN

Teaching Your Children about Money

"These commandments that I give you today are to be upon your hearts. Impress them on your children."

DEUTERONOMY 6:6-7

Our daughter, Hannah, currently attends college with several international students. Beyond the educational experience, more importantly she is observing the sacrifice these young adults are willing to make in order to receive a quality education. One precious young woman has given her all just to be able to fly to America and pay the tuition. She has been living on one meal a day for an entire year in order to stay in school and reach her ultimate goal—a degree.

By contrast, when Hannah recently went to a discount store to buy a new pair of shoes, the young American with her couldn't believe she would stoop so low as to wear those kinds of shoes and even refused to set foot in the store. At twenty-five it was beneath this person's dignity to consider the possibility that something good might come out of a discount store.

Today, grade school children carry Dooney & Bourke purses that cost two to three hundred dollars. Homecoming mums typically cost teenagers sixty dollars apiece. Prom dresses costing hundreds of dollars are worn only once. High school kids rent limousines, tuxedos, and hotel rooms for graduation night, potentially spending a thousand dollars or more as their "reward" for graduating. Average weddings cost ten thousand dollars, and extravagant ones can easily exceed twenty-five thousand. Today's young adults fully expect to step right out of their parents' home and into their own, forgetting that it took their parents thirty years or more to accumulate what they have. They have always received what they wanted when they wanted it. Having had so much, they value so little.

How different from the 1940s when people saved tin foil off gum wrappers and pooled their nickels and pennies to buy war bonds. Their consumption of bacon, butter, tires, silk stockings, gasoline, and sugar was rationed. In the face of hard times, these people were creative. An ad that appeared in a Sterling, Colorado, newspaper read "Wanted to rent. One pair silk stockings for one hour every Sunday morning to wear to church."[1] One enterprising manufacturer in those difficult days came out with leg makeup—a thick, flesh-colored liquid with a dauber applicator. It even included a pencil for drawing on the "seams" on the back of the legs. The novel idea, however, had a couple of flaws. The women had to shave their legs daily for a smooth application, and when it rained, the makeup ran down their legs like cheap mascara, ruining their shoes.

The deprivation of the 1940s generation produced a people who quite naturally desired to give their own children a better life than they had. This mind-set created a generation of super achievers. The times were right. The opportunities were many. And the next generation of children, commonly known as the Baby Boomers, quickly inherited an economic environment never before seen in history. These Baby Boomers of the late 1940s and early 1950s are now producing Baby Busters. Children born after 1964 are facing the tough reality that they will never have the wealth their parents had. How will they cope with the shrinking job market? How will they cope with the crises of the next twenty years? It is up to the parents to the best of their abilities to prepare them.

Ironically, one of the ways to instill a vision in children is to allow them to go through trials and pressures. Sometimes in our affluent society parents have to purposely set boundaries and limits in children's lives in order to produce character within them. Our children must be trained. Today's children are perhaps the least trained financially of any generation.

Many aren't prepared to make it on their own because their parents haven't given them the coping skills. We, as parents, have forgotten the injunction of Deuteronomy 6:6-7: "These commandments that I give you today are to be upon your hearts. Impress them on your children. Talk about them when you sit at home and when you walk along the road, when you lie down and when you get up."

One way for parents to fulfill this verse on a daily basis is by teaching their children biblical principles for handling money, and we can teach them in the same way Jesus did. Jesus lived in an agricultural society and used experiences common to that society to teach His disciples about Himself. Likewise, we can use our daily financial decisions to teach our children honesty, dependability, responsibility, reliability, and integrity. The focus of all child training, financial or otherwise, is to light a fire of desire in our children's heart to do the will of God. They must learn their lives are not their own; they have been bought with a price—the blood of Jesus. They and everything they own belong to God, and they are to be stewards, ready and willing to do the bidding of the King of kings and Lord of lords.

A woman we counseled was presented a wonderful opportunity to turn her five-year-old's heart toward God. This woman had taught her daughter well concerning long-range planning. By the age of five this little girl had already saved ninety dollars toward the purchase of a car. With every birthday and Christmas gift, as well as each allowance, she tucked some money away in a little purse. Then, to her dismay, she lost the purse. The mother and daughter searched every nook and cranny of the house, but it could not be found. Heartbroken, the child gave up.

To her surprise, the mother later found the money and asked us what to do. Should she hold the purse back, allowing the child to continue to feel her loss and learn a lesson in responsibility, or should she return it? We counseled her to return the purse quickly to her daughter and to share with her the parable of the lost coin. This gave the woman a tremendous opportunity to tell her happy five-year-old about how Jesus feels when those who are lost are found. That five-year-old found more treasure than her purse; she discovered something precious about Jesus. She understood how Jesus rejoiced when she was found. That mother used money to teach her daughter about Christ at an early age.

Know Your Child

In teaching your children about finances, it is important to understand their temperament. The delicate, sensitive child cannot be treated in the same way as the headstrong, willful child. The apprehensive, fearful child cannot be handled in the same way as the daring, aggressive child.

According to Beverly LaHaye, a child's temperament will be obvious by the age of two. Remember, everyone is a unique combination of at least two, and occasionally three, temperaments. At different stages of growth and development the child will react with some degree of variance because environment, inhibitions, and the influence of those around him can alter or subdue some of his basic temperament traits. Even so, a child's basic temperament is determined at birth—a sanguine is a sanguine, a choleric is a choleric.

Teach Your Child to Give

To young children, even money is a toy. When you give them a nickel to put into the offering plate, in their minds they are giving away a toy. When they are trained to drop it into the plate, they are learning to give. Sanguine children will be the most cheerful givers. On the other hand, parents will have to pry the nickel out of the tight-fisted phlegmatics' hands. Then there are the sanguine/choleric children. They cheerfully toss the nickel into the offering plate only to look around to see if anyone is watching as they reach into the plate to grab it back.

If children are not trained to be givers who hold all of life with an open hand, they will be miserable children indeed. The parents of phlegmatics will have the greatest difficulty teaching their children to give. While the children won't ask for much, they will want to keep their things forever.

They must be forced into the position of giving. When the parents see their little phlegmatics stuffing all their toys under their clothes or running to a corner to play quietly alone, they must encourage the children to come out and share. Parents must intentionally and repeatedly provide them the opportunity to give to others.

For sanguines, sharing is easy. They will meet their friends at the front door with all that they own. It is not uncommon for sanguine children to come home without their coat, their lunch box, and if possible, their shoes. Since these loving, giving children want to meet every need they see, the parents need to teach balance. Sanguine children must learn that there are times when it is not necessary to give everything to another person just because he or she wants it. The challenge to the parents of sanguine children will be teaching them not to give everything away but to discern true needs and how best to meet those needs.

Choleric children will give freely if it benefits them. It takes a wise parent to discern the motive behind the choleric giver. Giving only to gain something in return is not true giving. A choleric child must be taught to give unselfishly. One great opportunity is giving to a truly needy family at Christmas. Be certain that your choleric child is helping you distribute gifts to those people who are less fortunate than you.

One year when our family was struggling financially, we decided to focus not on the few presents we could provide our children but instead to give to a truly deprived family. When we explained this to our young children, they quickly entered into the spirit of giving as we planned, budgeted, went to the toy store, and picked out the gifts for this family. After discovering that neither parent was going to receive a gift, the children encouraged us to buy for the husband and wife also. Stretching our dollars a bit further, we bought their gifts, took all of the presents home, and wrapped them. Then at midnight on Christmas Eve our sleepy-eyed children crawled into the car with us, and we put the box of gifts on this family's porch. We had a twenty-four-hour answering service call them in the middle of the night to tell the family to go look on the front porch. In the meantime, our family had parked down the street, and our children got to watch that whole family come out in the middle of the night and find Christmas on their porch. That Christmas is our very most memorable Christmas ever. Our children had experienced the true reason for Christmas. They had been a vital part of our gift giving, and this experience changed their lives. From this point on, both children have been much more aware of other people's needs, and they respond unselfishly.

Teach Your Child Obedience

Start teaching your child at the age of one the first principle of all money management—no. "No, you may not touch." "No, that is not yours." "No, you may not have that." "No, I will not buy that." "No, don't open that until I pay for it." Why is this the foundation for managing money? Because this present generation has never learned the value of the word. The credit card companies say yes to everything we desire. But life is full of "no, you cannot have this." Maybe you can have it later; maybe you can never have it. Learning to accept no at the most selfish stage of life is the most important financial foundation stone.

When parents give in to children's cries and screams, they are unintentionally training them to cry loud and long in order to get what they want. This teaches children to become perpetual complainers who are never content with what they have, never willing to wait on God's timing. It also teaches them that there is no limit to the money supply. Why should they believe that money does not grow on trees since they eventually get what they want by using the right technique? Establish the power of your word early.

Susanah Wesley raised thirteen children, including Charles and John Wesley. She believed in teaching the child early the principles of life. She has been quoted as saying, "The worst form of child abuse is to allow a child to do something when he is very young that you are going to have to break them of later." In other words, if your child at age two is stealing cookies out of the cookie jar and you treat it merely as a humorous situation, you are allowing that child to establish patterns that may have serious repercussions and be virtually impossible to break when he is a teenager.

Choleric children will be the most difficult ones with which to cope. With their explosive, angry temperament they loudly declare their own desires, and they will test you severely to see how far they can go. They will be the children everyone hears screaming in the grocery store because you told them they could not have the candy bar. While sanguine children can scream too, they tend to use their charm and powers of persuasion to manipulate you and wear you down until you give in. Parents, stick to your no regardless. Stop the pattern before it becomes ingrained in the children that they can get their way by pushing the right buttons.

Teach Your Child Honesty

Regardless of the child's temperament, it is very important to develop honesty in every child. One mother we interviewed shared how she taught her child honesty. As she and her four-year-old son were out grocery shopping, he took a piece of candy without paying for it. On their way home from the grocery store, she smelled the definite odor of peanut butter candy wafting its way from the back of the van. Discovering what he had done, she immediately turned the van around, took her son back to the store, and had him ask forgiveness and make restitution to the store manager. What a lesson that little four-year-old will carry with him for the rest of his life. While it cost her time, that course of action laid a great chunk of honesty in her child's foundation.

Give Your Child a Sense of Value

Another principle that must be grafted into the child is a sense of value. What is something worth? Think of ways to demonstrate the worth in terms children will understand. Phlegmatic children will be the most difficult to train in this principle. Since they have little regard for what they wear, they will be unmindful of the way they care for their possessions. At the other extreme are melancholy children. They are painfully aware of every wrinkle in their clothes and every scuff of dirt on their shoes. Here the parents' challenge will be to teach them that they do not need the absolute best quality of everything they wear. With each temperament extreme the parent has to teach the balance of value.

Teach Personal Responsibility and Restitution

Personal responsibility must become a fact of life for all children, regardless of their temperament. If children break something, they need to make restitution by replacing the broken item. If they don't have money to replace it, give them extra chores. If they spill a drink, they should clean the mess. If they break another child's toy, they should give one of their own good toys in its place, which allows them to feel the same loss as the child whose toy was broken. If children continually leave their toys at a friend's house or at church, don't keep running back to get them. Let them experience loss at a young age. This is especially important with the forgetful sanguines and careless phlegmatics. They need some strong reminders if they are to overcome their forgetful tendencies.

Instill a Work Ethic

Having a work ethic is one of the most important financial principles for parents to teach their children. Paul says in 2 Thessalonians 3:10, "For even when we were with you, we gave you this rule: 'If a man will not work, he shall not eat.'" That's a strong statement. We must not create financially dependent children. While we desire that children be dependent and obedient when they are young, they must gradually make the transition to independence. They must become totally financially independent from their parents, while remaining absolutely dependent on God, trusting Him to meet all their needs.

Allowing your children to earn money is one way to teach them personal responsibility and a work ethic. However, children should not be paid for fulfilling their own responsibilities. For example, don't pay children for picking up their own toys, making their own bed, or clearing their own dishes. Not paying them for taking care of themselves underlines the fact that they must do some things just because those things have to be done. Further, whenever a job is not done properly, they should not get paid for it. However, allow them to earn money for doing work outside their responsibilities, which might be washing the family dishes or putting away a younger sibling's toys. The goal is to fairly compensate children for extra work without creating the impression that compensation is the only motivation for extra effort.

When children are young, commands such as "pick up your toys" must be obeyed, not halfheartedly or halfway, but properly and promptly. The impulsive sanguine children will often become distracted and forgetful, failing to follow through with their chores and your orders. Parents must be extremely consistent with these children, ensuring that they do as they have been told. The self-sufficient cholerics will need the fewest reminders of their personal responsibilities, unless they resist because they just don't want to do them. In fact, choleric children usually get paid the full amount for chores done properly because money motivates them. The detail-minded melancholies will take forever to get the chore done, but it will be done perfectly. All the toys will be stacked in color-coordinated order. You will not have to impress upon them the need to do it right, but you will have to impress upon them to do it quickly without wasting time or becoming distracted by their perfection. The easy-going phlegmatics, on the other hand, will drag their feet and drive you to distraction because they are absolutely content to live in a mess. They won't even care if they're paid because money means nothing to them. Parents must instill a reason for earning and saving money into these little phlegmatics. They have to see a point to what they are doing before they willingly head toward any goal. Find out what motivates your little phlegmatics, and use it for all it's worth!

Encourage Work Outside the Home

As children grow in their responsibilities at home, they also need to find work outside the home. We recommend they begin doing small jobs outside the home as early as eleven or twelve. The girl of eleven or twelve can go door-to-door, asking neighborhood mothers with younger children if they need a mommy's helper for an afternoon. As the young girl matures, she can become a baby-sitter or even a housekeeper, eventually establishing a clientele.

A young boy can mow lawns. Our son, Samuel, began mowing lawns when he was eleven. Because he was so young, we considered him an apprentice, and he charged an apprentice's wage that was less than what other neighborhood boys were charging. However, just because he charged less did not mean he could do a lesser job. To ensure that he did a quality job, his father inspected the lawns. We instilled into our son that we are to do everything as if we are working for the Lord, as Colossians 3:23 says.

We must train our children to please their earthly parents so that, as adults, they will desire to please their heavenly Father. After we inspected the lawn, our son would be paid for a job well done. The impact this had on our neighborhood was incredible. We were even able to share the Lord with unbelieving parents because our son did a great job on all of his lawns.

One of Samuel's clients owned a hair salon. Mona decided in order to be neighborly to go to him to have her hair cut. When she walked in, the neighbor called out, "This is Samuel's mom!" All the other hairdressers stopped and came into his work area, and he said, "This is the mother of the boy I have been telling you about who is such a hard worker. If my children turn out to be as good workers as her son, I will consider myself to have been a good father." When they asked how she had managed to raise such a responsible child, Mona was able to share the Lord with the entire group. The best evangelistic tool is still a godly family.

As Samuel grew older, he learned more valuable business principles. By charging less than the other neighborhood boys, he received more jobs than they and learned the first principle—the law of supply and demand. By doing a high quality job at each location, he learned that the person who does the best job keeps the job—a principle of job security. By keeping his prices lower and continuing to maintain a higher quality of work, he learned how much people appreciate an honest businessman and how to gain market share. Many times he found his pockets lined with tips from satisfied customers.

Teach Your Child to Keep Records

Children should have a book containing the names and numbers of clients, how much they made on each job, and what their expenses were. For example, Samuel kept a record of the cost of maintenance and gas for the lawn mower.

Once they begin working, children must have their own social security number and learn their responsibility to pay taxes to the IRS. This instills honesty. If they run their own small business, they must pay self-employment taxes. Children need to understand from the beginning their biblical and civil responsibility to obey the law. Over the years we have seen many households shipwrecked, including our own, because of irresponsible actions and misinformation conveyed to the government.

Prepare Them for the Future

As children grow older, they need to become reliable, dependable, and self-sufficient. Because of their earlier training, they should now take the initiative to do a good job because they realize people are counting on them. We believe that parents are ultimately responsible for equipping their children for a lifetime of work. Parents can teach their children how to fill out a job application. Parents should have mock interviews with them to teach them how to conduct themselves and how to respond to a potential employer's questions.

When Samuel was seventeen, he held down three jobs. One was a daytime construction job working for a Christian. This job was his choice and was very profitable. We made him keep his lawn jobs because he had found no replacement for his services. And in order to keep his word to his clients, he faithfully mowed their lawns after hours or on weekends. Finally, the last job he secured was for us. We wanted to ensure that he knew how to fill out a job application, how to interview, how to dress properly, and finally how to land the job. This he did, working part-time at a grocery store. Although this was a difficult summer for him because he was working over eighty hours a week, the skills he learned and the character-building processes he went through during those three months were invaluable. He called us from college a few weeks later to thank us for the valuable things he had learned through that process. As a result of such experiences, he is becoming an extremely responsible, independent young man yet one who has also learned to be dependent upon God.

First Timothy 5:8 states that anyone who "does not provide for his relatives, especially for his immediate family, has denied the faith and is worse than an unbeliever." The foundation for the child's work life can depend upon the parents' attitude toward work. We believe that part of providing for one's family is training our children with biblical principles for work and handling finances.

However, don't misunderstand. A work ethic is not a worth ethic. There is a fine line in developing balanced children. The identity of choleric children in particular can become entwined with what they do rather than who they are. At each stage of development, focus not on the achievements but on the children and who they are becoming in God's eyes. While they must be trained to do a good job, they are not to be judged solely on their work but on their character—their integrity, honesty, and reliability.

Teach the Importance of Saving

As they mature, children must learn how to save. They should be tithing 10 percent of their income and saving at least 10 percent of their income for the long run—college, cars, etc. When children are small, give them a see-through piggy bank. If a four-year-old can't see something, he thinks it's gone. So tell him the money is his. Let him watch his pennies grow. As he watches the money accumulate, he will see the reward for a job well done.

Today's children rarely know what truly is a need. Teaching them to wait allows them to have time to decide if what they desire that moment is something they really want. In one month's time desires change over and over.

Occasionally, let them spend some of the money they have saved on what they want. This begins to teach long-range planning. Teach them the joy of delayed gratification spoken of in Proverbs 13:12: "Hope deferred makes the heart sick, but a longing fulfilled is a tree of life." Real life has deferred hope laced all through it, but oh the joy when that hope is finally a reality. Let a small child experience that joy. When it comes from the labor of their own hands, your children will value the object of their deferred hope.

All through their life children should be saving for things they desire in the future. While they are young, teach them that they need a cushion for emergencies. Our children are both in college now. Since they have saved enough money in past years, neither must work during the school year but are able to focus entirely on their education. They can be single-minded because they learned the value of long-range planning.

Allow Them to Grow through Mistakes

Along the way, allow children to make mistakes. Mistakes are better made while children are at a correctable age rather than later when the mistakes could be life-threatening. For instance, sometimes allow children to fulfill their greed by spending their own hard earned money on a piece of junk that will fall apart in their hands. They will learn a good lesson on quality and will also experience the sting of greed.

Don't Bow to Peer Pressure

Using money as a tool, teach children to ignore peer pressure. Everywhere we go we hear the slogan, "Just say no!" How can children learn to "just say no" if they have never learned to obey your no? As children grow older, teach them to say no to name brands, which cuts across the very grain of peer pressure.

Sanguine children will be the most susceptible to peer pressure because they love people and love to gain new friends. They desire name-brand items because they're status symbols. Because sanguines need to be accepted, their appearance will be especially important to them. The parents' task is to direct children away from the value they place on things by focusing their attention on how valuable and important they are. Sanguines love praise. Rather than praising their outward appearance, praise their inner qualities, such as their giving heart and fun-loving nature.

Melancholy children also will be drawn to name-brand items, but not for the same reasons. Even as small children, melancholies love beauty and will reach out and touch lacy, intricate fabrics. They will hang on to their blanket the longest because they appreciate the feel. They simply love fine things. This love for finery is a good thing when it is controlled, but if it is not controlled, it can be a snare to them as they grow older.

Choleric children may desire the name brand because of the appearance of power they experience when they flaunt their expensive items. Cholerics are not driven by a need for approval or by a love of beautiful things. Their motive is control or pride, which is perhaps the most dangerous of all. They must be taught early on that God resists the proud.

Of all the temperaments, phlegmatic children are perhaps the least susceptible to name brands or peer pressure. They are secure in a few possessions. They don't value appearances or position or desire beauty. They just like to know that their possessions are theirs forever. The phlegmatics' ribbons, trophies, and fourth grade poems will drive a mom crazy as she tries to find a place for them. These children need to be continually put in a position of meeting other people's needs.

The reason we are so against the name-brand syndrome is that God promises to meet our needs, not our cravings. We must instill this principle into our children as well. Help children understand your opposition to the status symbols of this world system and you will help them control their desires. The pressure to look the part is not only difficult for children to withstand, it is also difficult for adults to withstand. With this principle as with others, we need to remember that "more ideas are caught than taught" in our children's lives. Children will observe our attitude toward things, and the attitude we portray in moderation is the attitude we risk our children showing in excess.

Teach Smart Shopping Principles

The principles of smart shopping are important for children as well as adults. Teach them to look sharp, attractive, and well dressed while making every penny count. One way to defuse the name-brand fight is to agree to pay for a nonname-brand item of equal quality. If children still want to buy the name-brand item, let them pay the difference in cost with their own money. This often takes the steam out of the fight quickly. When children have to pay the price, they must decide if the item is really worth the price. Another good idea is to show children the outlet stores, where it's not necessary to pay name-brand prices for name-brand items.

Teach them to improvise. Don't always run to get what they think they need. Give them time to figure out new ways to wear an old garment. Change its collar or give it a new cuff. Make an eyelet smock to cover a little girl's dress. Do anything to give longer life to an object, which in this disposable society is a major principle to teach your children.

Avoid fads. Every craze will fade away. Teach children to dress conservatively in clothing that will not become dated. Avoid faddish toys like Cabbage Patch dolls and Trolls which have a limited life span.

Most importantly, help children discern advertising gimmicks, even when they are young. Teach them to develop sales resistance. Let them watch you bargain at garage sales. But also teach the balance of this—not every cheap item is a bargain.

Teach them to avoid credit cards. One great way of doing this is not to loan children money. If you want to give children something, fine, but don't let them borrow from you. Teach them they must save for an item before they can get it. If this becomes an ingrained behavior when they are children, when they are adults, they won't find themselves in great financial difficulties.

Even young children can learn the value of careful spending. One sweet three-year-old choleric/sanguine found an ad for a toy she wanted for Christmas. She promptly tore the coupon out of the "mazagine" and gave it to her daddy. That little girl had already learned you can get what you want without paying the full retail price.

In Conclusion

What have we said by all of this? Everywhere you go, in all that you do, you are teaching and training your children in godly principles using daily illustrations from life. You are teaching your children about life. You are fulfilling Deuteronomy's injunction.

Train your children in the fundamentals of money management regardless of their temperament. When your children leave home, to your delight you will find they are able to live within their means rather than in bondage and slavery to their uncontrolled desires. Your children will understand value. Your children will take personal responsibility for their actions and their possessions and will have a talent for long-range planning. They will understand smart shopping principles, keep good records, and have a strong work ethic. They will not be greedy or selfish. On top of all of this, they will be givers. In their adult years, they will fully trust God with all that they are and have, and they will be equipped to face the challenges of adulthood.

CHAPTER EIGHTEEN

A
Final Word

"Well done, good and faithful servant."
MATTHEW 25:21

Our sincere hope is that this book has helped you do more than just treat the symptoms of your financial problems. We hope that you have been able to isolate and understand the root causes of your financial difficulties, for it is only in dealing with the causes that we will actually experience relief.

However, just getting motivated one time is not enough to change financial habits and behavior. Follow-through must occur in order to establish new habits, the right habits. We recommend that after finishing the book, you go back and highlight the parts that particularly apply to you. Also, take advantage of the aids in the Appendix. We've given you time-tested tools. Now you must do the work.

But the blessings are well worth the work. We believe that if you will consistently use the principles outlined in this book, you will discover:

• A clear vision of your financial goals in becoming a better steward of the assets God has entrusted to you.

• A step-by-step program which will allow you, over time, to incorporate the bite-size sections as needed rather than having "to eat the whole elephant in one bite."

• True financial success—success reflected by heart attitudes, motives, and behavior, not by the quantity of money. Some of us may be called to manage small assets, like the widow with the mite. Others may be called to manage large assets. Our success will be found in how well we manage what God has entrusted to us.

On that day when we look our Lord straight in the eye, may He say to each of us, "Well done, good and faithful servant." It is to this end that we have dedicated this book.

Appendix

Answers to Temperament Test

	TEMP. #1=MELANCHOLY		TEMP. #2=SANGUINE
	Perfectionist		Talkative, popular
	Analytical		Loud, sometimes brash
	Industrious		Emotionally volatile at times
	Musically inclined		Persuasive
	Enjoys art, music, things of beauty		Quick tempered
	Detail oriented		Colorful, exciting personality
	Precise, exact		Fun loving
	Introspective		Low self-control
	Self-sacrificing		Impulsive
	Excellent planner		Low sales resistance
	Supportive of others		Compassionate
	Self-disciplined		Emotionally responsive
	Serious		Warm friendly
	Gifted, multi-talented		Outgoing, extroverted
	Aesthetic		Enthusiastic
	Worrier, fearful		Loves people
	Critical and picky		Great encourager
	Indecisive		Not well organized
	Pessimistic		Loves approval of others
	Deeply emotional, moody		Restless
	Creative		Optimistic
	Sensitive		Sometimes late to appointments
	Loyal, faithful		Not good at details
	Frozen by fear, worry, depression		Sensitive
	Harbors resentment		Not well disciplined
	TOTAL		**TOTAL**

TEMP. #3=PHLEGMATIC	TEMP. #4=CHOLERIC
Calm, cool	Strong willed, determined
Laid back	Time is most valuable asset
Easy going	Driving personality
Quiet, reserved	Impatient—wants it done yesterday
Inactive, sometimes lazy	Sometimes bossy
Tendency toward passivity	Direct, forceful
Avoids and dislikes conflict	Values tasks over people
Slow to make decisions	Natural leader
Peaceable, peace loving	Likes to be in control
Quick, dry wit	Sometimes intolerant of others
Diplomatic in conflict resolutions	Decisive
Dependable, reliable	Strongly opinionated
Objective	Independent, hard working
Efficient	Self-motivated
Orderly	Confident
Agreeable, likeable	Self-reliant
Hard to motivate	Self-assured
Frequently waits until last minute	Goal oriented
Often indecisive	Aggressive driver
Fearful, worrier	Risk taker
Self-protective	Prone to anger
Saves everything	Sarcastic
Introverted	Argumentative
Stubborn	Insensitive, unsympathetic
Works well under pressure	Practical
TOTAL	TOTAL

Cash Flow Management

You may have tried to budget in the past with only limited results, or you may have a simple budget working now. Whatever your situation, you know that a budget is only as good as you make it. If you do not diligently work at your budget, or if you have made wrong assumptions, your budget will self-destruct.

Here is a budget that will work effectively throughout the year. It will also prove to be a valuable tool in preparing your income tax returns, since a record of spending has been kept all year.

Here are some appropriate amounts to designate in each category. Remember, these are only suggestions based on a family of four. These figures are a percentage of net spendable income (gross salary less tithe and tax). Your amounts may vary, but don't designate more than 100 percent.

If you have day care expense or Christian school tuition, your miscellaneous category will be higher than average, and you will have to adjust in other areas. Christian school tuition should not exceed 10 percent of net spendable income unless you are prepared to make sacrifices in other areas.

Housing	30-36%
Food	14-16%
Clothing	5%
Car	10-13%
Medical	5%
Insurance	7-9%
Savings	5-10%
Giving	3-5%
Entertainment and recreation	5-7%
Miscellaneous	7-10%
Credit	5%

HOUSEHOLD EXPENSE WORKSHEET   Month   Year

SALARY
His _____
Hers _____
Other Income _____
Gross Income _____
Tithe   10% of Gross Income _____ (1)
TAX
FIT _____
FICA _____
State _____
Total Tax _____ (2)
Net spendable income _____
HOUSING
Mortage (rent) _____
Taxes - Insurance _____
Electricity _____
Gas _____
Water - Sanitation _____
Telephone _____
Cable TV _____
Maintenance _____
Other _____
Total Housing ____ % _____ (3)
FOOD
Groceries _____
Lunches _____
Total Food ____ % _____ (4)
CLOTHING
Wardrobe _____
Laundry/Cleaning _____
Total Clothing ____ % _____ (5)
CAR(s)
Payments _____
Gas/Oil _____
License _____
Repairs _____
Maintenance _____
(tires, batt, etc.) _____
Total Car ____ % _____ (6)
MEDICAL
Doctor _____
Dentist _____
Medication _____
Other _____
Total Medical ____ % _____ (7)
INSURANCE
Life _____
Auto _____
Medical _____
Total Insurance ____ % _____ (8)

SAVINGS
Emergency Fund _____
Payroll Deduct. _____
Profit Sharing _____
Other _____
Total Savings ____ % _____ (9)
GIVING
Offering _____
Bldg. Fund _____
Benevolence _____
Missions _____
Other _____
Total Giving ____ % _____ (10)
ENTERTAINMENT/RECREATION
Eating Out _____
Vacations _____
Trips _____
Babysitter _____
Activities _____
Other _____
Total Entertain. ____ % _____ (11)
MISCELLANEOUS
Day Care _____
Christian Ed. _____
Special Ed. _____
Gifts (birthday, anniv., grad) _____
Christmas _____
Allowance _____
Personal Care _____
(beauty, barber, cosmetics, etc.)
Subscriptions _____
Cash (husband) _____
Cash (wife) _____
_____ _____
_____ _____
Total Misc. ____ % _____ (12)
CREDIT MANAGEMENT
Credit Cards (A) _____
(monthly payments) (B) _____
(C) _____
(D) _____
Personal Loans (A) _____
(B) _____
Total Credit ____ % _____ (13)

Add totals 1-13 to find your
total expenditures. ____ % _____

Divide the yearly totals by 12 to arrive
at your monthly amounts.

Reconciling Your Bank Account

An amazing number of people don't know how to reconcile their bank accounts. The problem most people have is that they have written checks since the date of their last statement and they haven't adjusted their account to reflect this.

By the time you receive your statement from the bank typically a week has elapsed since the statement was prepared and mailed. During that time, deposits may have been made and checks may have been written, which changes the actual balance in the account.

So the first step to reconciling your bank account is to write down the bank balance shown on the statement. Next, add in any deposits you have made since the date of the statement which are not reflected on that statement.

Once you have that total, subtract any checks that have not yet cleared the bank. This would include any checks you have written in the last few days, as well as any checks that may have been slow in clearing. Sometimes checks may take a month to clear the bank because the recipient may have misplaced the check or forgotten to deposit it. The best way to identify any checks that have not cleared your account is to go through your check register and put a check mark beside each check that appears on your statement. That means these checks have cleared the bank and have been paid. When you have determined which ones have not yet cleared the bank, add them up and subtract that amount from the total of the deposits and the previous balance. Also remember to subtract any service charges or withdrawals made from an automatic teller machine.

Once you have subtracted these amounts, you will have your actual balance, which should agree with your checkbook balance. Most checking account statements have this formula written on the back of the statement. If you have any problems with this system, be sure to take this information down to your local bank, and they will be more than happy to help you sort it out.

CREDITOR/ACCOUNT	PAY OFF	MONTHLY PAYMENT (MINIMUM)	AVAIL PAYMENT	PMTS LEFT	DUE DATE	% OF DEBT
TOTALS						

Miser Shopping

How to Save Percentages:

21%---------By driving 55 mph instead of 70 mph, save 21% on gasoline.

20-30%-----Properly insulate your house.

10%---------Caulk and weatherstrip doors and windows.

10%---------Have your furnace serviced once a year.

15%---------Put clear plastic film on doors and windows.

15%---------In the winter, set the thermostat at 68 degrees during the day and 60 degrees at night.

47%---------In the summer, set the thermostat at 78 degrees instead of 72 degrees.

35%---------Leave your credit cards at home.

10%---------Don't shop hungry. You will spend more.

10-12%-----Leave your husband at home when shopping. Men tend to buy more expensive items.

40-50%-----Buy store brand "generic" foods, which could save as much as $2,000 a year.

60%---------Choose the least expensive varieties of meats, fruits, and vegetables.

20%---------Buy bulk items such as flour and sugar in bags rather than boxes.

50%---------Shop seasonally for fruits and vegetables.

50-75%-----Pre-plan your funeral! Spare your family the emotional pain and avoid the advertising hype.

50%---------Avoid designer labels.

Save 30 to 50 percent by Shopping Off-Season

Anyone can save money by planning for future needs and shopping off-season when there is less demand for that item.

January and February:
Buy air conditioners, art supplies, appliances, bedding, bicycles, books, car seat covers, used cars, Christmas ornaments, Christmas paper and cards, Christmas gifts, clothes dryers, men's coats, costume jewelry, curtains, winter handbags and shoes, housewares, linens, lingerie, men's shirts, quilts, radios, large appliances, sportswear, storm windows, tablecloths, towels, toiletries, toys, water heaters, fabric, notions. Shop the Washington and Lincoln birthday sales.

March and April:
Buy coats (depending on geographical location), hosiery, infant wear, laundry appliances, luggage, children's shoes, skates, ski equipment, storm windows, men's winter suits, housewares, rainwear, soap, cleaning supplies, women's hats. Shop after-Easter clothing sales.

May and June:
Buy blankets, summer handbags (if on sale), linens, tires, typewriters, highly discounted winter wear, building materials (in June), housecoats, towels, school supplies, storm windows, furnaces, floor heaters.

July and August:
Buy air conditioners and fans (in August), bedding, baby carriages and supplies, drapes and curtains, furniture, hardware, housewares, winter lingerie, radios, tires (at the end of August), towels, lawn mowers, bathing suits (after July 4th), camping equipment (in August and September), new cars (in August and September), spring dresses, fuel oil (especially propane gas tanks in July), furs, home furnishings, lamps, men's summer shirts and clothing, refrigerators and freezers, colognes (in July), summer patio furniture and barbecue sets (in August).

September and October:

Buy batteries and mufflers, new cars, school supplies (at sales and in October), dishes, furniture, glassware, housecoats, piece goods, tools, bicycles, children's clothing (at sales), china, fishing equipment (in September), gardening equipment, hardware, paints, silverware, lawn mowers. Shop preholiday specials.

November and December:

December is the worst month to shop. Save as much as 50 percent by shopping in other months. The exception is December 26th, which is the biggest sale day of the year. Buy blankets, children's clothing, quilts, men and women's shoes, water heaters, used cars, ranges—after Christmas.

Additional Resources

Insurance Company Rating Services

Moody's Investor Service, Inc.
99 Church Street
New York, NY 10007-2787

Standard & Poor's Corporation
25 Broadway
New York, NY 10004-1064

Weiss Research, Inc.
P.O. Box 2923
West Palm Beach, FL 33402 (fee charged)

For more information on the different types of life insurance and what is best for you, send a $5 check—$3 for the report and $2 for shipping and handling—to Cornerstone Financial Services, 2000 E. Lamar, Suite 460, Arlington, TX 76006. Phone orders are not accepted.

Books on Temperament and Personal Growth

How to Develop Your Child's Temperament
by Beverly LaHaye, published by Harvest House

I Love You, But Why Are We So Different?
by Dr. Tim LaHaye, published by Harvest House

Your Temperament: Discover Its Potential
by Dr. Tim LaHaye, published by Tyndale House

Personality Puzzle
by Florence and Marita Littauer, published by Revell Division of Baker Books

On the Other Side of the Garden
by Virginia Fugate, published by Aletheia Division of Alpha Omega Publications

To take the Tim LaHaye Temperament Analysis Test, contact:
Dr. Tim LaHaye
370 L'Enfant Promenade SW #801
Washington, DC 20024
(202) 488-0700
The cost is $30.00.

Books on Buying an Automobile

N.A.D.A. Official Used Car Guide
National Automobile Dealers Assoc. Used Car Guide Company

Edmund's New Car Prices
Edmund Publications Corp.

Consumer Reports Used Car Buying Guide
Consumer's Union of United States, Inc.

For Additional Financial Information:

On Getting Out of Debt and Smart Shopping:

Mastering Your Personal Finances
(4 tape set) by Jerry and Mona Tuma
Cornerstone Financial Services, Inc.

2000 E. Lamar, Suite 460
Arlington, TX 76006-7338
Cost: $25.00
(Please write to order. We do not accept credit card phone orders for this tape series.)

On Mortgage Prepayment:

A Banker's Secret
by Mark Eisenson
Good Advice Press
Box 78
Elizaville, NY 12523
(800) 255-0899
Cost: $14.95, plus $3.00 for shipping. This book has excellent, detailed information on prepaying home loans. It could save you thousands of dollars by informing you on how to set up your prepayments properly.

The Banker's Secret Credit Card Software
Good Advice Press
Box 78
Elizaville, NY 12523
(800) 255-0899

The Cornerstone Report (monthly newsletter for investment advice by Jerry Tuma)
2000 E. Lamar, Suite 460
Arlington, TX 76006
(800) 327-4285
Cost: $79.00 year

NOTES

Chapter 3: Sanguines: The Last of the Big Spenders
1. Proverbs 19:2.
2. Proverbs 22:3, TLB.
3. Luke 14:28.
4. Galatians 5:22-25.
5. Proverbs 21:20.
6. 2 Peter 1:5-7.

Chapter 4: Cholerics: The Movers and Shakers
1. 1 Corinthians 9:27.
2. Proverbs 29:18, KJV.
3. 1 Peter 5:5, KJV.

Chapter 5: Melancholies: Balancing It to the Penny
1. Isaiah 61:1-3.

Chapter 8: The Lure of Our Culture
1. Galatians 5:22-23.
2. Florence and Marita Littauer, *Personality Puzzle* (Grand Rapids, Mich.: Fleming H. Revell, 1992) 149-157.
3. Hebrews 13:5.
4. Proverbs 15:16.
5. *The Banker's Secret Credit Card Software* (Elizaville, N.Y.: Good Advice Press, 1990).
6. 1 Corinthians 7:23, NASB.

Chapter 9: Gaining God's Perspective
1. Proverbs 10:4.
2. Proverbs 21:5.
3. 1 Timothy 6:9, AMP.
4. 1 John 4:18.

5. 1 Timothy 6:17.
6. Matthew 6:19-21, 25-34.
7. Ecclesiastes 2:1-11.

Chapter 10: He Owns It All
1. Exodus 20:17.
2. Exodus 20:14.
3. Matthew 6:19.
4. Matthew 25:21.

Chapter 11: Receiving God's Wisdom
1. Zephaniah 1:10-11.
2. 1 Corinthians 3:19.
3. James 1:5-6.
4. Proverbs 3:5-6, AMP.
5. James 4:6.
6. Philippians 2:6-8.
7. James 5:16, AMP.
8. Romans 8:5-6.
9. Romans 7:19.
10. John 15:5-7, KJV.

Chapter 12: Finding the Spirit's Direction
1. Haggai 1:4-6.
2. Romans 5:8.

Chapter 13: God's Principles of Money Management
1. Matthew 23:23.

Chapter 15: Advice for Family Finances
1. Virginia Fugate, *On the Other Side of the Garden* (Tempe, Ariz.: Aletheia Division of Alpha Omega Publications, 1992).
2. 1 Peter 3:6.

Chapter 16: Smart Shopping
1. Sue Goldstein, *Secrets from the Underground Shopper* (Dallas: Taylor Publishing, 1986), 7-43.

Chapter 17: Teaching Your Children about Money
1. *We Pulled Together and Won* (Greendale, Wis.: Reiman Publications, 1994).